Contents

Foreword

The rapid advances in medical science that have characterized the past two decades are clearly reflected in the greatly improved outlook for the newborn, especially the premature newborn. In no small way this improvement is due to the appearance and evolution of a new and hybrid offshoot of obstetrics and paediatrics – fetal or perinatal medicine. Whilst primarily concerned with the welfare of the fetus, this new specialty cannot afford to ignore the condition of the mother, as the interests of the pair are mutual and inseparable. This premise is recognized in the supremely important periods of fetal organization and growth. The following pages incorporate the work and thoughts over the past 10 years of a group of obstetricians and perinatologists working closely together in the practice and teaching of obstetrics.

Their book *Perinatal Medicine*, the first I believe of its genre, is intended for the guidance of all those medical students, pupil midwives and postgraduate doctors who are preparing themselves to undertake the care of pregnant women and their babies before, during and in the early period following labour. The authors have jointly dealt, chapter by chapter, with the problems that are faced daily in the wards of any busy obstetric hospital dealing with normal and abnormal obstetrics. Their aim is to establish an attitude of mind which accepts unhesitatingly the integration of the care of mother and fetus; for only in such a place can the pregnant woman and her baby flourish as we would all desire.

Professor J. H. M. Pinkerton
CBE MD DSc(NUI Hon) FRCOG FRCPI

Emeritus Professor of Midwifery and Gynaecology,
The Queen's University, Belfast

Preface

Our objective in writing this book is to give students of perinatal medicine a deeper understanding of the continuity of events that occur before and after birth. We think this is necessary because there are still many hospitals where obstetricians and paediatricians come into contact infrequently and where there is a great lack of understanding of the problems that each encounters. This can only be harmful to the mothers and babies and leads to divisions in the profession.

The practice of medicine is often concerned with making choices about means of treatment. Such decisions are made on the basis of scientific training and on the previous experience and skill of the clinician. There is often no 'right' way and we hope that this book may be helpful to those of you who will eventually have to make these decisions. We should at the outset encourage you to realize that knowledge is constantly changing, is not ossified and that we fully expect that much in this book will rapidly become out of date.

We hope that we have also conveyed in this text our attitudes to people. One failing is that textbooks of medicine describe patients as collections of symptoms and signs – a trap that we hope we have not fallen into. Patients are people with hopes and fears, with families and friends, and should be treated as such. This is sometimes called the 'holistic approach to medicine' – we prefer to believe that we are only human beings looking after others.

This book is not intended to be a handbook of obstetrics or of neonatal medicine. It is a statement of how and why we make our decisions; we hope it will be of help to others in this difficult area of medicine.

The late Dean of Medicine in Queen's University, Sir John Henry Biggart, used to remind us on the day of our graduation of the three great loves in medicine – the love of the art, the love of science and the love of people. We hope that in some small way we have conveyed these principles in this book.

We would like to thank Mr Brendan Ellis for illustrations and Lynda Thompson for typing the manuscript.

G. McClure
H. L. Halliday
W. Thompson

List of Contributors

James Dornan, MD, MRCOG Senior Lecturer in Obstetrics and Gynaecology, Queen's University, Belfast (Chapters 3, 4, 6, 8, 10, 15).

Henry L. Halliday, MD, FRCP(E) Consultant Paediatrician, Royal Maternity Hospital, Belfast (Chapters 2, 3, 4, 5, 8, 12, 14, 15).

Garth McClure, MB, FRCP(E) Reader in Child Health, Queen's University, Belfast (Chapters 1, 2, 3, 5, 7, 9, 10, 11, 13, 14, 15).

George Murnaghan, MAO, FRCOG Senior Lecturer in Obstetrics and Gynaecology, Queen's University, Belfast (Chapters 9, 11, 13).

Michael F. O'Hare, MD, MRCOG Consultant Obstetrician, Daisy Hill Hospital, Newry; late Senior Tutor, Royal Maternity Hospital, Belfast (Chapter 14).

Mark McC. Reid, MB, FRCP(G) Consultant Paediatrician, Jubilee Maternity Hospital, Belfast (Chapters 2, 6, 7, 8, 10).

J. W. Knox Ritchie, MD, FRCOG, FRCS(C) Professor of Obstetrics and Gynaecology, University of Toronto, Ontario, Canada (Chapter 5).

Maureen Scott, MD, MFCM Senior Lecturer in Community Medicine, Queen's University, Belfast (Chapter 1)

William Thompson, BSc, MD, FRCOG Professor of Obstetrics and Gynaecology, Queen's University, Belfast (Chapters 2, 11, 13, 15).

Anthony I. Traub, MD, MRCOG Senior Lecturer in Obstetrics and Gynaecology, Queen's University, Belfast (Chapters 7, 12).

1

Why Perinatal Medicine?

INTRODUCTION

In the past few decades there has been a revolution in understanding the physiology and pathophysiology of the fetus and newborn. The development of animal models has allowed the basic scientist to study perinatal physiology and biochemistry. More recently, new technology has permitted measurements to be performed on the human fetus and newborn, and pathologists have given added insight into the disease processes affecting pregnancy. Furthermore, obstetricians are becoming less worried about maternal health and increasingly concerned about the health of the fetus and about high perinatal death rates. Paediatricians are also enlarging their interest in this area as new techniques of care become available and a subgroup – the neonatologists – has begun to study and treat newborn infants exclusively.

The concept of perinatal medicine developed from obstetrics and paediatrics with the increasing recognition that events in pregnancy and the neonatal period were quite clearly interrelated and that the somewhat arbitrary division of responsibility for the delivery of care might have deleterious effects both on mothers and their babies. A combined obstetric/paediatric approach to the problems of high-risk pregnancy was thought to offer the best chance of a successful outcome.

The central problem facing those concerned with perinatal care was how to reduce perinatal death rates, which were intolerably high. More recently, the emphasis has changed with more importance being laid on the prevention and treatment of congenital malformation and on the prevention of handicap.

These changes in medical practice have not taken place in isolation but have occurred against a backdrop of social change. The population is generally

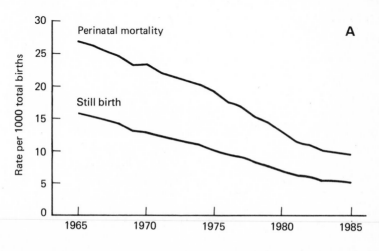

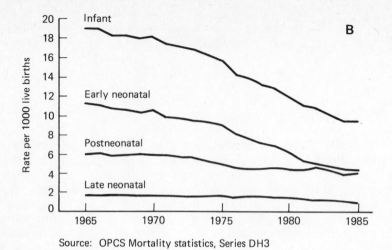

Source: OPCS Mortality statistics, Series DH3

Figure 1.1 (A) Perinatal mortality and stillbirth rates, England and Wales, 1965–1985. (B) Deaths in the first year of life, England and Wales, 1965–1985.

healthier and better educated, and so may require less medical attention. However, there is a recognized paradox that those who need most care, come from the most disadvantaged sections of the community and are least able to avail themselves of the services provided. One result is that the perinatal death rate, which has fallen dramatically overall (Fig. 1.1) remains highest in the lowest social classes (Table 1.1).

Any epidemiological study must define the condition or population to which observations relate and in this chapter the definitions are in accordance with those currently used by the Office of Population Censuses and Surveys for the derivation of national mortality statistics in the UK (see Table 1.2).

The perinatal period is legally defined as from the 28th week of intrauterine life until the end of the first postnatal week. This restrictive definition is no longer suitable because of various anomalies, such as the infant who survives after delivery at less than 28 weeks gestation and the infant who dies beyond the first postnatal week from some cause directly related to the perinatal period, for example whilst on a ventilator or as a result of congenital malformation.

Various factors may operate from the time of fertilization and during the period of embryogenesis leading to disease within the fetus and newborn. These factors, such as diabetes mellitus, may determine the outcome of the pregnancy

Table 1.1 Perinatal mortality by social class of father (England and Wales, legitimate births only)

Year	Social class		
	I and II *(professional)*	*III* *(skilled)*	*IV and V* *(semi-skilled and unskilled)*
1980	10.7	12.8	15.5

Table 1.2 Definition of mortality rates

	Definition	*Rate England and Wales (1985)*
Still birth rate	Late fetal deaths >28 weeks gestation/1000 live and still births	5.5
Perinatal death rate	Still births and deaths in first week/1000 live and still births	9.8
Neonatal death rate	Deaths in first 28 days of life/1000 live births	5.4
Post-neonatal death rate	Deaths at ages over 28 days and under 1 year/1000 live births	4.0
Infant death rate	Deaths at ages under 1 year/1000 live births	9.4

by causing congenital malformation before the 'perinatal period' has commenced. Clearly, then, perinatal medicine should encompass the period from pre-conception until the long-term outcome of the infant can be determined.

Still births are recorded on the basis of gestational age (over 28 weeks), which is of doubtful accuracy in a substantial number of cases, and live births are subject to no standard definition. The designation 'liveborn' may be influenced to varying degrees in different localities by certain factors, for example the place of delivery, the estimated gestational age, culture, religion and even the rules governing the payment of maternity financial benefits. Recognition of these influences casts doubt on the validity of comparisons of crude perinatal mortality rates from different areas or countries. To use comparative figures to make statements about the quality of obstetric and neonatal care or as a vicarious measure of the incidence of handicap in a population is to stretch them beyond their scientific usefulness. Sensitive to the absence of objective criteria for inclusion in perinatal statistics, the ninth revision of the International Classification of Diseases suggests the use of 500 g and 1000 g minimum birth weight standards for the preparation of data for national and international use, respectively.

Finally, it is insufficient merely to assess the success or failure of perinatal care only in terms of living or dying; long-term effects of perinatal disease must be assessed and considered when the efficacy of therapy is being quantified.

HISTORICAL REVIEW

Before the first census of 1801 and the nationwide collection of vital statistics which began with the implementation of the Registration of Births, Deaths and Marriages Act of 1836, reliable quantitative information about mortality did not exist. The only sources of information prior to this were the parish registers which had been recorded since the sixteenth century and the Bills of Mortality dating from the early seventeenth century. These undoubtedly provided underestimates of mortality because of geographical patchiness and omission of certain groups, for example non-Anglicans, the unbaptised and the illegitimate. From a study of a Shropshire population, it has been estimated that more than one-third of infant deaths were not recorded and that 10% of all births and deaths were not noted in parish registers during the sixteenth and seventeenth centuries. Of seventeenth-century England, it was stated that 'sometimes half the births were obliterated by disease and two fifths of the total deaths were in infants under two years' and that 'the high rate of infant mortality was due to the low status of public, domestic and personal hygiene'! The infant mortality rate was around 200 per 1000 live births in the century before national recording was introduced.

Birth was also associated with substantial hazard to the mother. In 1662, it was estimated from the London Bills of Mortality that 15 mothers per 1000 live births died within one month of confinement. In the late eighteenth century, a maternal mortality rate in the Westminster district of one in 39 deliveries in hospital, contrasts with the figure of one in 271 deliveries in the district as a whole. Hospital confinement was not common at that time and it is possible that those mothers who were admitted were those with established problems; it was suggested that the lower mortality among the poor was attributable to 'lack of harmful medical intervention'. Obstetric practice in the eighteenth century was held in low esteem, being largely in the hands of male midwives who had supplanted the female midwives of earlier years, but who were equally devoid of professional training and regulation. It was late in the nineteenth century before some medical examining boards added midwifery to their syllabuses, and in 1902 the Midwives Act saw the introduction of a system of training and examination for the practice of midwifery.

In 1841, when official statistics for mortality first became available, the infant mortality rate in England and Wales was 155 per 1000 live births and in the years 1847–54 maternal mortality stood at 5.4 per 1000 live births. Despite the great improvements in environmental conditions and the noticeable decline in the total mortality from infectious diseases associated with the passing of the Public Health Act of 1875, infant mortality rates did not show any obvious decline during the later years of the nineteenth century and in 1899 the infant mortality rate was 163 per 1000 live births. It has been suggested that a partial explanation may lie in the decline of infanticide. If a baby was killed shortly after birth, its birth and death were unrecorded. As the rate of infanticide decreased, a child might survive the neonatal period to die of natural causes later and then be registered. Further, the use of birth control techniques came into vogue among the upper classes, who had the lowest mortality rates. The number of births in this group declined so the overall mortality stayed constant. Infection was the leading cause of infant death in this period. Maternal mortality also remained high and in the quinquennium 1896–1900 was 4.69 per 1000 live births, almost half the deaths being attributed to puerperal sepsis.

One of the most remarkable happenings of this century has been the change in the age distribution of mortality statistics. Continuing improvements in housing, sanitation and nutrition, combined with medical advances on an unprecedented scale, have been the principal elements in reducing mortality. Infants and children have benefited most from these changes and the infant mortality rate fell by 88.7% between 1906 and 1978. Maternal mortality also improved dramatically. For the first third of this century the rate was stable at 4 per 1000 births but then began to fall rapidly and the most recent report on confidential enquiries into maternal death shows that the rate is around 0.1 per 1000 births. While improved maternity services have undoubtedly been the main contributor to this observed change, it is estimated that at least one-third of the fall can be accounted for by demographic changes, especially in the age and parity of the childbearing population.

FACTORS INFLUENCING PERINATAL MORTALITY RATES

1. Social Factors

Socio-economic adversity is associated with high perinatal mortality rates (Table 1.1). Poor social circumstances and educational disadvantage lead to a longer period of childbearing, with earlier, more frequent pregnancies. With increasing parity, the ability of the parents to provide adequate nutrition for themselves and their children may deteriorate and the ability of the mother to comply with the advice of the medical and midwifery professions may become even more limited. Poor social circumstances in the home may create additional pressures on the family which may lead to the mother seeking some medication to help cope with the situation. Such people are often less able to cope. They may suffer the additional disadvantage of a poor education and consequently have a limited understanding of the importance of adverse factors, such as smoking, which may affect their health.

The complex interaction of these factors is ill understood but the effects are striking. The medical and nursing professions are limited in what they can do to ameliorate these effects but they should be recognized and where possible attempts made to correct them. Advice should include discussion on contraceptive practice, diet and the availability of social welfare benefits.

There has been considerable debate as to the precise contribution of social changes to the fall in the perinatal mortality rate. Some have suggested that the role of the obstetrician in this area has been negligible and that the fall has been due to social change alone. That this is simplistic may be demonstrated by analysis of disease-specific mortality rates or birth-weight-specific mortality rates, which are perhaps more sensitive indicators of the effectiveness of medical care. The mortality rates in all such groups have fallen significantly, for example for antepartum haemorrhage, pre-eclampsia and low birth weight (Table 1.3).

2. Incidence of Congenital Malformation

Where the congenital malformation rate is high, the perinatal death rate will be high. In such areas, excluding low birth weight, congenital malformations are the most common cause of perinatal death.

Table 1.3 Disease-specific mortality rates, Royal Maternity Hospital, Belfast, UK

Year	Perinatal death rate (%)		Neonatal death rate (%) 'Prematurity'
	Pre-eclamptic toxaemia	Toxic antepartum haemorrhage	
1964	3.6	32.5	16.0
1972	3.5	41.4	15.2
1980	2.1	12.5	7.3

Neural tube defects are the most common single group of malformations with a high incidence in the Celtic races. Anencephaly is obviously a lethal defect, and spina bifida also carries an increased mortality and morbidity whether or not early operative intervention is undertaken. The aetiology of these defects remains obscure but there has been a natural fall in the incidence in the past decade.

The effect of supplemental vitamins is currently under investigation in the United Kingdom. There is considerable debate about the value of this means of therapy as the initial reports were not based on a randomized double-blind trial. This has necessitated the setting up of a Medical Research Council trial, the results of which are not yet available.

Congenital heart disease accounts for the second largest group of congenital malformations. In the majority of cases these defects are sporadic and therefore unexpected. Fortunately, with recent developments in neonatal cardiology and cardiac surgery, more of these defects are proving to be amenable to surgery so that the major problem is early recognition and referral to hospitals where investigation and treatment are available. It is also becoming possible with the development of more sophisticated ultrasonics, to visualize the fetal heart *in utero* and detect some types of defect. Where there is a strong family history of congenital heart disease, assessment of the fetus prior to birth is feasible, permitting immediate investigation and treatment soon after birth.

3. Unexplained still births

Still births account for a significant proportion of perinatal deaths and are particularly distressing to all concerned. The causes remain obscure even with careful review of all the available information. This reflects the limitations of our knowledge and methods of investigation.

4. Prematurity and low birth weight

In most developed countries the incidence of low-birth-weight (less than 2.5 kg) babies remains at about 5% of total births. The chance of survival of these infants is directly proportional to the gestational age and to the birth weight. Fortunately, by use of modern methods of intensive care both before and after birth, it is possible to reduce the hazards these infants face, although extremely small and immature infants still have a significant mortality. However, such techniques are not available on a worldwide basis, are invasive and costly and are not free from hazard.

LONG-TERM SURVIVAL

It is no longer acceptable in perinatal medicine to be concerned with mortality rates alone; quality of survival of the infants and children is becoming at least as important. It is clearly unreasonable to 'strive officiously to keep alive' every child who will end up handicapped, either mentally, physically or both.

Prediction and assessment of the quality of survival is essential in two quite separate and distinct groups of babies – those with congenital malformations and those of low birth weight who require intensive care. Where infants are born with a single, isolated congenital defect the medical treatment to be employed is usually clear. However, if the lesion which threatens the infant's life is part of a complex condition or a chromosomal defect such as Down's syndrome or Edward's syndrome, then parents and medical advisers must have regard for the long-term outcome when making decisions which have major ethical, moral and medical implications.

The smallest babies often present the largest problems. In general, these babies have the highest mortality rates, the highest risk of neurological problems and of other diseases such as broncho-pulmonary dysplasia. These problems will be discussed fully in Chapter 4 but it is timely to remember that by studying in detail those babies who have unfortunately developed serious mental or physical problems, a better understanding of the disease processes and of the results of treatment may be achieved.

One paradox in the area of handicap is the apparent willingness of those involved in the field to assume responsibility for the genesis of the handicap; the idea is that if a child has cerebral palsy then something must have gone wrong and that all handicaps are potentially preventable. This is clearly not the case as some infants develop cerebral damage well before the onset of labour. The precise numbers involved and the aetiology remain obscure but it is hoped that advances in neurological investigations may be revealing.

COMPONENTS OF A PERINATAL CARE SYSTEM

Epidemiological studies of perinatal problems should be carried out in each region. The incidence of disease clearly varies from place to place and it is unreasonable to plan any service without first deciding on what targets are to be set and the service designed to meet those specific needs.

Perinatal care of high-risk patients should be provided, where possible, in a major perinatal centre equipped and staffed to provide continuous care from fetal to neonatal life. Typically, a major perinatal centre will have ultimate responsibility for a large geographical area which will contain smaller specialist units. Both types of hospital should have obstetricians and paediatricians, but their roles differ in the two places.

In the smaller hospitals, the medical specialists can and should treat all but the very highest-risk patients and should have all the diagnostic and therapeutic means to provide this care. Patients such as those with twin pregnancies can be managed locally. Occasionally, for reasons usually related to gestational age or need for surgery, it may be necessary to transfer patients to the regional centre but it should be stressed that perinatal care in most pregnancies should take place as close to the patient's home as is medically possible.

In the local hospital, obstetricians, paediatricians and nursing staff should develop a team approach to perinatal care. Decisions about patient management should be based on the hospital experience of the given disease and upon the availability of resources within the hospital. These resources should include biochemical and ultrasonic fetal assessment, good provision for neonatal re-suscitation and the availability of short-term neonatal intensive care with blood gas monitoring and assisted ventilation.

Regional perinatal centres are usually based in large towns or cities; they provide care for the population in the immediate vicinity and also act as referral services for the larger geographical area. They should have the capacity to treat all types of disease, including surgical problems, in the neonatal period.

The good relationship between the regional centre and local hospital is one which requires attention and promotion. If this relationship deteriorates there may be unnecessary delays in referral of patients. Good relationships are promoted by such means as frequent inter-hospital meetings, early transfer of mothers and babies back to the local hospital and shared follow-up.

It is difficult to overestimate the effects of good nursing in the field of perinatal medicine. Nurses in these areas are highly skilled and motivated, and their views should be incorporated when planning a comprehensive perinatal service. All efforts should be made locally to encourage training of nursing staff by the provision of in-service training programmes, intensive-care courses and peri-natal discussion groups. Perhaps more importantly, attention should be paid to nursing and medical staff morale in all units. All too frequently nursing and medical staff who spend long periods of time working in intensive-care units become depressed or anxious because of the stressful nature of their jobs. These effects can be modified by rotation of staff from intensive care to special care, by 'complaint sessions' and by social gatherings.

RELATIONSHIP WITH PARENTS

The aim of the work of health professionals in the field of perinatal medicine is to ensure, as much as possible, that each family cared for is healthy, active and normal, before and after the birth of the baby. Many hospitals unfortunately lose sight of the fact that the patients treated are people and not just numbers. This has led inevitably to resentment and much justifiable criticism from mothers and fathers, usually directed at the attitudes of medical and nursing staff.

Having a baby should be made a pleasant and a happy experience for all the family. One major criticism frequently heard is that 'things were done but not explained'; a complaint which is often justified. Failure to explain what is happening generally arises for two reasons – either the time taken for explana-tion was too short and the conversation was truncated, or alternatively the language used in the conversation was so technical that the parents did not understand. In this situation, a little time and effort from the clinician will reap great rewards.

Perhaps the most important aspects are that the hospital staff should be seen to welcome people and provide an atmosphere of caring and comfort. It is unnecessary to have large antenatal clinics with droves of women waiting for long periods of time. The clinics themselves should be comfortable with provision for refreshments and for the caring of the young children who accompany their mothers. Fathers should be welcomed and encouraged to participate fully in the practical aspects of pregnancy and discussions thereon.

For most people, pregnancy is straightforward and uncomplicated. For a few, the situation may change radically and very often acutely. In these situations, they are confronted with problems of startling magnitude, presented to them by people that they may never have seen before and, occasionally, in hospitals that are foreign to them. The fear and bewilderment that they feel must be immense;

therefore kindness and explanations from the clinician are absolutely essential if these problems are to be overcome.

FURTHER READING

Budin, P. (1907) *The Nursling*. Caxton, London.
Chamberlain, R. *et al.* (1975) *British Births 1970*. Heinemann Medical, London.
Chard, T. and Richards, M. (1977) *Benefits and Hazards of the New Obstetrics. Clinics in Developmental Medicine* 64. Simp and Heinemann, London.
Silverman, W. A. (1980) *Retrolental Fibroplasia: A Modern Parable. Monographs in Neonatology*. Grune and Stratton, New York.
Usher, R. H. (1977) Regionalization of perinatal care. *Seminars in Perinatology* 1: 309.
Wigglesworth, J. (1980) Monitoring perinatal mortality: a pathophysiological approach. *Lancet* i: 684–689.

2

Normal Pregnancy

INTRODUCTION

Pregnancy is a normal physiological event that is only occasionally complicated by pathological conditions which may endanger the health of the mother and fetus. Doctors and midwives who undertake the care of pregnant women must understand the normal anatomical, physiological and biochemical changes that occur in pregnancy in order to explain them to mothers and to detect any significant abnormalities as early as possible so that appropriate action can be taken to minimize their effects.

Sex Education

The prevailing attitudes of the day have greatly increased the sexual awareness of young people, who are constantly subjected to a stream of information on human sexual experience in the popular media. At the same time, sex education in schools has become more widespread but has been largely restricted to the biology and mechanics of sexual reproduction taught in the science class as part of the curriculum. These two developments, together with the widespread availability of contraceptives, have allowed young people to enjoy sexual experience as an end in itself but with little understanding of the deeper emotional aspects. Unfortunately, such attitudes to sexuality may lead to emotional and physical problems at a later date, for example the steady rise in the rates of sexually transmitted disease, notably AIDS.

What would seem to be required is a much more thorough and deeper understanding of human sexuality in its widest sense. This would include the emotional and moral aspects, the responsibility of one person for the feelings of others and the development of the ability to see sex in the context of the rest of human experience. This will require a radical alteration in the content and methods of teaching in schools and there will have to be a marked increase in the contribution of parents who should be involved in this vital aspect of their children's lives. Teaching must not be restricted to the biology class but should be discussed whenever the occasion requires it. By developing this wider understanding, it is possible that young people may become happier, better balanced and more aware.

PRE-PREGNANCY COUNSELLING

Ideally all women should be seen by a medical practitioner prior to becoming pregnant. This allows for a full discussion of all the factors that may affect the pregnancy and advice can be given on any specific medical problems. Frequently, pregnancy is embarked upon with little awareness of its reality, or of the demands and changes that will have to be met. The level of understanding varies from family to family and many have little idea of the social and domestic consequences of pregnancy. The adverse effects of smoking, alcohol or drugs on the fetus may not be appreciated. Many women are unhealthy with inadequate or inappropriate diets and pay scant attention to their general physical condition. Such factors should be taken into account by the medical practitioner and advice given before conception. Pregnancy may be tiring and arduous, especially in the latter months, and the better the state of health at the outset, the more pleasant the experience will be.

Pre-pregnancy counselling is particularly important for women with diseases such as diabetes mellitus: the first four weeks of pregnancy is the phase of embryonic development and good control at this time will help to reduce the incidence of congenital malformations.

A comprehensive obstetric service should encourage the establishment of pre-pregnancy clinics and it must be recognized that women from the lowest socio-economic groups would benefit most but are least likely to take advantage of these services. Clinics have to be readily accessible to such groups, which implies that they should be available at a local level. This may mean that the clinics are provided as close to large deprived areas as possible, perhaps utilizing facilities which the women already use, such as local social clubs. The general practitioner has a central role in identifying those patients who would benefit most.

PHYSIOLOGICAL CHANGES IN PREGNANCY

Pregnancy affects all the bodily systems with changes occurring as early as six weeks. These changes are temporary and after pregnancy the mother is restored essentially to her pre-pregnancy condition. Maternal metabolism changes throughout pregnancy in order to meet the altering fetal and maternal needs and to create the optimum environment for fetal growth at different periods of pregnancy.

Many of the changes are discussed in more detail in Chapters 12 and 13 but will be summarized here.

The cardiac output rises in pregnancy because of an increase in the heart rate and stroke volume. There is an increase in the circulating blood volume primarily due to an increase in the plasma volume. The peripheral vascular resistance and the blood pressure are reduced. Total body water is increased by about 7.5 l, the majority of which (6 l) is accounted for by the growth of the fetus, uterus, placenta and liquor, but 1.5 l goes to the intravascular and extravascular spaces. Plasma protein concentration falls due to haemodilution, but there is also on overall fall in serum albumin level. There is an increase in the glomerular filtration rate which is maintained throughout pregnancy, in contrast to the renal blood flow which increases up to 28 weeks and then falls. The serum sodium is maintained to near normal levels by an increase in aldosterone secretion. Blood viscosity is reduced because of haemodilution; the white cell count rises from about 7500/mm^3 to about 12 000/mm^3 and the platelet count also increases. The ESR rises from 10 mm/hr to 55 mm/hr or more because of increased fibrinogen and globulin.

Metabolic activity increases in pregnancy. The resultant increased demand for oxygen is met by a rise in the tidal volume, probably due to an effect of progesterone. Total T_4 increases due to a rise in the thyroid binding globulin;

11

total T_3 also increases but free T_4 and T_3 are unchanged. There is considerable nitrogen retention in pregnancy, usually in excess of requirements. Blood total lipids increase due mainly to a rise in cholesterol and triglycerides, lipoproteins also increase and about 4 kg of fat is deposited.

Placental Hormone Production

These hormones are secreted by the trophoblast soon after implantation.

Human Chorionic Gonadotrophin (HCG)

This hormone is secreted in increasing amounts up to 60–80 days; the level then falls and stabilizes for the rest of pregnancy. Its major function is to maintain the corpus luteum which secretes oestrogen and progesterone. Additionally, it may regulate oestrogen production from the trophoblast and suppress maternal immunological reaction against the fetus.

Human Placental Lactogen (HPL)

This is secreted by the placenta and has a trophic action on the breast. It may also alter carbohydrate and lipid metabolism.

Oestrogen

Oestrogen, oestradiol and oestriol are all secreted by the placenta. They enhance RNA and protein synthesis and alter polymerization of mucopolysaccharides which reduces the adhesion of collagen fibres. This is particularly noticeable in the cervix. Oestrogen also helps the growth of the uterine muscle and its blood supply. In the breast, it causes duct and alveolar proliferation.

Progesterone

The main action of this hormone is to reduce smooth muscle excitability. This affects the uterus, urinary and gastrointestinal tracts and vascular smooth muscle. A further effect is to oppose the action of prolactin on the breast during pregnancy.

Uterine Changes

The uterus changes in size, shape and consistency during pregnancy. The weight increases from 50 g to about 1 kg and the capacity enlarges from 4 ml to 4 l. The uterine muscle increases by hyperplasia up to the 20th week of gestation and thereafter growth is due to hypertrophy. The uterus initially has a pear shape which is retained in the early weeks of pregnancy but becomes more spherical as the gestational sac enlarges. Subsequently the uterus enlarges and undergoes some degree of dextrorotation because of the presence of the sigmoid colon on the left side of the abdomen. The uterus changes in consistency; the lower part of the body of the uterus softens first, followed by the uterine fundus and the cervix.

As the overall dimensions of the uterus are changing, the pattern of the muscle fibres of the uterine wall is also changing. The middle layer of uterine muscle is comprised of two spiral systems of inter-digitating muscle fibres. This pattern is bilaterally symmetrical with the fibres in the fundus at right angles while, in the lower part of the uterus, the arch formed is much more oblique. As pregnancy develops, the arrangement of fibres in the upper part is unchanged while the lower part is stretched and the angle between the fibres become more acute.

The changes in the uterine isthmus are significantly different from the rest of the uterus. The isthmus lies between the dense connective tissue of the cervix and the muscle fibres of the corpus although its boundaries are ill defined. In early pregnancy the isthmus hypertrophies, elongates and softens. After 12 weeks, the isthmus opens out from above downwards and becomes totally incorporated in the body of the uterus, contributing to the formation of the lower uterine segment. The muscle fibres of the isthmus are circular.

Changes in the Cervix

The function of the cervix is to retain the conceptus during pregnancy and during labour to efface and dilate to allow the passage of the fetus. The cervix changes in pregnancy by becoming more vascular and oedematous. The collagen content of the connective tissue falls and is replaced by aminoglycan. This alters the mechanical properties of the cervix and is probably controlled by oestrogen and prostaglandin $F_2\alpha$.

The endothelium lining the endocervical canal is hyperactive and may protrude through the external cervical os. Additionally, there is hyperactivity of the squamous epithelium of the portio vaginalis. The cervical mucus increases in amount and becomes thick and viscous. It acts as a mechanical and bacteriological barrier to the uterine cavity.

Changes in the Vagina and Pelvic Floor

There is a marked increase in the vascularity of the vagina and pelvic floor. The vagina and its supports progressively loosen and become more distensible to allow passage of the fetus. The pH of the vagina is reduced since glycogen from shed vaginal cells is converted by *Lactobacillus acidophilus* to lactic acid. This inhibits the growth of most pathogenic bacteria, but promotes the growth of yeasts. The round, uterosacral and broad ligaments undergo marked hypertrophy.

THE DIAGNOSIS OF PREGNANCY

Clinical

The diagnosis of pregnancy is usually simple if a careful history and clinical examination are undertaken. The commonest symptoms are amenorrhoea, nausea, vomiting, breast tenderness and frequency of micturition. Fetal movements (quickening) are usually experienced by 20 weeks but can be detected as early as 16 or as late as 24 weeks.

The early signs of pregnancy are confined to the reproductive organs. Enlargement and vascular congestion of the breasts with characteristic dilatation of the superficial veins occurs about 6 weeks after conception. At a later stage, there is an increase in pigmentation of the areola and enlargement of the sebaceous glands (Montgomery's tubercles).

On speculum examination, the vagina and cervix are a deep bluish or purple colour, the result of congestion of the sub-epithelial venous plexus (Jacquemier's sign). On bimanual examination, the cervix is soft and the uterus enlarged and globular, its size consistent with the duration of the pregnancy (*vide infra*). Pulsation of the uterine arteries can sometimes be felt in the lateral fornices. After the 12th week of pregnancy, the uterus is usually palpable above the symphysis pubis. At 16–20 weeks, fetal parts may be detected on palpation (ballottement), especially if the woman is thin and the abdominal musculature relaxed. The fetal heart sounds may be auscultated from about 24 weeks.

Hormonal

The majority of pregnancy tests depend upon the detection of HCG in the urine. The recent introduction of HCG-B sub-unit assays has meant that the hormone can be detected on the ninth day following ovulation. For this test, the urine should be protein-free and have a specific gravity of at least 1.015, so that an early morning specimen of urine should be used. Such immunological tests are now widely available in simple kit form and provide a reliable, cheap and rapid assay procedure.

Ultrasound

Ultrasonic examination provides an alternative method of confirmation of early pregnancy; linear array real-time machines are particularly suitable for obstetric imaging in that they are small, relatively portable and can detect fetal movements. It is possible to identify the gestation sac at 6 weeks after the last menstrual period if the mother's bladder is full. Fetal echoes and heart action can be seen at 7 weeks and the fetal head becomes recognizable at 12 weeks gestation.

ESTIMATION OF FETAL MATURITY

The best time to establish the fetal maturity is at the first examination in the early months. As the date of the last menstrual period is usually used as the basis of calculation, the woman's menstrual history should be carefully reviewed, checking if the cycle was previously regular, that the last period was normal and no bleeding had occurred subsequently. For clinical purposes, the expected date of confinement (EDC) may be calculated using Naegele's rule. Seven days and nine calendar months are added to the date of the first day of the last normal menstrual period (LMP). The calculation is based on the assumption that ovulation took place about 14 days after the LMP, although this may vary. If the previous menstrual cycle was irregular or prolonged, no reliance can be put on this method. Furthermore, conception occurring during lactation or within

Table 2.1 Crown-rump length at various gestational ages

Length (mm)	Gestation age (weeks + days)
10	7
14	7 + 4
17	8
22	8 + 4
25	9 + 0
29	9 + 4
33	10 + 0
39	10 + 4
43	11 + 0
50	11 + 4
55	12 + 0
64	12 + 4
68	13 + 0
76	13 + 4
85	14 + 0

three months of discontinuation of the oral contraceptive pill can lead to errors in calculation.

Bimanual examination by an experienced clinician, performed during the first trimester, gives a reasonably accurate assessment of uterine size except when the body of the uterus is retroverted. Measurements of the height of the fundus in relation to the symphysis pubis or, in advanced gestation, the xiphisternum give only approximate estimates with an error of up to 4 weeks (Fig. 2.2).

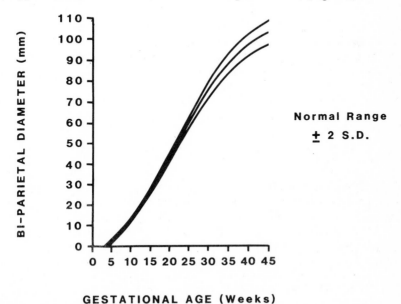

Figure 2.1 Curves of biparietal diameter against gestational age showing normal range ± 2 standard deviations. (After Campbell *et al.*, 1976.)

Ultrasonic measurement of the fetal size is the most accurate means of establishing fetal maturity and is one of the principal reasons for performing the investigation in early pregnancy. The crown-rump length of the fetus can be measured between 8 and 14 weeks and compared with standard growth curves (Table 2.1). Measurement of the biparietal diameter of the fetal head provides similarly accurate information about maturity between 14 and 20 weeks gestation and should be accurate to within one week of EDC; ideally two estimates should be made with an interval of 4 weeks to reduce observer error (Fig. 2.1). After 20 weeks, this method loses accuracy.

It is of vital importance to have an accurate estimation of gestational age early in pregnancy since it may be necessary later to deliver the mother early because of some fetal or maternal complication.

ANTENATAL CARE

Antenatal care is the keystone of good obstetric practice. The principal aim of antenatal care is to identify the high-risk patient so that the necessary care can be given to improve the outcome for mother and baby. Antenatal care also provides an opportunity to prepare the mother and father for childbirth and subsequent parenthood. In addition, in the antenatal clinics, large numbers of apparently normal women are seen regularly who would not otherwise be examined by a doctor. This affords an opportunity to screen a large population for other medical conditions.

All women should be seen for the first examination as early as possible in the pregnancy and certainly before the end of the first trimester. The antenatal clinic is often a woman's first introduction to the maternity hospital and the initial impressions gained can have a lasting impact on her attitudes. Childbirth may be an everyday event to doctors and midwives, but for the individual mother the experience is unique and sometimes frightening, attendants can become complacent and so the busy antenatal clinic should provide facilities to ensure that women are interviewed and examined in comfortable, pleasant surroundings with an acceptable degree of privacy.

At every antenatal visit the mother should be given the opportunity to ask questions. Furthermore, she should not be interviewed partially undressed and lying on the couch which, clearly, puts her at a disadvantage. Often, women may not discuss their problems for fear of being considered stupid or a nuisance. It is imperative that personnel working in the antenatal clinic develop skills to overcome this. In addition, there are many women from the ethnic minorities, for example Muslims, attending antenatal clinics; their religious and social attitudes require consideration in order that the care provided is not offensive to their ethics. In some areas with large ethnic populations it is advantageous to have members of the staff who can provide an understanding of the moral and language problems that such people confront.

The Booking Visit

At the first visit a careful review of all matters pertaining to the pregnancy is undertaken. A detailed history is obtained and the information recorded in a systematic manner.

General Medical History

It is important to ascertain if the woman has had any significant illness, including cardiac disease, hypertension, renal disease, metabolic disorders (diabetes), drug usage and psychiatric illnesses.

Previous surgical treatment, particularly abdominal and gynaecological operations should be noted.

Family History

Any disease with a hereditary tendency, such as diabetes, hypertension and congenital abnormalities, is recorded. A family history of multiple pregnancy may be significant; enquiry should also be made about tuberculosis, especially among recent immigrants.

Past Obstetric History

Accurate details of all previous pregnancies must be obtained, including antenatal complications, onset and duration of labour and the method of delivery. A history of third-stage complications is particularly important since these may recur. It is also essential to record in detail the outcome of previous pregnancies, particularly the birth weights and maturities of the babies. The cause of any still birth or neonatal death should be ascertained and every effort should be made to obtain the medical records of any previous complicated pregnancy. If there is a history of malformations in either the obstetric or family history, the patient should be referred for counselling to a paediatrician or a clinical geneticist (Chapter 6).

History of the Present Pregnancy

The menstrual history is obtained and the first day of the last menstrual period recorded. The history of contraception may be relevant, especially if this has been hormonal. Specific questions should be asked about bleeding in early pregnancy, alcohol and tobacco habits, drugs and infection.

General Examination

The height and weight are recorded. The teeth should be inspected and the patient referred to a dentist if necessary. The breasts are palpated to exclude tumours and the nipples are inspected to detect inversion. The heart and lungs are examined and the blood pressure is recorded.

Abdominal Examinations

A careful examination of the abdomen should be made and the height of the fundus is noted (*vide infra*).

Pelvic Examination

A bimanual assessment of the pelvic organs and speculum examination to visualize the cervix are made at the first visit. The position of the uterus and its size in relationship to the period of amenorrhoea are determined; any extra uterine abnormalities such as an ovarian cyst or uterine pathology (for example fibroids) may be detected. A cervical smear is obtained for cytological examination. Many women are anxious about pelvic examination in early pregnancy and, if fear is expressed, the procedure may be deferred until a subsequent visit.

Maternity Benefits

The doctor should outline the various statutory provisions made for the pregnant woman, such as maternity benefit, maternity leave, free prescriptions and free dental treatment.

Blood Tests and Screening Techniques

At the first visit, a sample of venous blood is obtained for determination of haemoglobin, ABO group, rhesus type, Australia antigen, atypical antibody, rubella immune status and the Venereal Disease Reference Laboratories (VDRL) test. If the patient is rhesus-negative, anti-D antibody should be measured (Chapter 10). In selected women, such as those of African origin, haemoglobin electrophoresis should be performed to detect haemoglobinopathies.

Serum alphafeto-protein as a screening test for open neural tube defects can be measured at 16–18 weeks gestation. The significance of this test must be explained to the mother before it is undertaken since if the serum level is raised it may be followed by tests to confirm a fetal abnormality. This will raise the question of termination of the pregnancy, which may not be acceptable to her.

Some clinics measure a random blood sugar level on all women at the booking clinic. If this is elevated then a glucose tolerance test is performed.

A mid-stream specimen of urine is tested for protein, sugar and significant bacteriuria (more than 10^5 organisms per ml).

An ultrasonic scan should be performed on all mothers at booking. This confirms fetal viability and is reassuring to a mother to see the early pregnancy and observe fetal movements. It also allows an accurate assessment of maturity and multiple pregnancy can be detected.

It is difficult to exclude even major fetal abnormalities when ultrasonic scans are performed before 12 weeks gestation. For this reason, it is advisable to perform a further scan for fetal abnormality at 16–18 weeks gestation.

Subsequent Visits

In normal pregnancy antenatal visits are made every 4 weeks until 28 weeks, every 2 weeks to 36 weeks and weekly until delivery.

Shared antenatal care between the hospital and the woman's general practitioner is preferable in normal pregnancies. This will save travelling, allows involvement of the general practitioner and community midwife and affords more time to be devoted to those with problems who attend the hospital clinic. Following the booking visit, the hospital visits take place at 28 and 36 weeks and weekly after the 39th week, the remaining visits being to the general practitioner.

A woman should be encouraged to discuss the progress of her pregnancy and any problems that may arise. Towards the end of pregnancy she should be told how to recognize when she is in labour and what arrangements are necessary for her transfer to hospital.

At each visit the woman is weighed, the blood pressure is checked and a specimen of urine is tested for protein, sugar and acetone. The haemoglobin should be checked at 28 and 36 weeks gestation; additional blood tests will be necessary in selected cases, for example rhesus-negative women with antibodies. In many hospitals pregnant women receive prophylactic iron and folic acid supplements which are started at 12 weeks. The abdomen is palpated to ascertain whether the uterus and fetus are growing as anticipated and the mother's legs and hands are examined for oedema. The date on which fetal movements were first felt (quickening) is recorded and after 28 weeks gestation the fetal heart is checked at every examination. Accurate records are essential, particularly when antenatal examinations on the same woman are performed by different attendants.

Abdominal Examination in Advanced Pregnancy

The objectives in performing abdominal examination are to assess the size of the uterus, the size and number of fetuses, the lie of the fetus, i.e. the relationship of the long axis of the fetus to the long axis of the uterus, the nature of the presenting part at the pelvic brim and its position in relation to the maternal pelvis, for example in vertex presentation if the occiput is anterior, the fetus is in the 'occipito-anterior' position. The fetal heart is also auscultated and the amount of amniotic fluid determined.

Inspection of the abdomen will determine the size and shape of the uterus and fetal movements may be seen. The uterus will appear larger than expected if there is multiple pregnancy, polyhydramnios or if the duration of pregnancy has been wrongly estimated. The uterus will appear wider than usual if the lie is transverse. If the back of the fetus is anterior, the uterus will have a smooth convex curve from the fundus to the symphysis; in the less likely event that the back is posterior, there will be flattening of the abdomen most marked below the umbilicus.

Four manoeuvres are used in palpation of the abdomen.

1. Fundal height. The patient is examined from her right side and the fundal height estimated by placing the ulnar border of the left hand at the highest point of the uterus (Fig. 2.2). The usual method of recording the fundal height is to judge its relationship to the umbilicus or xiphisternum depending on the uterine size. The examiner then decides if the fundal height is appropriate for the gestational age. Alternatively, the distance from the symphysis pubis to the fundus is measured in centimetres and this figure equates to the gestational age in weeks from 28 to 36 weeks (Fig. 2.2).

2. Lateral palpation. This is used to ascertain the lie of the fetus and the

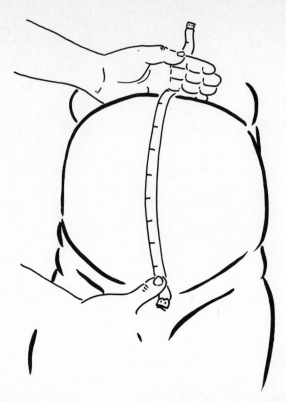

Figure 2.2 Fundal height is estimated by placing ulnar border of left hand at the upper uterine border and measuring in centimetres from the symphysis pubis.

position of the back in those cases where the lie is longitudinal. The hands are moved down the lateral aspects of the uterus and, with gentle pressure of the fingertips, the resistance of the back is looked for and its distance from the midline is noted (Fig. 2.3). The more laterally the back is felt, the more likely is the fetus to be in a posterior position. The fetal limbs may be detected on the side of the uterus opposite to the back as irregular and mobile bumps. The anterior shoulder is usually a prominent landmark and will assist in the determination of the position of the fetal head. If limbs are felt on both sides of the midline, this suggests that the fetus is lying with his back posteriorly.

3. **Reverse pelvic grip.** The hands are placed over the sides of the lower uterus, with the fingers directed towards the woman's feet (Fig. 2.4). The outline of the presenting part is palpated and its nature determined. The head is round, firm and ballottable, whereas the breech is irregular, soft and less ballottable. In cephalic presentations, an estimate of the degree of flexion of the head can be made by comparing the relative heights of the sinciput and occiput. The station, which is the level of presenting part within the true pelvis, is determined. If the greatest diameter of the fetal head has passed through the brim, it is 'engaged'. The 'rule of fifths' is a useful notation to describe the amount of head palpable above the pelvic brim (Table 2.2).

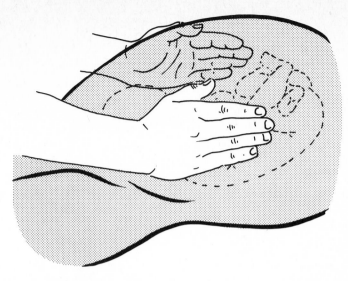

Figure 2.3 Lateral palpation of the abdomen to ascertain fetal lie and position of the back.

4. Pawlik's grip. The right hand, with the fingers well spread, should be placed in the suprapubic region (Fig. 2.5). Gentle pressure is applied with the thumb and middle finger. This should be done carefully as it may be painful for the woman but can be useful in distinguishing between a cephalic and breech presentation.

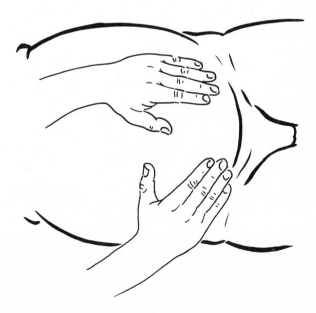

Figure 2.4 Reverse pelvic grip to determine presenting part and engagement.

Table 2.2 Rule of fifths

Fifths	Station
5	High, free head
4	Head entering brim
3	Almost engaged
2	Engaged
1 0 }	Deeply engaged

PREPARATION FOR LABOUR AND PARENTHOOD

In spite of a marked increase in mass media interest in childbirth, many women having their first baby know very little about pregnancy and the process of labour.

During pregnancy the woman and her partner should be encouraged to attend education classes which are now generally available at antenatal clinics. A simple explanation of pregnancy and labour will be given as this is important to allay anxiety, especially in primigravidae. It is helpful if the labour ward staff can meet the woman and give her a conducted tour of the hospital facilities. A comprehensive antenatal clinic also has the services of a dietician and a social worker.

Mothercraft classes also help prepare for the arrival of the baby and the responsibility of caring for him. Antenatal relaxation exercises can be given by a trained physiotherapist to help the woman later in labour. Mothers who wish to breast feed require additional help and encouragement during the antenatal period.

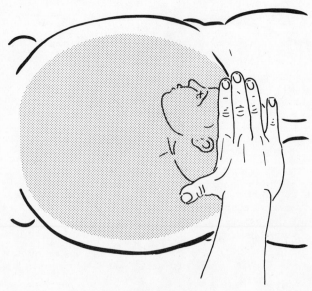

Figure 2.5 Pawlik's grip may help to determine the nature of the presenting part.

Preparation for labour is especially important as this is associated with anxiety about the pain and stress, and young women are often extremely apprehensive. Many of these fears can be allayed by honest explanations and the clinician should actively encourage the woman's partner to be present in the labour ward. No procedure should be carried out without full explanation of the reasons for doing it and what the woman should expect.

PLACE OF DELIVERY

The majority of deliveries in the United Kingdom are in hospital, which is favoured, as facilities and expertise to deal with any emergency are immediately available. Problems such as maternal haemorrhage, fetal distress or neonatal complications may arise in apparently normal pregnancies and urgent attention can be life-saving.

There has been a recent trend to encourage a return to domiciliary confinements in the belief that 'natural' methods are best. This situation has occurred for a variety of reasons, one of which is that hospitals were often too authoritarian and impersonal. However, it is possible to change the attitudes of hospital staff and to make the process of childbirth safe and pleasant. A friendly welcome and a willingness to discuss all that is going on will help to overcome the natural fear that many prospective parents have.

In addition, many unnecessary and institutionalizing procedures such as pubic shaving and enemas are being abandoned. Women should be encouraged to be mobile in the first stage of labour to aid their comfort and it is important that the delivery room should be as attractive, comfortable and non-threatening as possible. Medical and nursing staff should actively encourage mothers to adopt whatever position they prefer in the second stage of labour. Such simple changes will often transform a potentially unpleasant, regretful experience into one of considerable pleasure.

In Holland, there has been considerable success with domiciliary confinement coupled with a low perinatal mortality rate. Patient selection for such confinements is of vital importance and the ability to transfer the patient rapidly to hospital is mandatory if such policies are to be employed. To date, this system has found little favour in British obstetric practice because of fundamental differences in the health and social services and in the physical constitutions of the women.

LABOUR

Labour is one continuous process which is conventionally divided into three stages. The *first stage* occurs from the onset of labour until the cervix is fully dilated. This usually lasts from 6–8 hr in primigravidae and is much shorter in parous women. The latent phase of the first stage is an ill-defined period that commences at the onset of regular contractions and ends when the rate of cervical dilatation increases rapidly. It is followed by the active phase which usually starts when the cervix is more than 3 cm dilated and is marked by a dilatation rate of at least 1 cm/hr. The *second stage* of labour proceeds from full dilatation of the cervix until the baby is born. This usually lasts from 30 min to 2 hr, although it may be shorter. The *third stage* of labour extends from the birth of the baby until the placenta and membranes are delivered. This should take less than 10 min if oxytocics are given to the mother with the birth of the baby.

There are important differences between primigravid and multigravid labours. In the former, labour is longer because of inefficient uterine action and because the cervix and vagina have not been previously stretched. In addition, the primigravid uterus rarely ruptures. The parous uterus is efficient, the cervix and vagina have been stretched and uterine rupture may occur.

THE ONSET OF LABOUR

Labour usually begins with painful uterine contractions, a mucus discharge mixed with a little blood (show) or rupture of the membranes. The cervix begins to efface and dilate and the contractions become more frequent and stronger. The uterus contracts throughout pregnancy though such contractions are irregular and painless (Braxton-Hicks). However, in late pregnancy, some women, particularly multiparas, may be conscious of such contractions and assume that labour has commenced. The condition is termed 'false labour' and can be recognized by the absence of significant cervical dilatation.

The precise mechanism of the onset of labour is unclear, but many factors are known to influence it. Progesterone inhibits uterine activity during pregnancy and it was thought that a reduction of progesterone secretion may start labour. However, there is little evidence that progesterone secretion diminishes. The output of oestrogen does increase at this time and it may be this alteration in the relative amounts of oestrogen and progesterone that makes the uterus sensitive to other stimuli such as prostaglandins. These increase in the myometrium towards term, and prostaglandin E is known to increase uterine sensitivity and may be used to induce labour. Further, prostaglandins also cause release of oxytocin from the pituitary gland during labour.

Work on animals suggests that the fetal adrenal gland may have an important contribution to make in the initiation of labour by secreting increased amounts of corticosteroids, but as yet the situation remains to be clarified.

Mechanism of Labour

The pelvic floor is shaped like a sloping gutter directed forwards and downwards. This shape ensures that whatever part of the fetal head comes in contact with it first will be rotated anteriorly and directed downwards.

During labour, the pressure resulting from uterine contractions pushing the head into the pelvis (descent) causes the neck to flex (flexion), thus allowing the narrowest diameter of the fetal head to present; it then rotates (rotation) on the slope of the pelvic floor and extension follows as the head passes below the pubic arch. After the head is delivered, it rotates to allow restitution of the normal relationship between head and shoulders. This is followed by further turning of the head as the shoulder rotates within the pelvic cavity.

MANAGEMENT OF THE FIRST STAGE

On admission, inquiry should be made regarding the time when contractions started, their frequency, duration and intensity. The presence of a show, the state of the membranes and fetal heart rate should be noted. The woman's antenatal record should also be reviewed.

In every case, the woman's general condition is assessed, her pulse rate and blood pressure recorded and her urine tested for protein, sugar and ketones. The abdomen should be examined carefully as previously outlined. Particular attention is paid to the relation of the presenting part to the pelvic brim and the strength, duration and frequency of uterine contractions. The fetal heart is auscultated immediately following a contraction and the rate recorded.

A vaginal examination with attention to asepsis is then performed. The introitus is inspected, noting the presence of discharge or bleeding. The cervix is palpated and its consistency, degree of effacement and dilatation in centimetres ascertained; the presenting part is felt and a note is made of its application to the cervix. The membranes are palpated and, if ruptured, the nature of the liquor is observed. Additional information about the presenting part, including its nature, position, degree of flexion, station (relation to ischial spine plane), presence of caput and the degree of moulding of the skull bones, should be recorded.

An estimate of the size of the pelvic cavity should be made. In a normal pelvis, the sacral promontory cannot be reached by the examining fingers, the sacral curve is deep, the ischial spines are not prominent, the sacrospinous ligaments accept at least two fingers and the subpubic angle is more than 90°.

If the history and findings on examination suggest that the patient is established in labour, with the cervix at least 4 cm dilated and well applied to the presenting part, the membranes should be ruptured. This allows the quantity and colour of the liquor to be observed and may also accelerate labour. If the liquor is meconium stained, electronic monitoring of the fetal heart should be commenced and fetal scalp pH measured (Chapter 3).

Vaginal examination is repeated every 2 hr during the course of labour and the findings recorded in graphic form – the partogram (Fig. 2.6). This plots cervical dilatation and descent of the presenting part at successive vaginal examinations. If the woman is only in early labour she should be encouraged to relax, or walk around.

During labour it is important that regular observations on the condition of the mother and fetus and of the progress of labour are made. It is customary to record the woman's respiratory rate and temperature every 4 hr or more frequently if either is elevated. The pulse rate is recorded hourly and the blood pressure every 2 hr unless elevated. The fetal heart rate is counted every 30 min in the first stage of labour and more frequently in the second stage. It should be regular and have a rate of 120–160 beats/min. Early in the first stage the duration, strength and frequency of contractions are recorded hourly; every 30 min late in the first stage, and every 15 min in the second stage. A fluid balance chart is kept and the urine tested for ketones.

If the head is engaged, there is no need for the mother to remain in bed during early labour and she should be encouraged to walk around or sit in an armchair. Oral feeding is best avoided but the mother may be given a cup of tea in early labour.

A simple alkaline mixture such as magnesium trisilicate is given to neutralize gastric acidity thereby reducing the risk of Mendelson's syndrome if general anaesthesia is required urgently. H_2 blockers such as ranitidine may also be used in women at high risk of needing Caesarean section. If the first stage of labour is

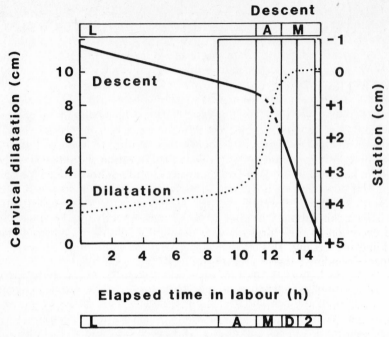

Figure 2.6 The partogram showing cervical dilatation and descent of the presenting part during the second stage of labour. L = latent, A = accelerating phase, M = maximum slope, D = decelerating phase, 2 = second stage. (After Friedman, 1954.)

prolonged or if ketones appear in the urine, an intravenous infusion of 5% dextrose and 0.18% saline should be commenced and 500 ml given.

The mother should be encouraged to empty her bladder frequently during labour but retention of urine can occur and catheterization may be necessary, particularly in women with an epidural *in situ*.

Augmentation of Labour

The progress of labour may be poor as a result of weak and infrequent contractions, causing the rate of dilatation of the cervix to be slow, less than 1 cm/hr. Careful abdominal and vaginal examination should be performed to exclude major cephalo-pelvic disproportion or malposition; if these are not present labour should be augmented by an oxytocin infusion and artificial rupture of the membranes, if spontaneous rupture has not already occurred. This is commonly practised in the management of labour in primigravidae and may be cautiously done in multiparous patients if there is no evidence of disproportion and the dose of oxytocin is carefully adjusted in relation to uterine response. The drug is used initially in a low dose (for example 8 units of oxytocin diluted in 500 ml of 5% dextrose/saline at 2 drops/min) which is doubled every 20–30 min until a satisfactory response is obtained as indicated by uterine contractions lasting 45 sec with relaxation for 2–3 min. Augmentation of labour is usually combined with external or internal monitoring of the fetal heart with measurement of uterine contractions either internally using a fluid filled catheter or externally using a pressure transducer strapped to the abdominal wall.

PAIN RELIEF IN LABOUR

In the early stages of labour, pain relief can be achieved by the use of intramuscular analgesic drugs which may be supplemented by inhalation analgesia in the late first and second stages. Pethidine in a dose of 100 mg intramuscularly is commonly used. The initial injection should be given before the pain becomes severe as the optimum effect will not be obtained for up to 30 min. The most serious unwanted side-effect is respiratory depression in the newborn because of placental transfer. The maximal depressant effect is seen if the baby is born about 2 hr after administration of the drug. Fetal metabolism and excretion of these drugs is very slow and can have an adverse effect on suckling and feeding. This effect may last for up to 48 hr after delivery and may influence bonding between mother and baby.

The most commonly used inhalational analgesic in hospital practice is Entonox, a mixture of 50% oxygen and 50% nitrous oxide. It is administered by face mask, the gas being released from a demand valve only if there is a negative pressure within the mask. If the mother becomes drowsy, she will release her hold on the mask, so that the pressure falls and release of the gas ceases. Mothers should receive antenatal instruction in the use of this apparatus to help overcome apprehension and ensure that the correct method is used. Nitrous oxide is relatively insoluble in body tissues and is rapidly excreted when inhalation stops so that its effect is not cumulative. During the first stage of labour, inhalation should commence 20–30 sec before each uterine contraction to ensure maximum analgesic effect before the height of a contraction. The midwife can time the contractions and instruct the woman when to commence using the face mask. Deep slow breaths may cause alkalosis and maternal tetany and thus should be avoided.

Epidural analgesia is now increasingly available and is the most effective way of obtaining pain relief in labour. A local anaesthetic such as bupivicaine 0.5% is introduced into the epidural space using a fine plastic catheter whenever labour is established. If successful, epidural analgesia will provide complete relief from pain and the patient will have no impairment in consciousness, in contrast to the effect of narcotic analgesics. Once the catheter is *in situ* the patient must be confined to bed and should be nursed on her side to avoid inferior vena caval obstruction and hypotension. Epidural analgesia is contra-indicated if there is a local skin infection, skeletal abnormality, coagulation defect, hypovolaemia or bleeding, active neurological disease or if the patient has an allergy to local anaesthetic agents.

The immediate maternal risks are accidental injection into the subarachnoid space which may lead to paralysis of the diaphragm, hypotension, motor paralysis leading to a reduction of maternal expulsive efforts and toxic reaction. Delayed risks include severe headache, urinary retention and sepsis. The second stage may be delayed (by up to 2 hr) as a result of loss of perineal sensation, but this distresses neither mother nor fetus and instrumental delivery is not usually necessary.

MANAGEMENT OF THE SECOND STAGE

The second stage of labour may be divided into two phases. The first commences with full dilatation of the cervix and is the period when the head descends and rotates within the pelvic cavity. The second phase begins when the head is clearly visible on the perineum and is complete with the birth of the baby.

Following full dilatation of the cervix, the head will descend onto the pelvic floor and the mother will usually have an overwhelming desire to push. She should be encouraged in these efforts. With each uterine contraction and expulsive effort, the head descends and the perineum will gradually distend with pouting of the anus. Delivery of the baby should take place with the mother assuming the position she finds most comfortable, provided the attendants are able to control the delivery of the head, have access to the nose and mouth of the baby and can protect the perineum from tearing. A minority of women will want to give birth in the squatting position or even 'sitting' upright, and birthing chairs are now available for this purpose. The vulval area should be swabbed with an antiseptic solution and sterile drapes placed beneath the patient and on the abdomen. As the head advances the left hand of the midwife is placed so that the fingers are spread over the vertex to maintain flexion of the head. The right hand (holding a gauze pad) is placed on the perineum in order to control the rate of delivery and detect the position of the chin (Fig. 2.7). Flexion is maintained until the greatest diameter of the head has passed through the vulval outlet and the mother should then be discouraged from bearing down. The head may now be delivered slowly by extension of the neck.

The perineum is pushed back below the fetal chin as the head emerges.

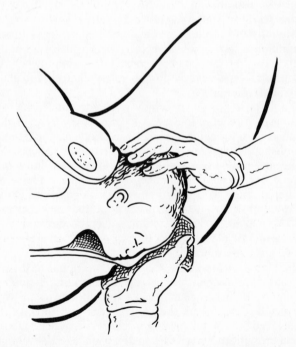

Figure 2.7 Management of the second stage of labour.

Immediately the head is born, a finger is inserted under the pubic symphysis to feel if a loop of cord is round the neck. Provided the loop is loose, it can be slipped over the baby's head; if this cannot be achieved, the cord is clamped with two artery forceps and divided between them.

The head rotates spontaneously through 90° and, with the next uterine contraction, is grasped between the fingers of each hand and is gently drawn posteriorly so that the anterior shoulder is released from under the pubic symphysis. The posterior shoulder is delivered by drawing the baby slowly upwards. After birth, the infant is laid between his mother's thighs and the cord is clamped and divided. He is then wrapped up in a warm towel and given to his mother.

MANAGEMENT OF THE THIRD STAGE

The third stage of labour is the time of separation and delivery of the placenta. It is expedited by giving an oxytocic drug such as one ampoule of Syntometrine (0.5 mg ergometrine/5 units syntocinon) with delivery of the anterior shoulder which helps to reduce the risk of post-partum haemorrhage. When separation of the placenta occurs, the umbilical cord appears to lengthen, the uterus rises up in the abdomen and assumes a more globular shape and there is often a small gush of blood.

When these signs are seen the placenta is delivered by the Brandt–Andrews method (Fig. 2.8). With the woman lying on her back, the attendant places the left hand over the anterior surface of the uterus just above the symphysis pubis and the umbilical cord is held taut with the right hand. The uterus is then gently pressed upwards with the left hand. If the cord does not retract into the vagina, separation of the placenta has occurred and gentle controlled traction of the

Figure 2.8 Management of the third stage of labour using the Brandt–Andrews method.

cord in a downward and backward direction helps the placenta to descend into the lower vagina where it is removed. If the membranes are ragged or follow slowly, they may be teased out with an artery forceps. At the completion of the delivery the fundus is palpated to ascertain that it is well contracted. The mother should remain in the delivery ward for at least 1 hr and the blood pressure, pulse and uterine fundus checked before transfer to the postnatal ward.

It is essential that the placenta and membranes are inspected for any defects such as a succenturate lobe or a missing cotyledon. If the latter is found, the uterine cavity should be explored in order to remove the missing cotyledon and avoid post-partum haemorrhage.

EPISIOTOMY

This is a planned incision of the perineum, carried out when the head is crowning, i.e. is easily visualized and is distending the perineum, to prevent an uncontrolled tear. It is advisable for the birth of the premature infant as it will allow better control of the head and reduce the risk of intracranial haemorrhage. The direction of the incision is usually mediolateral, beginning in the midline to avoid damaging the duct of Bartholin's gland and aimed posteriorly and laterally to avoid the anal sphincter. A midline episiotomy has the advantage of making repair easier and of lessening post-partum pain, but extension into the anal canal may occur.

The line of the incision should be infiltrated with up to 20 ml of 0.5% lignocaine at least 2–3 min before the procedure is performed. The episiotomy scissors are directed into position between two fingers inserted into the vagina to guard the fetal head. At the height of a contraction a single cut is made through the perineal skin and muscles. When the procedure is properly timed immediate delivery of the head should follow. The repair of the wound should be undertaken as soon as possible after completion of the third stage of labour.

THE PUERPERIUM

Traditionally, the puerperium is defined as the first six weeks after delivery. During this period the mother's body gradually returns to the pre-pregnancy state. The uterus undergoes involution and returns more or less to its original size by the time the first menstrual period has occurred. Throughout this time the mother is relatively but not totally infertile.

While in hospital, the mother should be encouraged to be out of bed soon after she has had a rest following her delivery. This promotes a feeling of well-being and helps prevent venous thrombosis. There is normally a slight vaginal loss of blood (lochia) which becomes brown in the first several days after delivery.

The essential element at this time is that the mother and baby get used to each other. They are relative strangers so they should be encouraged to get to know each other by simple procedures like rooming in. The staff of the ward should be careful about interfering at this time unless there is obviously something going wrong.

All non-immune rhesus-negative mothers with rhesus-positive babies should be given anti-D (Chapter 10). Rubella vaccination should be given to non-immune women together with advice not to get pregnant for the first three months following vaccination. There is no firm evidence that a fetus conceived by a woman who has just been vaccinated will come to any harm, but it is better to be cautious. All women should be offered contraceptive advice. The haemoglobin is checked routinely prior to discharge.

Care should be given to the breasts of women who do not wish to breast feed. They often become engorged and painful and are treated by giving adequate breast support and simple analgesics. Bromocriptine may also be useful if these measures fail.

At six weeks, the mother should attend her general practitioner for a postnatal check to be sure that all has returned to normal.

THE NORMAL NEWBORN

Adaptation at Birth

The birth of an infant transposes him from the warm contentment of the uterine environment, where he is totally dependent on his mother for his well-being, to the outside world, where he must be capable of an independent existence. The baby must be able to make this sharp transition swiftly, and in order to achieve this a series of adaptative functions have been developed to accommodate the dramatic change from the intrauterine environment to the outside world.

Cardio-respiratory Changes

Until the time of delivery, the fetus depends upon maternal blood gas exchange via the maternal lung and the placenta. Following the sudden removal of the placenta after delivery, very rapid adaptation takes place to ensure continued survival. Prior to delivery, the fetus makes breathing movements and the lungs will have matured both biochemically and anatomically to produce surfactant and have adequate numbers of alveoli for gas exchange. While the main mechanisms responsible for the initial breath at birth are known, their relative importance is not. However, they certainly include the following.

1. Thermal. Cooling is a marked stimulus to respiration. This has been confirmed by the experimental production of apnoea when heat loss is prevented.

2. Chemical. The process of birth is associated with hypoxaemia, hypercapnia and acidosis. Chemo-receptors present in the aorta and carotid arteries influence respiratory efforts by neural input to the mid-brain and the respiratory centres. In addition, there is a rise in systolic blood pressure following clamping of the cord which stimulates the aortic baro-receptors and sympathetic nervous system.

3. Tactile. Handling and decompression following birth help to initiate respiration as do visual stimuli.

Prior to birth, the fetal lung is full of fluid which is secreted by the lung itself. During birth, this fluid leaves the alveoli either by being squeezed up the airways and out of the mouth and nose or by moving across the alveolar walls into the pulmonary lymphatic vessels and thence to the thoracic duct, or to the lung capillaries.

These respiratory changes occur in concert with the cardiovascular changes. Before birth, pulmonary arterial blood is shunted away from the lungs to the aorta via the ductus arteriosus. This means that the pulmonary venous return to the left atrium is low and left atrial pressure is also low. This allows passage of blood from the right atrium to the left atrium across the foramen ovale. Following the first breath, there is diminution in pulmonary arterial resistance with a consequent increase in pulmonary blood flow. At the same time, the ductus arteriosus starts to constrict in response to increased oxygen tension, further increasing the pulmonary blood flow. Increased blood flow returning from the lungs via the pulmonary veins causes an increase in left atrial pressure and closes the foramen ovale. In addition, when the umbilical cord is severed, the aortic blood pressure increases which further inhibits ductal flow. It should be noted, however, that the ductus may not close totally for 3–4 days and, during this period, hypoxaemia or acidosis may cause reopening of the vessel. In preterm or ill babies, ductal constriction may be delayed.

Temperature Control

Eighty years ago Pierre Budin in Paris recognized the importance of avoiding hypothermia, when he correlated rising mortality with increasing hypothermia in infants of low birth weight. The importance of this observation remains today.

The newborn infant is at a disadvantage compared to the adult in so far as he has a higher surface area to body mass ratio, thus facilitating loss of heat by radiation, by convection and, to a lesser extent, by conduction at greater rates than seen in older children. Most importantly, he is born wet and if fluid is allowed to evaporate, pronounced cooling will occur. Heat loss in the infant is reduced by a layer of insulating fat beneath the skin. Heat is generated by muscle activity and by brown fat which is thermogenic and lies between the scapulae and around the adrenals. The low-birth-weight infant is particularly disadvantaged because of reductions of insulation and brown fat, and a paucity of muscle activity. Sedative drugs given to the mother may cause reduced muscular activity and β-blockers impair non-shivering thermogenesis by altering brown fat metabolism. The ill-effects of hypothermia include hypoglycaemia, metabolic acidosis, hypoxaemia and lethargy. To avoid these, the infant should be delivered into a warm environment, dried after birth to reduce heat loss and, once the infant's cardio-respiratory system has stabilized, wrapped in a warm, dry blanket and returned to the protection and warmth of his mother's bed and embrace.

Assessment at Birth

All babies should be assessed immediately after birth. Most infants are in perfectly good condition when they are born and require only to be kept warm and given to their mothers to be cuddled and inspected. It is customary to estimate the Apgar score in all babies (Table 2.3). This is a rapid, easy method of assessing the condition of the infant at birth and serves as a useful basis on which to plan treatment.

The Apgar score is recorded at 1 min after birth and again at 5 min. The first score enables the attendant to decide on what, if any, treatment is needed; the

Table 2.3 Apgar score

	Score		
	0	1	2
Heart rate	Absent	<100	>100
Respiratory rate	Nil	Slow, irregular	Regular
Muscle tone	Limp	Some tone	Active
Reflex irritability	Nil	Grimace	Cry
Colour	Pallor or generalized cyanosis	Body pink, blue extremities	Pink all over

second score correlates better with the child's long-term prognosis as well as indicating how effective any treatment has been. In clinical practice the two most important points of the Apgar score are the heart rate and respiratory rate. Generally speaking, infants with a good heart rate who are breathing well do well; those with a bradycardia and poor respiratory effort require urgent assistance. Birth asphyxia and its management are discussed in Chapter 3. Soon after birth, 1 mg of vitamin K should be given to all babies to prevent haemorrhagic disease of the newborn. Babies at higher risk, such as preterm and small-for-dates, and those to be breast fed should be given the vitamin K intramuscularly; others may have it orally.

Psychological Adaptation and Development

There has been increasing interest and awareness of the psychological development of mother and child over the past decade. Although the major field of investigation has been in the mother/child relationship, the role of the father and other members of the family with regard to the development of the infant have also been the subject of investigation.

The acceptance of pregnancy by the mother in the first trimester changes in the second trimester through appreciation of fetal movement, as she begins to recognize the fetus as a potential human being. The responses of mothers vary greatly. In some, the pregnancy is unwanted and will only lead to further economic and emotional burdens. At the other end of the scale, many babies are loved from the moment of conception. Such responses may obviously be modified by the attitudes of the fathers and of the rest of the family.

Many women may be frightened by the physical process of birth and of having the responsibility for bringing up and caring for an infant. Others do not know how they will feel towards their babies after birth. They know that they will be expected to love their babies – all the magazines and television programmes say they will – but many people have worries about their own feelings. These can be reduced by sympathetic handling and it should be explained to expectant mothers that feelings of anxiety and apprehension, as well as those of pleasure and hope, are normal rather than abnormal.

Recent studies have shown that the infant can hear, see, smell and respond to speech, often with synchronized movements. The infant would appear to be in a particularly alert state in the first hour after delivery, following which he may enter a period of quiet sleep. This period of increased awareness coincides with the natural curiosity and inclination of the mother to touch, stroke and examine the infant in considerable detail. This process of maternal examination of the infant is presumably to reassure her that the infant is perfectly formed. In addition the baby will react to her stimuli by eye-to-eye contact which may convey an immensely complex emotional interchange.

While it has not been shown that infants are adversely affected by the absence of immediate maternal contact due to transfer to a special-care baby unit after birth, mothers have been shown to have increased difficulty in managing these babies and developing a close relationship with the infant where access has been limited in the first few hours of life.

For these reasons, as soon as the infant's condition is stable and there is no medical condition requiring urgent treatment, the baby should be given to his mother so that she can nurse him. There is physiological evidence to show that if the baby is allowed to suckle, although the baby itself may receive no food and only lick the nipple, this will cause the release of maternal oxytocin. This, in turn, will cause an increase in uterine contraction and tone, leading to more rapid involution of the uterus reducing the incidence of retained placenta and post-partum haemorrhage.

Examination of the Newborn Infant

All infants should be examined soon after birth as an apparently normal pregnancy does not always result in the birth of a normal infant. This first examination should be brief and the baby returned to the mother as soon as possible. Care should be taken to keep the baby warm and not to alarm the mother. The examination should take place close to the mother and the examiner should explain what is happening.

There are three aims in the initial examination. The first is to ascertain that the infant has adapted to extrauterine life satisfactorily, the second is to examine the infant for the presence of any congenital malformations and the third is to make sure the infant is of the appropriate size for his gestational age. A second examination should be carried out prior to discharge from hospital.

The examination should be carried out systematically in the presence of the mother or, preferably, both parents; by so doing they can watch the examination and be reassured of their infant's well-being. At the same time, they have an opportunity to question the examiner about the infant's condition, as minor problems may have caused anxiety.

It is useful to have a check-list or diagrammatic representation of the baby in the infant's notes to ensure that no part of the examination is inadvertently omitted. The second examination before discharge is aimed at detection of minor problems which may not have been apparent at birth, or which may have developed subsequently.

The first important step is to look closely at the infant. These first few moments of close inspection of the infant are the most revealing to the expert observer. The second important point is that the observer should be an opportunist able to alter the examination routine to suit the baby. If the baby opens his eyes, that is the time they should be looked at; if he moves around, that is the time to observe the range and normality of these movements. However, it is best to ausculate the chest early if it looks as if the baby may cry.

Major problems such as Down's syndrome are frequently obvious at first glance from the recognizable pattern of abnormalities (p. 136); sometimes the baby may just look slightly peculiar with no obvious stigmata. In these circumstances a quick look at the parents may reveal family traits!

The next thing to note is the colour of the baby. Pallor, jaundice and cyanosis are easily observed in adequate light. Peripheral cyanosis of the hands and feet is frequently seen in normal newborn infants and is of no significance, but central cyanosis of the lips, tongue and mucous membranes is always pathological.

The scalp should be examined for the presence of abrasion, cephalhaematoma or caput. The size and tension of the fontanelles should be assessed. The eyes should be examined when they are open for the presence of any local infection, cataract or anomaly of the iris. The ears should be examined to ensure that the external auditory meatus is patent, for the presence of accessory auricles or the rare downward displacement and flattening of the ear as may be seen in Potter's syndrome.

Defects of the palate can be observed if the baby cries, and a finger should be gently inserted into the mouth and run along the palate to exclude the presence of a cleft, and of any neonatal teeth. The rooting and sucking reflexes can also be examined at this time. Defects of the nose and lips should be obvious on examination of the facies. The facies should be critically examined for the presence of abnormalities such as those of Down's syndrome or other trisomies and less obvious anomalies such as those of the fetal alcohol syndrome (Chapter 6). The baby's neck should be examined to ensure that the clavicles are intact, particularly after an instrumental or difficult delivery. At the same time the neck is examined for the presence of sinuses, redundant skin folds or cystic hygroma.

Examination of the chest should include observation for symmetry of chest movement, the presence of normal musculature and the respiratory rate should be counted. Auscultation of the lungs should be carried out although this may not be very rewarding, even in the presence of fairly gross pathology. Cardiac auscultation should be performed to determine the presence of murmurs, arrhythmias or major cardiac displacements. The femoral and radial pulses should be palpated. The blood pressure should be measured if there is any suspicion of cardiac abnormalities.

The abdomen should be inspected for any distension and palpated with a warm hand to feel for the presence of any enlarged organ. The umbilicus should be examined for the presence of an omphalocele or a vitello-intestinal duct. The testes should be palpated in the scrotum and the presence of herniae or hydroceles noted. The penis should be examined to ensure that the urethral orifice is in the correct position. The female genitalia should be observed for clitoral enlargement which may occur in congenital adrenal hyperplasia. There is often a mucoid vaginal discharge which is normal. Any swelling or palpable lump in the labia should be noted as this may be a testis as seen in the testicular feminizing syndrome.

The limbs should be examined to exclude the presence of such abnormalities as polydactyly, syndactyly, talipes, bowing, the presence of constriction bands and shortening.

The baby should be placed prone and the back examined for the presence of a neural tube defect, sacral dimple and the correct positioning of the anus. Any asymmetry of the skin creases on the backs of the thighs should be noted.

When this is done, the baby is again placed in the supine position. The head circumference and length should be measured and plotted on centile growth

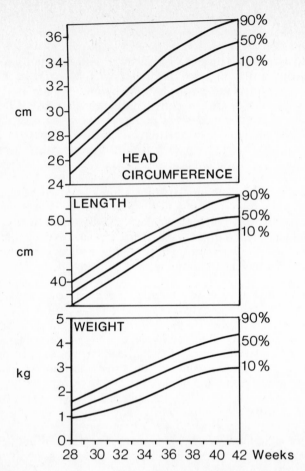

Figure 2.9 Centile growth charts of head circumference, length and weight from 28 to 42 weeks.

charts (Fig. 2.9). Babies whose weight is below the 10th centile for postnatal age are small for gestational age (SGA) (see Chapter 10). If birth weight is above the 90th centile, the baby is large for gestational age (LGA) (see Chapters 8 and 12). All babies with weights between the 10th and 90th centiles are said to be appropriate for gestational age (AGA).

The infant's eyes may now be open and can be examined. If they are not the observer should turn the baby's face towards a diffuse light or lift the baby into a vertical position; the eyes will then open.

The examination is concluded by assessing the baby's hearing by noting the response to noise. The Moro reflex should be tested making particular observation of symmetry of movement. In this reflex, the baby is held horizontally in the examiner's hands and the head is allowed to drop about 10° below the level of the body. The arms are extended, the fingers spread, then close, and the arms are flexed. Finally, the infant is examined for the presence of congenital dislocation of the hips (CDH) (*vide infra*).

At the end of the examination, the infant should be wrapped up and given back to the mother for the consolation of both.

The examiner should now spend some time with the parents discussing any abnormal findings and listening to any worries. It is useful at this time to discuss the development of the child in the first few months with special regard to feeding, bowel movements and sleep patterns as these are generally the functions which most concern young parents with their first baby. He should also ensure that the screening tests for metabolic disease (Chapter 6) have been performed prior to the infant's discharge from hospital.

Congenital Dislocation of the Hip

CDH may be detected in 1–2% of babies in the neonatal period. There may be a family history or the baby may have another postural deformity such as talipes. It is associated with breech presentation and oligohydramnios. In most infants, the hip is dislocatable rather than dislocated and in the majority the hip will rapidly become stable. However, it is not possible to decide which will become normal and which will not. Early diagnosis and treatment is of paramount

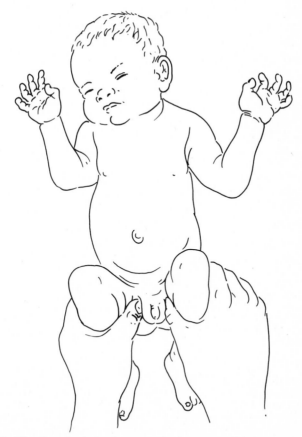

Figure 2.10 The Ortolani–Barlow test for congenital dislocation of the hip.

importance since early treatment is simple and effective whereas management of the child presenting late is difficult.

CDH is diagnosed in the neonatal period by the Ortolani–Barlow manoeuvre (Fig. 2.10). The baby lies on his back with the hips adducted and fully flexed. The examiner's warm hand grasps the baby's lower limbs with the thumbs inside the thigh opposite the lesser trochanters, the tips of the middle fingers over the greater trochanter and the legs in the palms of the hands. In this position, a gentle attempt is made to push each femoral head backwards and forwards into or out of the acetabulum. The thumbs push backwards on the head of femur in an attempt to dislocate the head out of the acetabulum. If there is movement with or without a 'clunk' the hip is dislocated. The middle fingers now press on the greater trochanters in an attempt to move a posteriorly dislocated head into the acetabulum. At the same time, the thighs are gently abducted. Dislocation is diagnosed if there is a definite movement of the femoral head with or without a 'clunk' and suspected if there is limitation of abduction.

If an abnormality is found, the infant must be reviewed by a consultant paediatrician or orthopaedic surgeon who has a special interest in this condition. Ultrasound scanning of the hip at birth may be helpful, but radiographs are often negative until 3–4 months of age (see Chapter 6).

INFANT FEEDING

Inexperienced mothers are often concerned about feeding their infants. This concern may arise before and after the baby's birth and often the young mother is confused by conflicting advice from a variety of sources. The process is fundamentally simple provided the parent has a little basic knowledge and follows a few simple rules.

The nutritional requirements of any infant alter with the age of the baby and his physical well-being, and there is considerable variation amongst healthy babies.

On average, the fluid requirement of a baby is 150 ml/kg/day, which is usually achieved by the fifth day after birth. Fluid is lost from the body in the urine which is produced at a rate of 1–3 ml/kg/hr and by insensible water loss through respiration, stools and sweating which accounts for one-third of the total body fluid loss.

The energy intake of a normal full-term infant is 110 cal/kg/24 hr. This intake is required for growth, resting caloric expenditure and to compensate for losses through activity and to the environment. It is not usually achieved till the fifth day of life because of the comparatively small fluid intake, and during this period the baby relies on his body stores of glycogen and fat. For this reason, there is a weight loss of up to 10% of the body weight, but thereafter the baby gains weight at a rate of approximately 1% of the body weight per day (approximately 30 g/day in a term infant).

The nutritional needs of any normal infant may be provided by an adequate supply of maternal milk or suitably modified cow's milk formula. Human milk is the superior feed, and, if feasible, all newborn infants should be fed with their mother's milk. The advantages of breast feeding should be explained early in pregnancy and possible worries discussed with the parents-to-be, but at no time should the practitioner attempt to impose his views. Such attempts invariably fail and only cause unnecessary anxiety. Whichever form of feeding is chosen, the goal is to make the mother happy and the baby contented and well nourished. This may be achieved by using either breast feeding or proprietary milk preparations.

Breast Feeding

During pregnancy, the breasts radically alter under hormonal influences. Oestrogen increases the size and numbers of the duct system while progesterone causes proliferation of the alveolar cells. Fat deposition occurs in the breast under the influence of progesterone. Prolactin causes the alveolar cells to secrete milk, but this is inhibited in pregnancy by oestrogen and progesterone. After birth, with removal of the placenta, the supply of these hormones ceases and the effect of prolactin is unimpeded.

Prolactin continues to be secreted after birth by the anterior pituitary. This secretion is thought to be caused by neural impulses arising in the breast, generated as the baby suckles and empties the breast, although the precise nature and route of these neural impulses remain in doubt. Prolactin production is also dependent on the mother's emotional state and can certainly be inhibited by anxiety. This may be mediated by a prolactin-inhibiting factor from the hypothalamus.

When the baby is put to the breast, his cheek should be allowed to rest against the nipple. This initiates the rooting reflex which causes the baby's head to rotate to the side of the stimulus, turning his mouth to the nipple. The breast should be offered into the baby's mouth so that the areola is engulfed. As suckling commences, neural impulses are generated which cause the release of oxytocin by the posterior pituitary. This, in turn, causes contraction of myoepithelial cells around the alveoli, propelling milk along the ducts into the baby's mouth (the let-down reflex). This reflex may also be inhibited by maternal anxiety.

For the first few days, the breast produces colostrum. This has sufficient energy for these few days and also contains large quantities of immunoglobulins and maternal white cells. After a few days, breast milk secretion is established.

Breast feeding was the norm at the turn of the century in Western countries, but the development of breast milk substitutes and modifications of cow's milk led to the decline of breast feeding in most industrial countries and also in many developing countries. In the past decade the many unique qualities of breast feeding have been increasingly recognized, especially the effects on mother/ infant bonding, and its antibacterial properties, so its use should be advocated especially in developing countries where it may be life-saving.

The main advantages of breast feeding are:

1. Sterility and anti-bacterial affects. Breast milk presented to the baby is sterile or contains only contaminants of the mother's skin. It also enhances the resistance of the infant to infection by the provision of immunoglobulins, lactoferrin and macrophages. In addition it enhances the growth of lacto-bacilli and thus prevents overgrowth of the infant's intestine with pathogenic bacilli.

2. Nutritional advantages. Although there is great variation in the nutritional composition of human milk, breast milk is suitable for normal growth if the intake is adequate.

3. Financial aspects. Breast milk is inexpensive, a particularly important point for those living in developing countries and/or those living in poverty.

4. Psychological aspects. Breast feeding carried out successfully enhances mother/infant bonding to the advantage of both and may also help in the longer term to reduce the likelihood of breast cancer.

The contraindications to breast feeding are few. Many arguments are advanced but the majority of these reasons are specious.

1. Drug treatment to the mother. Many drugs are known to be secreted in breast milk and may cause harm to the newborn infant; some of the more commonly used are listed (Table 2.4). In other cases, the drugs are present in breast milk in amounts too small to be harmful. The secretion of some drugs in breast milk is not known and these should be avoided until more information has been gathered (see also Table 13.12, Chapter 13).

2. Malformation. Breast feeding cannot be accomplished in the infant with major malformations of the gastrointestinal tract until the malformation has been corrected. Babies with cleft palates may be able to breast feed eventually if the mother is encouraged to express her milk in the early weeks when feeding by artificial means may be necessary.

3. Severe maternal disease. Breast feeding is contraindicated in severe disease of the mother such as cancer of the breast, active tuberculosis, severe sepsis and post-partum psychosis.

4. Metabolic disease of the infant. There is a small number of infants with

Table 2.4 Some drugs to be avoided or used with caution in breast feeding mothers (modified from the British National Formulary, 1986)

Cardiovascular system
    Beta-adenoreceptor blocking drugs
    Phenindione
Respiratory system
    Aminophylline
    Cough mixtures containing iodine
Central nervous system
    Hypnotics and anxiolytics
    Alcohol
    Benzodiazepines
    Antipsychotic drugs
        Lithium salts
        Phenothiazine derivatives
    Narcotic analgesics
Antibiotics
    Chloramphenicol
    Tetracyclines
    Nalidixic acid
Endocrine system
    Oral hypoglycaemic agents
    Carbimazole
    Corticosteroids
    Oestrogens
Cytotoxic drugs

---

metabolic disease who require special milk formulae or substitutes because they accumulate toxic metabolites when fed on breast milk. These conditions include phenylketonuria, galactosaemia and primary lactose intolerance.

The maternal decision regarding the method of infant feeding is based on cultural, emotional and environmental factors and is seldom based on scientific principles. Improvement in the rate of breast feeding requires alteration of these attitudes, which is perhaps best achieved by the non-medical media.

The reasons given for refusal or discontinuation of breast feeding generally fall into three categories. The mother may dislike the concept of breast feeding. This is a problem which will not be overcome at the time of the infant's birth and may only be diminished by adequate education and counselling during pregnancy and sensible management of the post-partum period. The reasons for reluctance to breast feed may have a complex psychological background, often associated with feelings of embarrassment about the function of the breast. If one is to maintain the trust and confidence of the mother who does not wish to breast feed, despite adequate explanation of the advantages, it is far better that she bottle feed well rather than be forced into breast feeding with consequent conflicting emotions of anxiety, annoyance and hostility, involving herself, the baby and medical attendants.

Some mothers may express anxiety about the possible adverse affects of breast feeding on the eventual shape and contour of their breasts. It should be explained that the eventual change in breast shape is a consequence of pregnancy and age as distinct from lactation and suckling. Mothers may also be worried about the possibility of discomfort from engorgement and breast abscesses when they are preparing for delivery in the antenatal period. Adequate breast care during pregnancy and frequent breast feeds should reduce the risk of occurrence of these complications.

Some mothers find that breast feeding is inconvenient. Certainly many mothers soon return to work where the baby may not be permitted and where no provision is made for privacy. The let-down reflex may prove embarrassing with consequent wetting of her clothes. In these situations the physician should be realistic rather than idealistic when offering advice.

The infant should be allowed to suckle at the breast for 5-min periods. This stimulates the production of milk, allows the infant adequate quantities and enables the mother to accustom herself to feeding the baby. Frequent small feeds stimulate prolactin production during suckling and enhance oxytocin release which causes propulsion of the milk from the alveoli into the ducts around the nipple. Avoidance of excessive maternal analgesia during labour is important since if the baby is too sleepy to feed adequately, the breast may become engorged and tender. The mother herself may still be drowsy and have a diminished let-down reflex.

Most infants who are breast fed will become restless and hungry every 2–3 hr. They will establish a fairly regular pattern of feeding after 7–10 days, by 3 months will only require occasional feeds at night and usually sleep from 10.00 p.m. to 6.00 a.m. The baby should be fed as often as he requires and, generally, it is unrewarding to ask an infant in the first few days to obey any schedule! The baby will gradually set his own pattern of feeding which usually will emerge in the first days of life.

Table 2.5 Comparison of human milk, cow's milk, a standard infant formula and a humanized milk formula

Amount per 100 ml	*Human milk*	*Unmodified cow's milk*	*Standard formula*	*Humanized formula*
Carbohydrate (g) (lactose)	7.4	4.7	7.2	7.3
Fat (g)	4.2	3.8	3.6	3.6
Saturated (%)	52	63	47	44
Unsaturated (%)	48	37	53	56
Protein (g)	1.3	3.4	1.5	1.5
Casein (%)	40	82	82	40
Lactalbumin (%)	60	18	18	60
Energy (kcal)	70	65	65	65
(kJ)	285	275	275	275
Renal solute Load (mOsm/l)	86	225	100	96

Artificial Feeding

In spite of the persistent advocacy by health professionals of breast feeding, there are still many mothers who elect to feed their babies artificially. For the majority of infants born in the Western world, this proves to be entirely successful for all concerned; clearly in many parts of the developing world this is not the case.

The differences between human milk and cow's milk are listed in Table 2.5.

The differences are significant but nonetheless most infants will thrive perfectly well if fed on a modified cow's milk formula. The role of the attendant is to ensure that the infant's intake is adequate and that the milk is prepared properly and cleanly. In general, milk feeds are prepared using one level scoop of milk powder to 30 ml of water. However, many mothers add additional powder, thus making the milk too concentrated. In addition, many have the habit of putting additional foods like rusks into the bottle, thus rendering the feed unsuitable. The other major problem is the achievement of sterility. Many mothers do not clean the bottles properly, sometimes leave the teats unrinsed and often leave the packets or tins of milk uncovered, thus enhancing the possibility of the feed becoming infected. Bottles and teats should be washed and sterilized using dilute sodium hypochlorite solutions. Neither of these two problems need arise provided the mother is well taught and is prepared or is able to carry out such instructions.

CONCLUSION

Most mothers have normal pregnancies and deliver normal, healthy babies. The role of a mother's attendants is to observe the pregnancy and birth to ensure that all goes well for her and her infant, to give advice and encouragement when possible and to promote the happiness of all concerned with this unique event. Each mother and infant is special, and should be made to feel so.

FURTHER READING

Budin, P. (1907) *The Nursling*. Caxton, London.

Campbell, S. (1976) Fetal Growth. In Beard, R. W. and Nathanielsz, P. W. (eds), *Fetal Physiology and Medicine*. W. B. Saunders, London, pp. 271–301.

Friedman, E. A. (1954) The graphic analysis of labor. *Am. J. Obstet. Gynecol.* **68**: 1568.

Halliday, H. L., McClure, C. and Reid, M. (1985) *Handbook of Neonatal Intensive Care*, 2nd edn. Baillière Tindall, London.

Jelliffe, D. and Jelliffe, E. (1978) *Human Milk in the Modern World*. Oxford University Press, Oxford.

Klaus, M. H. and Kennell, J. H. (1982) *Parent–Infant Bonding*, 2nd edn. Mosby, St Louis, MO.

DHSS Guidelines (1986) *Screening for the Detection of Congenital Dislocation of the Hip*. DHSS, London.

Stern, L. (1984) *Drug Use in Pregnancy*. Adis Health Science Press.

Wald, N. J. (1984) *Antenatal and Neonatal Screening*. Oxford University Press, Oxford.

3

High-risk Pregnancy

INTRODUCTION

Over the past 50 years significant reductions have occurred in both maternal and neonatal mortality rates. These have been due to a complex variety of changes in the social circumstances and reproductive habits of parents, as well as to many significant advances in perinatal medicine.

Overall, the population of this country is healthier, better educated and more informed. Young couples now have the ability to plan their families, often making their choices on an economic basis leading to smaller, more prosperous family units who are healthier, better nourished and fitter than ever before. Thus health problems, including those of pregnancy, are becoming less frequent.

Coincidental with this social revolution have been major changes in perinatal medicine. The ability to investigate the fetus, improvements in anaesthesia and the development of neonatal care are a few examples of advances made in this area.

Most pregnancies are entirely normal and the role of the doctor is one of watchfulness, but there remains a hard core of pregnancies where either the mother, the fetus or both are threatened – the high-risk pregnancy. A high-risk pregnancy is one that is complicated by reason of maternal illness, or drug therapy, and from which one may anticipate an ill or immature baby.

IDENTIFICATION OF THE HIGH-RISK PREGNANCY

Identification of the high-risk pregnancy is usually done at the booking visit to an antenatal clinic or the general practitioner. However, those patients at greatest risk because of social disadvantage and ill health are often the least able or willing to avail themselves of the services provided.

Pre-pregnancy Counselling (see Chapter 2)

Any woman in good health, embarking on a planned pregnancy, has a better chance of a successful outcome than those less well prepared, such as the very young, the single or the socially disadvantaged. In ideal circumstances patients should be counselled before pregnancy occurs. The adverse effects of poor nutrition, smoking, alcohol and addictive drugs have all been recognized and given extensive publicity and yet many women fail to heed these warnings.

Pre-pregnancy counselling assumes even greater significance when the mother has a chronic disease such as diabetes mellitus or hypertension. Harley (1982) states that 'this is particularly important where it is considered that an alteration in treatment before conception will result in a better prognosis for mother and baby, and in addition problems already present or those that may occur can be discussed fully with the prospective parents and their anxieties allayed'.

The goal of pre-pregnancy counselling is laudable but this luxury is seldom afforded to the general practitioner or obstetrician.

During Pregnancy

Every prospective mother should be encouraged to attend her doctor as soon as she suspects that she is pregnant. At the first antenatal visit a careful history and examination are performed, on the basis of which risks can be identified (Table 3.1).

If risk is identified, shared care between general practitioner and consultant should only take place when there are exceptionally good communications between them. For patients with particular medical problems such as diabetes, many larger maternity hospitals have special clinics with physicians in attendance.

SUBSEQUENT ANTENATAL CARE

Antenatal care of the high-risk pregnancy requires frequent, regular assessment of both mother and fetus to detect any deterioration in the clinical condition of either. Routine observations as outlined in Chapter 2 form the basis of such care, and it is preferable that these women see one senior obstetrician regularly since this provides continuity as well as making the visit more pleasurable and rewarding for the mother. In addition to such observations, it may be necessary to investigate serially the condition of the fetus using other means.

ASSESSMENT OF FETAL WELL-BEING

Clinical Assessment

This provides basic information which may indicate that the patient should be further investigated using more sophisticated techniques.

Maternal Weight Gain

All women are weighed at each antenatal visit and a weight gain of less than 0.5 kg per week after the 16th week of pregnancy suggests that the fetus may not be

Table 3.1 Pregnancy risk factors

Primigravida
Age <16 or >35 years
Maternal weight at booking <45 kg or >90 kg
Grande multiparity
Medical complications
Previous obstetrical complications
History of perinatal death, prematurity or serious neonatal problems
Complication developing in present pregnancy

growing satisfactorily. There is some controversy about this, but a poor weight gain in the third trimester merits further investigation. Women who are either overweight or underweight at the outset of pregnancy have a higher incidence of problems.

Uterine Growth

It has been traditional to relate the gestational age to the position of the uterine fundus relative to the pubic symphysis, umbilicus or xiphisternum but such estimates are inaccurate in the third trimester of pregnancy. A better estimate of uterine growth is obtained by direct measurement of the fundal height above the pubic symphysis (Chapter 2).

Estimate of Fetal Weight

It is possible to estimate fetal weight by abdominal palpation. This degree of expertise is only achieved with considerable practice and each obstetrician should test his estimate against the actual weight of the baby at birth in order to improve his accuracy.

Amniotic Fluid Volume

It is possible to gain a rough estimate of the amniotic fluid volume (AFV) by abdominal palpation, feeling how much space the fetus has inside the uterus and how easy it is to ballotte fetal parts. Alterations in AFV are associated with a variety of fetal problems (Table 3.2) and merit further investigation.

Fetal Activity Counts

When it is suspected that the fetus may be compromised, an estimate of fetal well-being may be obtained by asking the mother to record the fetal movements she feels. If the movements are diminished the fetus may be compromised. The method usually employed is to have the mother record the time taken each day for the first ten movements she feels. These would normally be felt by the end of

Table 3.2 Altered amniotic fluid volume

Oligohydramnios	Fetal growth retardation
	Potter's syndrome
	Amniotic fluid leakage
Polyhydramnios	Twins
	Diabetes mellitus
	Neural tube defects
	Intestinal obstruction
	Swallowing defects/neuromuscular disorders
	Severe rhesus incompatibility

the morning and certainly before 12 hr have elapsed. One of the disadvantages of this method is that it is subjective and mothers may wrongly interpret an intra-abdominal movement as a fetal movement. This pitfall may be avoided by allowing the mother to correlate fetal activity with movements seen on an ultrasonic scanner.

These observations are only of value if they are recorded serially when any alteration in fetal activity may be significant.

Biophysical Assessment

Ultrasonic Examination

Real-time ultrasound scans in early pregnancy are now performed routinely in many hospitals. This procedure has several purposes: the gestational age can be confirmed (Chapter 2), multiple pregnancy diagnosed and many major congenital abnormalities can be recognized, particularly those of the neural tube.

Biparietal Diameter (BPD). The BPD may be used to monitor growth in pregnancy and normal growth rate curves are widely used (Chapter 2). Two types of abnormal pattern have been described by Campbell (1976) (Fig. 3.1). In the more common variety (Fig. 3.1A) the rate of head growth is normal until the last trimester when it slows excessively. This is called 'late flattening' or asymmetrical growth retardation and is seen in placental insufficiency, as in pre-eclampsia. In the less common type (Fig. 3.1B) head growth is slow from the second trimester. This is called 'low profile' or symmetrical growth retardation and is associated with intrauterine infection, fetal malformation or chromosome abnormality although it may be seen in normal small fetuses.

Abdominal Circumference (AC) and Abdominal Transverse Diameter (ATD). AC and ATD are measured at the level of the ductus venosus which is found by identifying the fetal spine, visualizing the aorta which lies anteriorly and rotating the transducer head through 90°. A reduction in these values may be seen in growth retardation because of the reduction in hepatic glycogen stores.

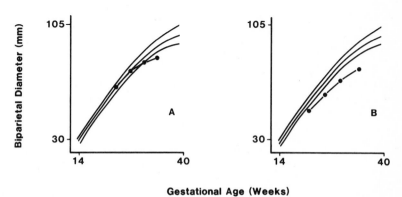

Figure 3.1 Biparietal diameter growth curves showing (**A**) 'late flattening' and (**B**) 'low-profile' types.

BPD/ATD Ratio. The BPD/ATD ratio is of value in later pregnancy in distinguishing between asymmetrical and symmetrical growth retardation. At 37 weeks in normal pregnancy this ratio is 1:1. After this time, trunk growth is greater than head growth so the ratio falls, for example 0.8:1. Failure of the baby to grow after 37 weeks will be detected if the ratio remains high or even increases. This may also be seen in asymmetrical growth retardation prior to 37 weeks; in symmetrical growth retardation the ratio usually remains 1:1.

Fetal Weight. A method for calculating fetal weight from the abdominal circumference has been devised (Table 3.3). This is replacing the less-accurate method of estimating fetal weight from the abdominal trunk diameter. It is especially useful when clinical palpation is made more difficult by a reduced amniotic fluid volume or if the mother is obese.

Amniotic Fluid Volume (AFV). AFV can be estimated ultrasonically and is useful in the third trimester when a pool of liquor of 3 cm or greater should be seen at the fundus and around the cord insertion at the umbilicus.

Placental architecture. Changes in placental architectural appearance which are related to fetal lung maturity can be seen with ultrasound (Fig. 3.2). These changes are due to the laying down of calcium and fibrin in the placenta. They do not seem to relate to gestational age but grade 2 and 3 appearances are said to be associated with mature fetal lungs as shown by a lecithin/sphingomyelin area ratio (LSAR) of 2.0 or more in greater than 80% of cases. This method is still experimental but has obvious potential if the clinical accuracy of this observation is confirmed.

Fetal Breathing Movements (FBM). Real-time ultrasound allows the observation of fetal chest wall movements. The nature and significance of these movements has yet to be fully elucidated but it is suggested that compromised fetuses show atypical rhythms and rates.

Fetal Body Movements. Gross movements may be observed directly with

Table 3.3 Weight prediction by abdominal circumference (AC)

AC (cm)	Weight (kg)
21.0	0.90
22.0	1.03
23.0	1.18
24.0	1.34
25.0	1.51
26.0	1.68
27.0	1.87
28.0	2.08
29.0	2.28
30.0	2.48
31.0	2.70
32.0	2.90
33.0	3.10
34.0	3.30
35.0	3.48

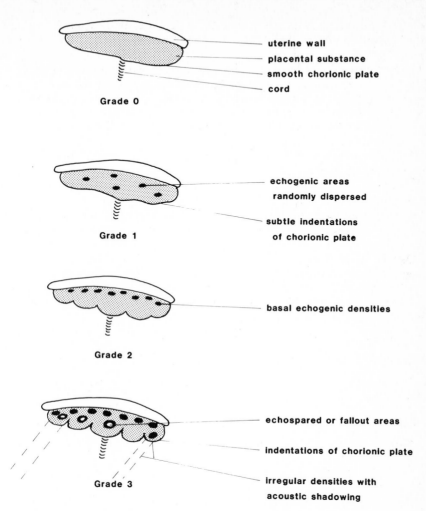

GRADES OF PLACENTAL MATURITY

uterine wall

placental substance

smooth chorionic plate

cord

Grade 0

echogenic areas
randomly dispersed

subtle indentations
of chorionic plate

Grade 1

basal echogenic densities

Grade 2

echospared or fallout areas

indentations of chorionic plate

irregular densities with
acoustic shadowing

Grade 3

Figure 3.2 Placental maturity on ultrasound examination. (After Hobbins *et al.* 1979).

ultrasound. The observation of at least two movements in 20 min is taken as normal.

Umbilical Artery Blood Waveforms. It has recently become possible to assess fetal umbilical artery blood waveforms using Doppler ultrasound. This technique is still experimental but derangements can be detected, especially in growth-retarded fetuses (Chapter 5).

Antenatal Cardiotocography

By antenatal cardiotocography fetal heart activity is detected using an ultrasonic device attached to the mother's anterior abdominal wall at the point where the fetal heart is most easily auscultated. The antepartum cardiotocogram (CTG) has developed along different lines in Europe and North America. In Europe, the non-stress test is most commonly used. This assesses the changes in the fetal heart in response to fetal movements and spontaneous uterine activity (Braxton-Hicks contractions). If the fetus is healthy there should be acceleration in the fetal heart rate in response to these movements. Fetal compromise is indicated if there is a lack of acceleration or a deceleration in response to such activity. Loss of variability may also indicate fetal compromise. However, the response may be altered by fetal sleep state, maternal sedation and by some fetal abnormalities. Fetal heart rate accelerations are uncommon in normal fetuses prior to 32 weeks gestation.

In North America, the oxytocin challenge test (OCT) has been used most commonly. Uterine activity is stimulated by an intravenous infusion of oxytocin and the effects of uterine contractions on the FHR are assessed. Decelerations similar to those seen in labour (*vide infra*) suggest fetal hypoxia.

Neither method is particularly satisfactory and both overdiagnose fetal compromise; however, improved results may be achieved if the test is performed serially.

Biochemical Assessment

Blood and Urine

Blood and urine tests have been widely used but to some extent have fallen into disrepute because of misleading results. Central to the problem is the fact that the feto-placental unit is an uncommonly complicated biochemical structure and it is difficult to see how simple biochemical investigations could be rewarding.

The two most commonly used investigations are estimations of serum human placental lactogen (HPL) and plasma and urinary oestriol levels. The former is used as a measure of placental size; the latter is an estimate of function of the feto-maternal unit.

HPL is secreted at a rate of 0.5 g/100 g of placental tissue in 24 hr at term. Maternal venous blood HPL rises from 2–5 µg/ml at 20 weeks to 11–22 µg/ml at 38 weeks before falling slightly at 40 weeks.

Oestriol is derived from dehydroepiandrosterone sulphate (DHEAS) which comes mainly from the fetus. The DHEAS produced by the fetal adrenal is aromatized in the placenta to form oestrogens, especially oestriol. Urinary oestriol levels rise from 2–10 mg/ml in 24 hr at 20 weeks to 10–40 mg/ml in 24 hr at term. Oestriol levels of less than 5 mg/ml in 24 hr late in the third trimester suggest fetal compromise. However, the daily output varies widely within individual patients, making the test of doubtful value. Serial measurements may be more helpful and suggest a diagnosis of placental sulphatase deficiency if they remain low without fetal compromise.

Amniotic Fluid

Amniocentesis involves the needle aspiration of amniotic fluid and is described in Chapter 6.

Table 3.4 Incidence of respiratory distress syndrome (RDS) by LSAR value

LSAR	RDS (%)
>2.5	1
>2.0	2
1.5–2.0	40
<1.5	75

In fetal assessment, amniocentesis is particularly useful in the management of rhesus incompatibility where the amniotic fluid bilirubin content reflects the degree of fetal haemolysis (Chapter 10). The fluid may also be used to assess fetal lung maturity prior to induction of labour before term. This is estimated by measuring the LSAR or by measurement of phosphatidyl glycerol (PG). An LSAR of greater than 2 indicates that the fetal lung is mature, and less than 1.5 indicates fetal lung immaturity (Table 3.4). The presence of PG in amniotic fluid indicates fetal lung maturity. Two problems of amniocentesis are that labour may be initiated and bleeding from the placenta may occur if it is inadvertently damaged. However, with use of ultrasound to guide the needle, these risks may be kept to a minimum. This is of particular importance in rhesus-negative mothers where fetal rhesus-positive cells may cause sensitization. For this reason, a Kleihauer test to detect the presence and quantity of fetal cells in the maternal circulation should be performed in all rhesus-negative women after the procedure and anti-D immunoglobulin given (Chapter 10).

The colour of the amniotic fluid may be observed non-invasively by amnioscopy. A flexible instrument is inserted through the cervix and the constituents of the liquor observed. The finding of any meconium prior to 40 weeks gestation and thick meconium after this time must be considered evidence of fetal compromise.

Fetal Blood

In certain specialist units the practice of sampling fetal blood by cordocentesis is becoming more widespread (Fig. 3.3). A needle is inserted into the cord under ultrasound control and the blood obtained can be used to measure the oxygen content, group and haemoglobin. Additionally, the haemoglobin type and enzyme assays may be performed. The procedure is not without risk and should only be performed by an experienced operator.

PLACE OF ASSESSMENT

Pregnancies at risk are managed initially in a special fetal assessment clinic. At this clinic, a group of doctors regularly perform assessment of fetal well-being as

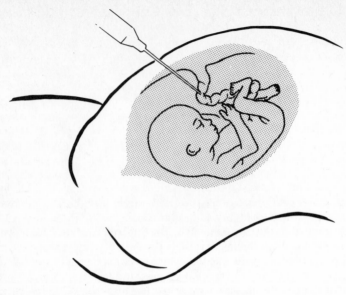

Figure 3.3 Fetal blood sampling by cordocentesis under ultrasound guidance.

outlined above. Such a system enables a considerable degree of expertise to be brought to bear on this relatively small number of women.

If there is evidence of deterioration in the health of either the mother or the fetus, immediate hospital admission is advised so that assessment can continue on a daily basis.

TIMING OF DELIVERY

Clearly this depends upon a number of factors which vary from individual to individual. Any decision should be made with full knowledge of the baby's potential for survival if delivered, and this may vary from hospital to hospital. In general, babies who have gestational ages of greater than 32 weeks have about a 5% mortality rate, while those less than 28 weeks face a risk of death of 30–50%. It must be stressed, however, that these figures vary from country to country and hospital to hospital (see Chapter 4).

ROUTE OF DELIVERY

There is a considerable debate about the best method of delivering mothers of babies at high risk; some favour elective Caesarean section, while others employ induction of labour in almost all circumstances. It is important not to be dogmatic. In general, if the condition of the fetus is seriously compromised, if there is malpresentation or if it is thought that labour will not be completed in 6 hr, it is better to effect the delivery by Caesarean section. If the fetal condition is less severe, and the cervix is favourable, induction of labour may be performed, but both mother and fetus should be carefully monitored during labour.

PLACE OF DELIVERY

It is foolhardy to deliver electively babies who are at risk in hospitals with poor facilities for looking after them. When possible, high-risk pregnancies should be cared for in large hospitals where perinatal intensive care is available.

The successful conduct of a high-risk delivery demands the closest possible co-operation between obstetrician and paediatrician. In these situations, there is a dynamic, ever-changing balance of risks to the fetus, and often to the mother, which requires regular reappraisal.

The obstetrician is responsible for both mother and fetus and has to balance these risks. The paediatrician can be of assistance by informing the obstetrician of the risks to the baby if born at a particular gestational age and weight and of the problems which may result from a particular maternal disease. To this end, it is important that each maternity unit constantly reappraises its results so that accurate, up-to-date information is available.

It is also important that the paediatrician who will look after the baby talks to the parents about the problems that the baby may face. Further, these meetings allow the parents to meet the paediatric team so that they realize that the baby will be looked after by people they know. A visit by the parents to the neonatal unit to meet the nursing staff and see the equipment may also be helpful. What worries parents most is the thought of their infant facing unimaginable difficulties in the care of unknown people. Discussion and preparation of the parents prior to the birth may help to allay these fears.

MANAGEMENT OF THE FETUS DURING LABOUR

High-risk fetuses are in danger of developing fetal distress in labour because they are already in jeopardy due to the hostile intrauterine environment. If vaginal delivery is attempted, every effort must be made to detect and correct fetal distress.

Signs of Fetal Distress

Meconium-stained Liquor

Meconium-stained liquor is always of concern, especially when the meconium is fresh, as denoted by its bright green colour, or when it is thick and associated with a low amniotic fluid volume. Asphyxia may lead to gasping and aspiration of meconium during or immediately after birth. The incidence of meconium-stained liquor increases post-term due to increased maturation of bowel motility. It is rare in a fetus of less than 34 weeks unless there is infection such as listeriosis.

Meconium staining is also common with breech presentation. In advanced labour, this is of doubtful significance but, in early labour, suggests fetal distress. Very occasionally, meconium-staining may be confused with bile staining secondary to gastro-intestinal obstruction or with altered blood in the amniotic fluid from previous amniocentesis or placental abruption.

Fetal Heart Rate

Auscultation of the fetal heart rate has long been a method of detecting fetal distress. Bradycardia, especially when associated with meconium-stained liquor, suggests that the fetus is in jeopardy.

Continuous monitoring of the fetal heart by a scalp electrode or by Doppler ultrasound has improved the detection rate of abnormalities of the fetal heart and its variability. Such monitoring in low-risk pregnancies is unrewarding, leading to increased Caesarean section rates, but if the technique is applied only in high-risk situations, clinically useful information is obtained.

The best method of monitoring the fetal heart in labour is to apply a fetal scalp electrode for the fetal ECG and to insert an intrauterine pressure catheter to record uterine contractions.

Changes in Baseline Rate. The normal baseline rate is between 120 and 160 beats/min. A consistent increase in rate above 160 beats/min may occur in the very preterm fetus, in fetal supraventricular tachycardia or in association with maternal pyrexia or drugs, e.g. ritodrine. Bradycardia, or a persistent heart rate below 120 beats/min may be due to congenital heart block, and occasionally occurs in the post-term fetus. Bradycardia occurring suddenly is associated with profound vagal stimulation and is ominous when prolonged. Fortunately it is most commonly seen in the second stage of labour when delivery can be expedited.

Variability. The time between successive heart beats (the beat-to-beat interval) varies in the healthy fetus. The variation in the beat-to-beat interval can only be calculated accurately from computer analysis of the interval between each R wave in the ECG complex. Baseline heart rate variability, which is a close approximation to this, may be discerned from the change in rate with each beat recorded by the pen of the chart recorder; as variability is lost, the trace becomes flatter (less reactive).

Normal variability depends upon the two components of the autonomic system. The sympathetic system tends to keep the baseline heart rate high while

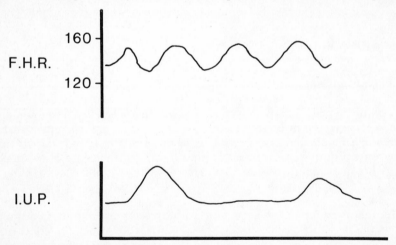

Figure 3.4 Sinusoidal fetal heart rate (FHR) pattern. Two uterine contractions are shown. IUP = intrauterine pressure.

the parasympathetic system phasically slows it down. Variability is less in the preterm fetus, but increases as the autonomic nervous system develops. It is also reduced by centrally depressant drugs such as narcotic analgesics, sedatives and local anaesthetic agents, all of which cross the placenta. Hypoxia, when prolonged and severe, also reduces heart rate variability. Occasionally, particularly when fetal anaemia is present, variability may be lost and replaced by regular slow oscillations of 3–5 cycles/min – the sinusoidal pattern (Fig. 3.4) – which is an ominous sign.

Periodic Changes with Uterine Contractions. Accelerations in fetal heart rate are associated with uterine contractions and fetal movement, and indicate a reactive, healthy fetus.

Decelerations or transient falls in fetal heart rate are not uncommon during labour and occur in three distinct patterns. The first two are consistently uniform in configuration while the third is variable. Occasionally mixed patterns may occur.

Early decelerations (Fig. 3.5) have a characteristic, uniform, V-shaped pattern which is coincident with the uterine contraction. The nadir of the deceleration occurs at the same time as the peak of the contraction and often is in proportion to the intrauterine pressure. This pattern may be seen in the late first stage of labour and is thought to be due to head compression mediated by pressure of the cervix on the anterior fontanelle. The consequent rise in intracerebral pressure stimulates the vagus nerve causing a slowing of the heart rate. The pattern is often transient and occurs most commonly when the fetus is in the occipito-posterior position. When early decelerations are persistent, severe or prolonged, or occur in association with the passage of meconium, the scalp blood pH should be measured and delivery expedited if the pH is below 7.20 (*vide infra*).

Late decelerations (Fig. 3.5) are thought to be due to hypoxia and acidosis resulting from utero-placental insufficiency which is exacerbated by the uterine contraction. The lowest fetal heart rate occurs after the peak of the contraction has passed, and recovery to the baseline does not occur until after the intra-uterine pressure has returned to the resting level. In the less severely affected fetus, the heart rate may temporarily overshoot the baseline, probably due to catecholamine release. Tachycardia between contractions or failure of the fetal heart rate to return to the baseline indicates progressive deterioration in the fetal condition. On occasion, this pattern may be caused by overstimulation of uterine action by an oxytocic infusion and may be corrected by stopping this. Hypotension in association with epidural anaesthesia may also precipitate this pattern, and should be corrected by intravenous infusion of fluids and ensuring the mother is nursed on her side.

Variable decelerations (Fig. 3.5) are variable both in shape and in their timing relative to the onset of contractions, and are due to umbilical cord compression. The change in heart rate is normally abrupt and is due to reflex changes in vagal tone caused by alterations in fetal blood pressure detected by the baroreceptors. Cord compression leads to transient hypertension and consequent slowing of the heart rate.

The possibility that compression is due to cord prolapse should be excluded by vaginal examination. Transient variable decelerations during labour are common and often disappear when the maternal position is altered. When the pattern persists, or a mixed pattern (see below) develops, a scalp blood pH should be performed or the mother delivered.

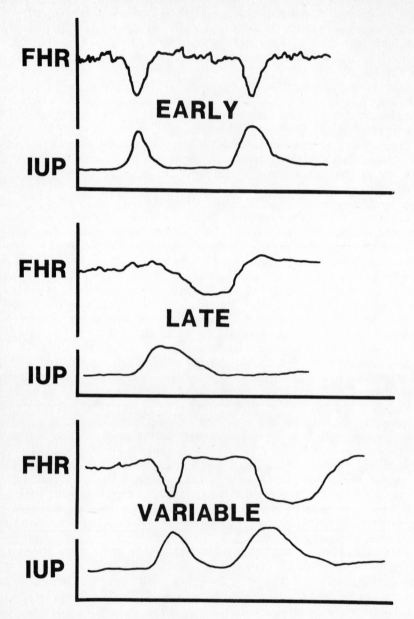

Figure 3.5 Fetal heart rate (FHR) patterns of early, late and variable decelerations. IUP = intrauterine pressure.

Mixed pattern: when variable decelerations are prolonged, recovery to the baseline heart rate may be slow, suggesting increasing fetal distress.

The most ominous pattern is a combination of late deceleration and poor baseline variability.

Fetal Blood Sampling

The measurement of the pH of fetal scalp blood can detect significant acidosis. This technique is used to help evaluate abnormal fetal heart rate patterns or meconium-stained liquor.

A pH of 7.20 or below indicates severe acidosis, in which case immediate delivery is the rule. When the pH is between 7.20 and 7.25, the test is repeated within an hour if labour is progressing normally and no other problems are anticipated. A pH greater than 7.25 is considered normal and permits further careful observation of the labour.

Blood can readily be obtained from the fetal scalp when the cervix is more than 3 cm dilated by using an amnioscope passed through the cervix. Blood is obtained by incising the fetal scalp with a guarded knife blade on a long handle and collected into a heparinized capillary tube (Fig. 3.6). The procedure should

Figure 3.6 Fetal scalp blood sampling for pH measurement.

be carried out with the mother in the lateral position to minimize the effect of vena caval compression and the resulting hypotension. Fetal scalp blood sampling should be a regular procedure being carried out in all cases with an abnormal fetal heart rate. Only when the procedure is carried out carefully, correctly and often can the results be trusted by all the labour ward staff.

Management of Fetal Distress in High-risk Pregnancy

Management of fetal distress in high-risk pregnancy is essentially the same as when distress appears in a normal labour with one major proviso – the fetus may already be compromised prior to the onset of the hypoxic episode and thus his tolerance is considerably more limited. The reaction of the perinatal team must therefore be even more prompt.

In general, the rule is to deliver the mother as quickly as possible by whatever method is appropriate. The route will depend upon the stage of labour and the presentation of the infant.

NEONATAL MANAGEMENT

It is possible to anticipate and prevent many of the problems that may arise in the newborn if sufficient attention is paid to the history of the mother, the pregnancy and the labour. The prevention of disease is often simple and free from risk, whereas treatment may be unsuccessful. One example is in the small-for-gestational age infant where the risk of hypoglycaemia is high. Regular measurement of blood sugar levels and early feeding should detect hypoglycaemia and prevent convulsions. However, if the baby develops hypoglycaemia, irreversible brain damage may occur.

The second principle is that diagnosis and treatment of these babies must be prompt since the margin of tolerance is narrow. Medical practitioners treating newborn infants for the first time are often amazed by the speed at which an apparently well infant can become gravely ill.

The third principle is that senior medical staff should be available at all times to look after these infants. Important decisions having huge significance for the infant and his family should only be made at senior level.

When there has been consultation prior to the onset of labour, the neonatal team will be in a position to carry out any appropriate treatment necessary. Specific disease problems of pregnancy and the neonatal period are discussed in subsequent chapters so particular discussion, apart from birth asphyxia, is inappropriate here.

BIRTH ASPHYXIA

Asphyxia is a major problem in high-risk pregnancy because of fetal compromise prior to the onset of labour. It is important as a cause of death and irreversible brain damage, but the effects on other organs such as the heart, kidney and gut should not be ignored.

Pathophysiology

The major physiological changes in birth asphyxia are summarized in Fig. 3.7. In birth asphyxia, both respiratory failure and circulatory failure may occur so that the blood supply to all organs of the body is reduced in quantity as well as quality. Since respiration is impaired, the arterial oxygen tension (P_{aO_2}) falls, the arterial carbon dioxide tension (P_{aCO_2}) rises and a respiratory acidosis develops. As circulatory failure occurs, perfusion falls, and there is an accumulation of lactic acid thus making the acidosis worse.

In addition to these, there may be failure of adaptation of the normal circulatory changes which occur at birth. There may be persistent pulmonary vasoconstriction with poor pulmonary perfusion. The vasoconstriction leads to an increase in the right atrial pressure while the reduced pulmonary flow leads to a fall in left atrial pressure. These two effects lead to right-to-left shunting of blood at atrial level. In addition, the pulmonary artery pressure may be greater than the aortic pressure causing further right-to-left shunting of blood across the patent ductus arteriosus. These two events constitute the syndrome of persistent fetal circulation.

The resistance of the neonate to asphyxia is greater than that of the adult because of the increased neonatal cardiac glycogen stores and also because the

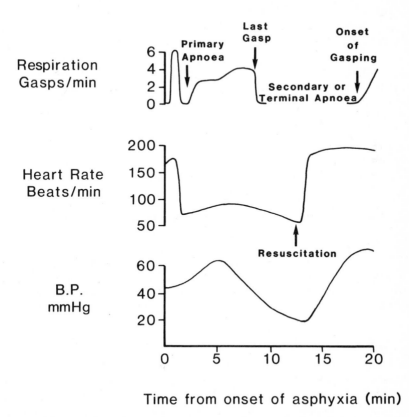

Figure 3.7 Physiological changes in birth asphyxia.

neonatal brain can utilize fatty acids as energy sources. In addition, the cerebral blood flow may be maintained because of the vasodilatory effect of carbon dioxide on the neonatal cerebral circulation.

Treatment of the Infant with Birth Asphyxia

The birth of an infant who has been at risk *in utero* should always be attended by a medically qualified person experienced in neonatal resuscitation. Preferably, this person should be a paediatrician since the further, longer-term management of the infant will rest with him. However, in many cases this is not possible so all those concerned with the labour room care of babies should be familiar with the standard methods of resuscitation. There are two cardinal rules which should be obeyed at all times by inexpert medical personnel:

1. **Get help.**
2. **Keep going until a senior doctor says 'Stop'.**

The main essential in the treatment of an infant with birth asphyxia is that the procedure is carried out in a logical and calm manner, using readily available equipment. The first priority is to dry the baby and to keep him warm. This is easily achieved in a few seconds by drying the baby with a prewarmed towel and placing him below a radiant heat source. The next step is to decide what treatment is necessary. The Apgar score is the routine method of assessing the clinical condition of a newborn at birth (Chapter 2). This method is useful to the relatively inexperienced clinician and provides a guide to further treatment. If the infant is pink and active with a good cry, clearly no further treatment is necessary. If the baby is breathing poorly but is pink and has a heart rate greater than 100, gentle peripheral stimulation, suctioning of the airway to remove blood or secretions and bag and mask ventilation using either an anaesthetic bag or a recoil bag (Laerdal or Ohio) will usually prove to be sufficient. The major difficulty encountered by inexperienced staff is an inability to ventilate effectively using a bag and mask. The usual problem is that the seal between the infant's face and the mask is not firm enough. Ventilation may be aided by slightly extending the infant's neck.

If there is continued deterioration or if the infant is born apnoeic and shocked, endotracheal intubation is necessary. This is done under direct vision using a laryngoscope and an appropriate size of endotracheal tube (2.5 mm for infants less than 1000 g, 3.0 mm for infants 1000–2000 g and 3.5 mm for infants greater than 2000 g).

The cardiac output of the baby may remain low with a pronounced bradycardia even when effective ventilation has been established. Such infants require external cardiac massage if the heart rate is less than 50–60 beats/min, and volume expansion using salt-poor albumin. Intravenous sodium bicarbonate may be given via an umbilical venous catheter and intravenous adrenaline is sometimes necessary. Naloxone may be given if it is felt that the infant has been depressed by narcotic analgesics.

On occasion, in spite of these measures, the infant fails to respond. This may be due to a variety of problems such as the development of a pneumothorax, the presence of a diaphragmatic hernia or of pulmonary hypoplasia or may be due to technical problems such as the application of an insufficient inflation pressure. However, one problem that may be overlooked is that of fetal blood loss. If the infant remains pale in spite of the application of the measures given above and if the history is suggestive of the possibility of fetal blood loss such as placental abruption, a transfusion of Group O negative blood should be given.

Subsequent Problems and their Management

Infants who have been severely asphyxiated should be admitted to an intensive-care nursery for observation and management.

Immediate attention is devoted to the detection and management of problems that may make the prognosis worse. It is necessary to measure the blood gases, the blood sugar, the blood pressure and packed cell volume in all such infants and to correct any abnormalities by infusions of sodium bicarbonate, dextrose and blood. Additionally, if the infant is still having significant respiratory difficulties, intermittent positive pressure ventilation may be necessary. Whenever the condition of the infant has been stabilized, further investigation and treatment are directed at the possible effects of the asphyxial insult on the major organ systems.

Hypoxic-ischaemic Encephalopathy

This is the most important consequence of asphyxia since damage to the brain may lead to death or irreversible damage. The infant may be comatose, unresponsive to stimuli and may develop periodic respiration or apnoeic attacks. The infant may exhibit decerebrate posturing. Dysconjugate eye movements and fixed, dilated pupils may be seen. Clonic seizures may occur but convulsive activity may be subtle, for example lip smacking and eye jerking. Hypotonia is common. Other infants may be less severely affected. They are irritable, tend to be hypertonic and have high-pitched cries. Respiratory problems and seizures are less common in these babies.

A method of assessing the degree of encephalopathy in common usage is that of Sarnat and Sarnat (1976) (Table 3.5). Infants are grouped into three stages, essentially on the basis of level of consciousness, autonomic activity, muscle tone, reflexes and the presence of seizures. Those in stage 1 generally have a good prognosis for life and neurological function, those in stage III nearly always do badly and for stage II the prognosis is variable (Table 3.6).

The management of these infants is extremely difficult; many methods of treatment are employed but there has been little systematic study of the effects of such treatments.

Dexamethasone for 48 hr is often used to treat cerebral oedema, but the effects are questionable. The same may be said for the use of diuretics and mannitol. Hyperventilation is frequently used in the most severely affected infants in an attempt to control cerebral oedema, but its effects are probably short-lived. Phenobarbitone has been used to control seizures and to prevent extension of haemorrhage, especially in the preterm infant, but this latter use has been recently called into question.

What does seem sensible is to maintain such essential functions as respiration and cardiac output and to try to prevent such secondary phenomena as hypoglycaemia which are known to increase cerebral damage.

Table 3.5 Sarnat scoring system for hypoxic-ischaemic encephalopathy

	Stage I	*Stage II*	*Stage III*
Level of consciousness	Hyperalert	Lethargic or obtunded	Stuporous
Neuromuscular control			
Muscle tone	Normal	Mild hypotonia	Flaccid
Posture	Mild distal flexion	Strong distal flexion	Intermittent decerebration
Stretch reflexes	Overactive	Overactive	Decreased or absent
Segmental myoclonus	Present	Present	Absent
Complex reflexes			
Suck	Normal	Weak or absent	Absent
Moro	Strong, low threshold	Weak, incomplete high threshold	Absent
Oculovestibular	Normal	Overactive	Weak or absent
Tonic neck	Slight	Strong	Absent
Autonomic function	Generalized sympathetic	Generalized parasympathetic	Both systems depressed
Pupils	Mydriasis	Miosis	Variable: often unequal; poor light reflex
Heart rate	Tachycardia	Bradycardia	Variable
Bronchial and salivary secretions	Sparse	Profuse	Variable
Gastrointestinal motility	Normal or decreased	Increased; diarrhoea	Variable
Seizures	None	Common; focal or multifocal	Uncommon (excluding decerebration)
Electro-encephalogram findings	Normal (awake)	Early: low-voltage continuous delta and theta. Later: periodic pattern (awake). Seizures: focal 1–10 1.5-Hz spike-and-wave	Early; periodic pattern with isopotential phases. Later: totally isopotential
Duration	<24 hr	2–14 days	Hours to weeks

Cardiovascular Complications

Infants who have suffered severe birth asphxia may develop myocardial ischaemia leading to cardiac failure. This, in turn, may cause hypotension and further tissue hypoperfusion. The diagnosis is suspected in an asphyxiated infant who develops pulmonary oedema, hepatomegaly and poor peripheral perfusion. It is confirmed by observing cardiomegaly on a chest radiograph and ECG changes of myocardial ischaemia.

If the infant is hypotensive, the blood pressure should be corrected by a

Table 3.6 Sarnat score and adverse outcome (death or handicap)

Sarnat score	Adverse outcome (%)
Stage I	0
Stage II	40
Stage III	>95

Royal Maternity Hospital Belfast (1985)

transfusion of blood or albumin, and a diuretic such as frusemide should be given when the blood pressure is normal. Dopamine may raise blood pressure and improve renal perfusion.

Pulmonary Complications

Meconium aspiration syndrome and persistent fetal circulation may occur (Chapter 8).

Renal Problems

In birth asphyxia, the renal blood flow may be seriously reduced, leading to renal cortical or medullary necrosis. The infant later develops oliguria with proteinuria and haematuria. When this occurs, a diuretic may be given to try to force a diuresis but if this fails fluid restriction is mandatory.

Intestinal Complications

Occasionally, infants who have been asphyxiated develop necrotizing enterocolitis (NEC). This condition is discussed in Chapter 4.

Metabolic Complications

Birth asphyxia is often associated with hypoglycaemia which is corrected by infusion of dextrose. Hyponatraemia may also occur because of an inappropriate secretion of antidiuretic hormone (ADH) and is treated by fluid restriction.

Haematological Problems

Disseminated intravascular coagulation (DIC) and haemorrhagic disease of the newborn may both occur in the asphyxiated infant. If bleeding occurs in such infants at venepuncture sites or heel pricks, a blood coagulation profile should be carried out. In haemorrhagic disease, the prothrombin time is prolonged but the platelet count, thrombin time and fibrinogen titre are normal. Treatment is with vitamin K. In DIC, the prothrombin and thrombin times are prolonged, the platelet count is low and fibrinogen degradation products are increased in the blood. Treatment is by infusion of fresh frozen plasma or fresh blood.

It should be clear by now that treatment of the asphyxiated infant may be extremely complicated; there are often conflicting requirements – for example, if the infant is hypotensive and in cardiac failure, the treatment of the former may make the latter worse. Such infants require expert supervision with treatment planned to correct abnormalities of all organ systems.

Outcome in Severely Asphyxiated Infants

This is one of the most worrying areas in perinatal medicine as it is extremely difficult to be sure if severe irreversible brain damage has occurred and that intensive therapy should be withdrawn.

The Sarnat score is helpful; the longer the infant remains in stage II the worse the outlook and stage III is almost invariably associated with poor outcome; persistent seizure activity or apnoeic episodes are also of grave significance.

In such infants the EEG may be isoelectric or only show seizure activity, there may be elevation of the brain specific isoenzyme of creatine kinase in the spinal fluid and computer axial tomographs (CAT scan) may show areas of haemorrhage, ischaemia or necrosis; ultrasonic examination of the infant's brain is of limited value in the term infant. Further information may be gleaned from such techniques as cerebral blood flow studies using Doppler ultrasound, auditory and visual evoked responses and power spectral analysis of the EEG, but these are still experimental and are not widely available.

The decision to withdraw life-support systems can only be made when all the information has been acquired and when two consultant paediatricians agree that the evidence points to irreparable damage. The parents should be fully informed, and must give their consent before the baby is allowed to die in their arms.

FURTHER READING

Campbell, S. (1976) Fetal growth. In Beard, R. W. and Nathanielsz, P. W. (Eds), *Fetal Physiology and Medicine*. W. B. Saunders, London.

Dawes, G. S. (1968) *Fetal and Neonatal Physiology*. Chicago Year Book Medical, Chicago.

Finer, N. N., Robertson, C. M., Peters, K. L. and Coward, J. H. (1983) Factors affecting outcome in hypoxic-ischemic encephalopathy in term infants. *Am. J. Dis. Child* 138: 21.

Halliday, H. L., McClure, G. and Reid, M. (1985) *Handbook of Neonatal Intensive Care*, 2nd edn. Baillière Tindall, London.

Harley, J. M. G. (1982) Foreword – pre-pregnancy counselling in obstetrics. *Clin. Obstet. Gynaecol.* 9: 1.

Hobbins, J. C. (1979) Ultrasound in perinatal medicine. In Gluck, L. (Ed.), *Obstetric Decisions and Neonatal Outcome, Report of the 78th Ross Conference on Pediatric Research*. Ross Labs, Columbus, Oh. p. 83.

Lissauer, T. (1981) Neonatal resuscitation. *Hosp.* Update 7: 109.

Pearson, J. F. (1982) Monitoring high-risk pregnancy. In Bonner, J. (Ed.), *Recent*

Advances in Obstetrics and Gynaecology. Churchill Livingstone, Edinburgh, Vol. 14, pp. 3–24.

Sarnat, H. B. and Sarnat, M. S. (1976) Neonatal encephalopathy following fetal distress. *Arch. Neurol.* **33**: 696.

Quilligan, E. J. (1979) Update on fetal monitoring. *Clin. Obstet. Gynaecol.* **6**: no. 2.

4
Preterm Birth

INTRODUCTION

It has been realized for many years that babies who are born before term may die or become handicapped and today these babies still account for about 70% of the deaths occurring in the perinatal period.

A few decades ago the general view was that all that should be done for the preterm baby was to handle him as little as possible and keep him warm and nourished. Recently, developments in perinatal medicine have led to a much more aggressive approach in the management of the preterm baby with a consequent reduction in the morbidity and mortality rates.

Definition

An infant is said to be preterm when delivery occurs before the end of the 37th week of gestation.

AETIOLOGY OF PREMATURITY

The majority of babies are born preterm because of some complication of pregnancy such as antepartum haemorrhage, hypertension or cervical incompetence. In approximately 30%, delivery has occurred following spontaneous preterm labour which has happened for no known reason. Since the causes of the preterm birth vary, the effects on the fetus and newborn also differ. For example, an infant born as a result of placental abruption may suffer from respiratory distress syndrome, hypoxia and shock. In contrast, a baby delivered after prolonged rupture of the membranes may have mature lungs but suffer from infection. Analysis of the events in each case allows prediction of possible problems, prevention of some of them and preparation to deal with the remainder after birth.

PRETERM LABOUR

The trigger mechanism for spontaneous preterm labour is uncertain. In animals, a rise in plasma corticosteroids from the fetal adrenal occurs about 7 days before labour, leading to an increased production of oestrogens by the placenta. This in turn causes the release of prostaglandin precursors which directly stimulate the myometrium. In humans, these hormonal events do not seem to occur in the same manner, but local release of prostaglandins may be an important final event.

There are a number of factors associated with preterm birth which predispose to this event (Table 4.1). These have been used as the basis of scoring systems to detect the mother at risk of preterm labour.

Table 4.1 Factors associated with preterm labour

Low social class, poverty and low maternal age
Cervical incompetence/uterine abnormality
Polyhydramnios
Antepartum haemorrhage
Infection and fever
Trauma
Smoking and alcohol
Previous preterm labour
Multiple pregnancy

CLINICAL PRESENTATION

Preterm labour is often diagnosed late because the mother may not recognize the significance of her abdominal pains or the diagnosis may be mistaken by her attending doctor. Characteristically, the pains increase in strength, duration and frequency, features which help to differentiate preterm labour from Braxton-Hicks contractions. Urinary tract infections especially may closely mimic preterm labour but can also initiate contractions. A 'show' may occur or the membranes rupture prior to admission to hospital. Some women have few symptoms until very late and only present in advanced labour.

MANAGEMENT

The first requirement is to determine whether labour has commenced or not. When the membranes are intact, the diagnosis should be confirmed by a vaginal examination which will demonstrate cervical dilatation and effacement. If the membranes are thought to be ruptured, a speculum should be passed so that the condition of the cervix may be inspected. Any liquor seen in the posterior fornix should be aspirated and the 'fern' test carried out. In this test, a drop of fluid dried on a microscope slide shows characteristic fern patterns confirming the fluid to be liquor. The remainder of the fluid should be sent for estimation of lecithin/sphingomyelin area ratio (LSAR), Gram stain and culture.

The next requirement is to determine the duration of the pregnancy since the chance of survival of the baby depends largely on its gestational age (Fig. 4.1). In about 60% of women the gestational age may be known because the mother is sure of her dates, but in the remainder there is uncertainty because of unknown dates, irregular menstrual cycles or the use of the oral contraceptive pill within 3 months of conception. In these circumstances, early pregnancy records with clinical and ultrasonic estimation of gestational age will prove invaluable. Unfortunately, it is often those women who deliver prematurely who do not attend antenatal clinics early.

If there is uncertainty, an estimate of the fetal size may be obtained by abdominal palpation and ultrasonic examination of the fetus but it must be recognized that such results may be inaccurate and not correlate well with gestational age (Chapter 3). The ultrasonic scan is also important to confirm the presentation and to exclude major fetal abnormality or multiple pregnancy.

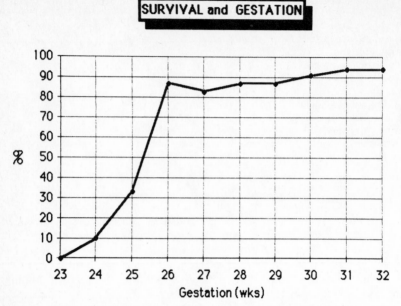

Figure 4.1 Survival rates by gestational age for babies born in the Royal Maternity Hospital, Belfast, 1981–1983. Babies with lethal congenital anomalies and those not resuscitated in the labour ward have been excluded from the analysis.

Table 4.2 shows the correlation of weight at birth with rates of survival and handicap.

Once the gestational age and fetal size are known further management depends on whether or not the membranes are intact (Fig. 4.2).

Intact Membranes

If the woman is not in labour and the cause of her symptoms has been elucidated, she is allowed home or given appropriate treatment. If she is in labour, this is allowed to progress if the fetus is of more than 32 weeks gestation and at least 1500 g estimated weight, and good neonatal facilities are available.

Table 4.2 Survival and handicap rate by birth weight

Birth weight (g)	Overall survival (%)	Handicap (%)	Intact survival (%)
501–750	14	33	9
750–1000	49	13	42
1001–1250	80	8	74
1251–1500	81	4	87

Royal Maternity Hospital, Belfast, 1981–1983.

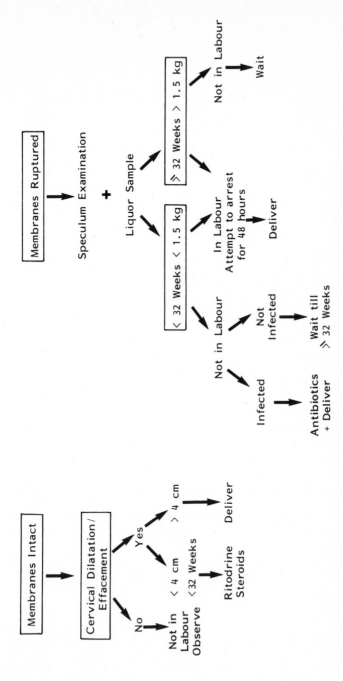

Figure 4.2 Management of preterm labour depending upon whether membranes are intact or have ruptured.

If the gestational age is less than 32 weeks and the cervix is less than 4 cm dilated, a beta-adrenergic agonist such as ritodrine is given. If the cervix is more than 4 cm dilated, the drug is usually ineffective and labour is allowed to progress. There is considerable discussion on its value in preterm labour. Certainly, the initial expectations were too high but it would appear that unless there are contraindications, such as antepartum haemorrhage and severe hypertension, the use of ritodrine is justified. Many patients experience unpleasant feelings such as palpitations and sweating. Steroids are also given to accelerate fetal lung maturation and help prevent hyaline membrane disease. Again, this means of treatment is not accepted by all but the general consensus is that steroids should be used. Betamethasone is given in a dose of 4 mg intramuscularly, every 8 hr for 48 hr, repeated every week until 32 weeks is reached. The most dangerous side-effect of treatment with ritodrine and steroids is acute pulmonary oedema.

Where good neonatal facilities do not exist, the mother and fetus should be transferred to a major centre if this is feasible. Ritodrine may be used during transfer provided the patient is accompanied by an experienced doctor.

Ruptured Membranes

If the patient is not in labour, she should rest in bed. Evidence to suggest the development of maternal infection such as fever, a rise in the white cell count or an increase in C-reactive protein should be sought and the patient delivered if infection occurs. Antibiotics in labour will reduce the incidence of serious neonatal infection but large doses are needed, for example ampicillin 2 g intravenously. If the patient remains well and uninfected, she should remain in hospital until spontaneous labour occurs. Throughout the period of stay in hospital evidence of fetal compromise should be sought (Chapter 4) and the fetus delivered if it is found.

A major problem arises when spontaneous rupture of the membranes occurs before 22 weeks. It is not quite clear how this situation should be managed but information is accumulating that the outcome is poor irrespective of the treatment employed because of the likelihood of pulmonary hypoplasia.

If the patient is in labour and the gestational age is less than 32 weeks, ritodrine should be used for 48 hr to try to stop labour unless there are signs of intrauterine infection. Steroids should not be used because they increase the risk of such infection. If the gestational age is 32 weeks or more, labour should be allowed to progress.

DELIVERY

If preterm labour is not preventable, it is important to have experienced personnel supervise both labour and the immediate care of the newborn infant. Vaginal delivery is preferred in vertex presentations provided the condition of the fetus can be closely monitored and the labour conducted by an experienced obstetrician. Ideally, delivery should be performed under epidural anaesthesia. A generous episiotomy aids the control of the head by the operator's hands, prevents the rapid release of the constricting effect of the vulval ring and so helps prevent intracranial haemorrhage. Delivery is aided by gentle fundal pressure and, immediately after birth, the baby should be held at the level of the placenta until the cord is clamped. Unless the baby is obviously asphyxiated, this should be done after the first breath and allows transfusion of placental blood to the baby. Early clamping or elevation of the baby above the plane of the mother's abdomen may lead to a significant reduction in the baby's blood volume; late clamping or keeping the baby dependent may lead to polycythaemia and jaundice.

If fetal distress occurs in labour, Caesarean section should be performed unless the fetus has been deemed non-viable, for example if the estimated fetal weight is less than 700 g or the gestational age less than 25 weeks.

The delivery of the preterm breech is a vexed question in obstetrics. Many advocate Caesarean section but this should not be undertaken lightly. The lower uterine segment may be extremely ill-formed and it may be necessary to do a classical Caesarean section. This may be traumatic to the mother and fetus and predisposes to uterine rupture in subsequent pregnancies. However, Caesarean section may be justified if the estimated fetal weight is between 1000 and 1500 g.

If a decision is made to allow vaginal delivery, an experienced obstetrician must be present to supervise this. The main danger is that the baby may be born through an incompletely dilated cervix which allows passage of the body but, then, traps the head and neck. If this arises, it may be necessary to incise the cervix but this situation is usually preventable if the mother is not allowed to bear down until the cervix is fully dilated. In addition to this major risk, cord prolapse and compound presentation are much more common in the preterm breech both of which require expert immediate attention. In such deliveries, a balance must be struck between handling the baby too much which may traumatize him or too little with imperfect control of the delivery which can allow the head to suddenly deliver and cause intracranial haemorrhage.

Many babies are born after a complication of pregnancy such as severe pre-eclampsia (Chapter 9) or antepartum haemorrhage (Chapter 11). In these circumstances delivery is almost invariably by Caesarean section unless spontaneous labour has begun or the cervix is favourable and the fetus in good condition.

RESUSCITATION OF THE VERY LOW-BIRTH-WEIGHT INFANT

Perinatal asphyxia is an important determinant of outcome in the low-birth-weight infant. The detrimental effects of asphyxia are seen in the brain, lungs, kidney, gastrointestinal tract and heart, and exacerbate the pre-existing physiological immaturity. Resuscitation of the very low-birth-weight infant should proceed as described for the full-term asphyxiated infant (Chapter 3) though some special requirements are needed, such as a smaller endotracheal tube, that is size 2.5 and 3.0 mm and smaller umbilical vessel catheters, 3.5 FG.

The very low-birth-weight infant is often intubated electively for resuscitation. This technique requires skill and should be performed by the most experienced person available. Heat loss is pronounced in the tiny baby so resuscitation must take place under a good radiant heater in a warm labour ward. When stable, the infant should be immediately transferred to the special-care or intensive-care baby unit, after the parents have been allowed a short period with their infant.

ADMISSION OF THE PRETERM BABY

The assessment of the baby should be in a warmed environment either under a radiant warmer or in a servo-controlled incubator. Certain infants, especially those of very low birth weight, may need help very early, but many larger babies do very well with minimal treatment.

The gestational age of the infant may be known from the menstrual history or from scan measurements but a clinical estimate of gestational age is mandatory in any baby born prematurely. Normally, formal estimation of the gestational age is done using the Dubowitz assessment scale (Figs 4.3–4.5) but the complete examination is not performed until the second day of life when the infant has recovered from labour, and only then if the infant is well and not requiring intensive care. It is possible to obtain a rough estimate of the gestational age by observation of the superficial signs as listed on the Dubowitz scale, such as the distribution of lanugo hair or the presence of skin creases on the soles of the feet (Fig. 4.3). Such assessment is necessary since it is known that infants of lowest gestational age generally need most intensive care and fare least well since they are physiologically and biochemically very immature. The accuracy of the assessment is ±10 days and it is of less value in infants of below 28 weeks gestation. For babies of very low gestation, the presence of fused eyelids or of marked bruising are often associated with a poor outcome.

PHYSIOLOGICAL PROBLEMS OF THE PRETERM INFANT

The preterm infant is at a significant disadvantage when compared to the full-term infant because of immaturity affecting all bodily systems.

Temperature Control

The preterm infant has difficulty in maintaining body temperature because of excessive heat loss as a result of reduced subcutaneous fat and large surface area to body weight ratio. In addition, there is reduced heat production because of inadequate amounts of brown fat, and an inability to shiver.

Respiratory System

Deficiency of pulmonary surfactant may lead to the respiratory distress syndrome (*vide infra*). As a result of poor gag and cough reflexes and uncoordinated sucking and swallowing, there is an increased risk of aspiration pneumonia. The pliable thorax and weak respiratory musculature of the preterm infant result in less efficient ventilation and may lead to patchy atelectasis so that oxygen requirements may be increased for the first few weeks of life. Periodic breathing and apnoea may result from immaturity of central chemoreceptors.

Nutrition and Gastrointestinal System

Before 34 weeks gestation, babies have poor sucking and swallowing reflexes and have decreased intestinal motility which may lead to abdominal distension. In addition, the intestine has reduced digestive and absorptive capacity for fats

EXTERNAL SIGN	SCORE				
	0	1	2	3	4
OEDEMA	Obvious oedema hands and feet; pitting over tibia	No obvious oedema hands and feet; pitting over tibia	No oedema		
SKIN TEXTURE	Very thin, gelatinous	Thin and smooth	Smooth; medium thickness. Rash or superficial peeling	Slight thickening. Superficial cracking and peeling esp. hands and feet	Thick and parchment-like, superficial or deep cracking
SKIN COLOUR (Infant not crying)	Dark red	Uniformly pink	Pale pink; variable over body	Pale. Only pink over ears, lips, palms or soles	
SKIN OPACITY (trunk)	Numerous veins and venules clearly seen, especially over abdomen	Veins and tributaries seen	A few large vessels clearly seen over abdomen	A few large vessels seen indistinctly over abdomen	No blood vessels seen
LANUGO (over back)	No lanugo	Abundant; long and thick over whole back	Hair thinning especially over lower back	Small amount of lanugo and bald areas	At least half of back devoid of lanugo
PLANTAR CREASES	No skin creases	Faint red marks over anterior half of sole	Definite red marks over more than anterior half; indentations over less than anterior third	Indentations over more than anterior third	Definite deep indentations over more than anterior third
NIPPLE FORMATION	Nipple barely visible; no areola	Nipple well defined; areola smooth and flat diameter < 0.75 cm	Areola stippled, edge not raised diameter <0.75 cm	Areola stippled, edge raised diameter > 0.75 cm	
BREAST SIZE	No breast tissue palpable	Breast tissue on one or both sides 0.5 cm diameter	Breast tissue both sides; one or both 0.5–1.0 cm	Breast tissue both sides; one or both 1 cm	
EAR FORM	Pinna flat and shapeless, little or no incurving of edge	Incurving of part of edge of pinna	Partial incurving whole of upper pinna	Well-defined incurving whole of upper pinna	
EAR FIRMNESS	Pinna soft, easily folded, no recoil	Pinna soft, easily folded, slow recoil	Cartilage to edge of pinna but soft in places, ready recoil	Pinna firm, cartilage to edge, instant recoil	
GENITALIA MALE	Neither of testis in scrotum	At least one testis high in scrotum	At least one testis right down		
FEMALES (With hips half abducted)	Labia majora widely separated, labia minora protruding	Labia majora almost cover labia minora	Labia majora completely cover labia minora		

(Adapted from Farr *et al.* (1966). Develop. Med. Child Neurol. **8**, 507)

Figure 4.3 External criteria for Dubowitz score to assess gestational age.

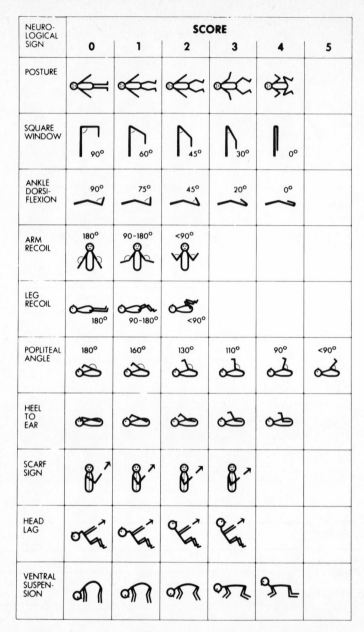

Figure 4.4 Neurological criteria of the Dubowitz score.

and fat-soluble vitamins. Lactase in the intestinal brush border is deficient before term but this enzyme may be rapidly induced once oral feeding has begun. Body stores of calcium, phosphorus, protein, vitamins A, C, D, E and K, trace elements and iron are less than at term and deficiencies of these nutrients may develop with postnatal growth. Hepatic function in the newborn is less than

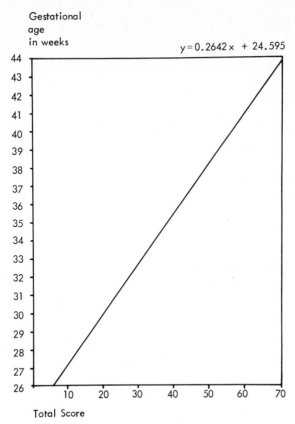

Figure 4.5 Chart for calculating gestational age from Dubowitz score, that is combined external and neurological criteria scores. (After Dubowitz *et al.*, 1970.)

optimal in that there is impaired conjugation and excretion of bilirubin which may result in significant jaundice. In addition, there may be deficiency of the vitamin-K-dependent clotting factors.

Renal System

The kidneys of the preterm infant resemble those of the adult with mild renal failure. The baby is unable to excrete large solute loads and produces a relatively dilute urine. For this reason, fluid and electrolyte balance may prove difficult and metabolic acidosis tends to occur because of the accumulation of inorganic acids.

Immunological System

The preterm infant has a reduced ability to combat infection as a result of both reduced humoral and cell-mediated immunological activity. The larger immunoglobulins (IgM and IgA) do not cross the placenta so the newborn infant must rely on the presence of maternal IgG as the major antibody in his fight against infection. In addition, the preterm infant has reduced phagocytosis, which is probably the result of inadequate circulating opsonizing antibody, and a relatively blunted inflammatory response (*vide infra*).

Nervous System

The periventricular area of the brain is highly vascular but poorly supported. Perinatal stresses such as hypercapnia and hypertension may predispose to bleeding in this area (periventricular haemorrhage), which may rupture into the ventricles (intraventricular haemorrhage). Periventricular leucomalacia, areas of softening and liquefaction of the white matter, may result from such haemorrhage or may be caused by ischaemia due to hypotension. Immaturity of the respiratory centre probably plays a part in the attacks of recurrent apnoea and bradycardia that occur in most very low-birth-weight infants.

CLINICAL PROBLEMS IN THE PRETERM INFANT

The most important early problem is the respiratory distress syndrome.

Respiratory Distress Syndrome (Hyaline Membrane Disease)

Definition

Respiratory distress syndrome (RDS) is an acute pulmonary condition of the newborn occurring as a result of surfactant deficiency. Clinically the baby presents with respiratory distress comprising tachypnoea (respiratory rate greater than 60/min), grunting and subcostal indrawing. Surfactant deficiency is more likely to occur in babies born preterm or those whose mothers have diabetes or rhesus isoimmunization.

Incidence

The incidence of RDS varies according to gestational age (see Table 4.3). For babies of less than 1000 g birth weight an incidence of about 80% is found, while for all those less than 1500 g about 65% will develop RDS.

Table 4.3 Incidence of RDS with gestational age

Gestational age (weeks)	Incidence (%)
28	70+
30	65
32	50
34	25

Table 4.4 Pathways of surfactant synthesis

Cytidine diphosphate choline (CDP choline) + D-α, β-diglyceride → lecithin   (choline incorporation pathway)

Phosphatidylethanolamine (PE) + $2CH_3$ → lecithin   (methylation pathway)

Pathogenesis

Surfactant is a mixture of phospholipids and protein which is produced by the alveolar type II cells of the lung. The major phospholipids are phosphatidyl choline (lecithin), phosphatidyl glycerol and phosphatidyl inositol. Surfactant acts by reducing alveolar surface tension and so prevents collapse of the alveoli in expiration. If surfactant is deficient, the lungs will tend to collapse causing a reduction in lung volume, decreased lung compliance and ventilation/perfusion abnormalities. The acute hypoxia produced will cause intense pulmonary vasoconstriction which is potentiated by acidosis. This may lead to right-to-left shunting of blood which will further impair surfactant production and cause a vicious cycle of events.

Surfactant is produced by two pathways (Table 4.4) – the choline incorporation pathway (CDP choline pathway) and the methylation pathway. This latter appears early at about 24 weeks but is extremely sensitive to changes in temperature and pH. The CDP choline pathway becomes active at about 28–30 weeks and from 35–37 weeks increases its production of surfactant. This pathway is more resistant to alterations of pH, temperature and hypoxia. Certain hormones are known to have controlling influences on this pathway. Both corticosteroids and thyroxine tend to stimulate the production of lecithin whereas insulin is known to inhibit it. This provides the basis for the treatment of mothers in preterm labour with steroids. As surfactant is produced by the fetus, it is able to spill from the lungs into the amniotic fluid where it can be estimated by measurement of the LSAR.

However, the quality of surfactant as well as its quantity appears to be important. One of the phospholipids that makes up surfactant appears to be important for adequate lowering of surface tension in the alveoli. This is phosphatidyl glycerol (PG) and when this is present in amniotic fluid, the infant is unlikely to develop RDS even though the LSAR may be less than 2 : 1 (Table 4.5).

Table 4.6 shows some factors that alter the risks of RDS.

Table 4.5 Pulmonary maturity by LSAR and presence of phosphatidyl glycerol (PG)

LSAR	RDS if PG present (%)	RDS if PG absent (%)
≥2.0	0	0
<2.0	3	86
all	<1	83

After Whittle *et al.* (1982).

Table 4.6 Factors affecting the incidence of RDS

Increased risk	Decreased risk
1. History of RDS in siblings	1. Prenatal steroids
2. Maternal diabetes	2. Prolonged rupture of membranes
3. Rhesus isoimmunization	3. Pre-eclampsia
4. Male sex	4. Heroin addiction
5. Second twin	5. Chronic intrauterine stress
6. Elective Caesarean section	6. Black races
7. Birth asphyxia	
8. Antepartum haemorrhage	

After birth, the baby with RDS will develop chronic hypoxaemia from ventilation/perfusion imbalance. This hypoxaemia may lead to cellular anaerobic glycolysis, accumulation of lactic acid and a consequent metabolic acidosis. Respiratory acidosis may also be present because of hypoventilation leading to retention of carbon dioxide. This combination of acidosis and hypoxaemia will reduce myocardial contractility, cardiac output and blood pressure. Perfusion of kidneys, gastrointestinal tract and other non-vital organs will be reduced and oedema and electrolyte disturbances will occur. For these reasons, the management of RDS is complex and involves more than just support of ventilation. If, however, one can correct the underlying hypoxaemia and acidosis, many of the other complications of RDS will be reduced.

Clinical Features

Many infants who subsequently develop RDS have evidence of perinatal asphyxia with delayed onset of respiration at birth. Others, however, may appear to be pink and active at birth and only develop symptoms after the first hour of life. The very low-birth-weight infant may present with respiratory failure from birth and require early assisted ventilation. The larger preterm infant will more usually present with a rapid respiratory rate (over 60/min), grunting and subcostal indrawing. Auscultation of the lungs is rarely helpful, although breath sounds may appear to be reduced over both lung fields. Tachycardia (160–170/min) is often present and heart rate variability will be reduced.

As the infant becomes more distressed he may develop progressive hypoxaemia and acidosis with reduced peripheral perfusion. At this stage he may often appear to be grey/blue in colour and will develop progressive oedema. The urinary output is usually poor for the first 2–3 days after birth.

A chest radiograph is necessary to confirm the diagnosis and blood gas analysis will detect the presence of hypoxaemia and acidosis. The major differential diagnoses are congenital pneumonia (often due to group B beta-haemolytic streptococci), transient tachypnoea of the newborn, heart disease and pneumothorax.

Investigations

Chest Radiograph. The early picture is usually characteristic with areas of collapse appearing as a fine diffuse reticulo-granular mottling and with air in the

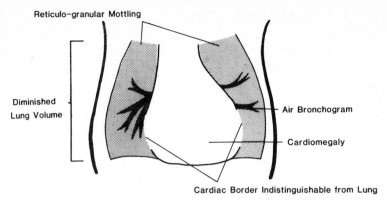

Figure 4.6 Schematic representation of chest radiograph in RDS.

major bronchi contrasted against the background of the lungs as an 'air bronchogram'. This is usually present beyond the border of the heart extending out into the periphery of the lung fields (Fig. 4.6). A large thymus is almost invariably present. In very severe RDS, the radiograph may be completely granular with the lungs appearing totally white. The radiological picture of congenital pneumonia may be identical to that of respiratory distress syndrome. However, with pneumonia, the mottling may be coarser and less uniform. In transient tachypnoea of the newborn, the radiograph shows overinflation of the lungs with increased pulmonary vascular markings and fluid in the horizontal fissure and the costophrenic angles (Fig. 4.7). The infant with congestive heart failure may have a radiograph which shows cardiomegaly (cardio-thoracic ratio greater than 0.6), increased vascular markings and pulmonary oedema.

Blood Gas Analysis. Arterial blood gas and pH values will depend upon the stage of the disease and on its severity. There is hypoxaemia of varying degree and retention of carbon dioxide leading to respiratory acidosis. Additionally, metabolic acidosis may occur because of impaired perfusion; this is indicated by an increased base deficit.

Examination of Gastric Aspirate. The gastric aspirate is used for three purposes. The LSAR or shake test may be performed, Gram stain can be done and

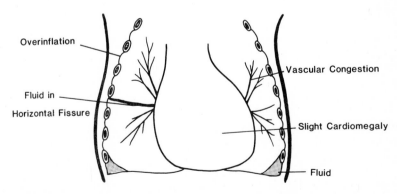

Figure 4.7 Schematic representation of chest radiograph in TTN.

bacterial culture is carried out. In the shake test, the gastric aspirate is mixed with ethanol to remove contaminants such as proteins, bile salts and free fatty acids. If the fluid is stained heavily with meconium or blood, it should be discarded. Then 0.5 ml of the fluid is added to 0.5 ml isotonic saline in a clean test tube with the addition of 1.0 ml of 95% ethanol. The tube is capped with a clean stopper, shaken for 15 sec and left to stand for 15 min. If bubbles form a complete ring at the surface the test is positive, i.e. little risk of RDS; if no bubbles are present, the test is negative and the risk of RDS is high. Gastric aspirate that is heavily contaminated with organisms and polymorphs suggests a risk of congenital infection and warrants treatment with antibiotics. The fluid should be cultured so that the precise nature of any infecting organisms may be identified.

Other Investigations for Infection. These include blood culture, blood film for white cell count and platelet count, immunoglobulin M (IgM) and C-reactive protein (CRP) measurement. An initial white cell count outside the range of 6–30 000 mm^3 and a platelet count below 100 000 mm^3 are suggestive of intrauterine infection. IgM and CRP are raised in cases of congenital infection.

Clinical Course

The clinical course of infants with RDS is of gradual deterioration for the first 2–3 days with worsening of hypoxia, hypercapnia and acidosis. During this time, the infant requires intensive observation and care. Recovery is often heralded by an increase in the urinary output and of the infant's muscle activity.

Treatment of RDS

The infant with RDS has a condition that not only affects respiratory function but also the circulation, renal function, temperature control and metabolic status. It is essential that in management one does not concentrate solely on improving respiratory status but treats the baby as a whole.

The baby should be placed in an incubator in the neutral thermal environment (NTE) or under a radiant warmer. The NTE is that range of environmental temperature over which heat production, oxygen consumption and nutritional requirements for growth are minimal provided the body temperature is normal. The NTE on the first day ranges from 35–37°C for infants of 1 kg to 32–33°C for infants of 2.5 kg or more. In some cases it is necessary to insert an arterial catheter for blood gas monitoring using either the umbilical artery or the radial artery. It is important to correct hypoxia and acidosis and to detect hypercarbia. This means fairly frequent blood gas estimations, perhaps as often as every hour until the infant's condition is stable. The baby should have his respiratory and heart rate monitored and a transcutaneous oxygen electrode or pulse oximeter applied to monitor his oxygen needs.

Air/oxygen mixtures are warmed and moistened and given to the infant in a perspex headbox. The oxygen concentration is monitored in the headbox with an oxygen analyser placed close to the infant's face. At the same time, it is important to keep the infant warm and provide him with fluids and nutrition.

Dextrose (5 or 10%) with small amounts of added amino acids may be given into a peripheral vein. Electrolytes, calcium, bilirubin, blood glucose and urinary output should be serially assessed. Observations should be repeatedly made to detect the development of any of the *acute* complications listed in Table 4.7.

It is customary to use continuous positive airways pressure (CPAP) when the arterial oxygen tension is less than 8 kPa (60 mmHg) in 60% oxygen. CPAP may be applied by endotracheal tube, face mask or nasal prongs. The essence of CPAP is that a positive pressure applied to the upper airway prevents the alveoli from collapsing at the end of expiration, making the work of inspiration less. During CPAP, the baby is breathing spontaneously. Should respiratory failure occur, with progressive hypoxaemia and hypercapnia causing acidosis, intermittent positive pressure ventilation (IPPV) is required. Penicillin should be given because of the marked similarity between RDS and streptococcal pneumonia.

The blood pressure and haematocrit should also be measured routinely and a blood transfusion is usually given if the haematocrit or the systolic blood pressure fall. Surfactant replacement therapy is currently under evaluation and may play a significant role in the prevention and management of this disease (Chapter 15).

Acute Complications of RDS

Pulmonary Air Leaks

This term includes pneumothorax, pneumomediastinum and pulmonary interstitial emphysema.

Incidence. The incidence of pneumothorax in infants with RDS is 10%. If treatment with assisted ventilation is given, the incidence increases to 15–30% and in 10% of these infants, the pneumothorax will be bilateral.

Pathogenesis. Following alveolar rupture, gas escapes along the bronchovascular space to the mediastinum and thence to the pleural space. As the gas dissects along the bronchovascular space, it may cause a reduction in lung compliance and impede gas exchange. This condition is called pulmonary interstitial emphysema (PIE). If gas has reached the pleural space, the usual consequence is a tension pneumothorax. If the dissection of air is massive, a pneumopericardium may develop producing cardiac tamponade. Gas may also pass from the anterior mediastinum across the diaphragm into the peritoneal cavity causing a pneumoperitoneum. Only rarely does the air dissect superiorly to the tissues of the neck and give rise to surgical emphysema.

Clinical Presentation. The usual sequence of events is that the infant with RDS, who may be having assisted ventilation, suddenly deteriorates. The infant may become cyanosed and shocked; if the blood pressure is being monitored, the

Table 4.7 Complications of respiratory distress syndrome

Acute	Pneumothorax, pulmonary interstitial emphysema, pneumopericardium, patent ductus arteriosus, intraventricular haemorrhage
Chronic	Bronchopulmonary dysplasia, post-haemorrhagic hydrocephalus
	Cerebral palsy, retrolental fibroplasia, subglottic stenosis

infant will develop hypertension followed by hypotension. Clinically, there may be a shift of the mediastinum (the apex beat) away from the side of the pneumothorax and reduced breath sounds may be detected on the affected side. However, in severe RDS, the lungs are very non-compliant so that a major shift of the mediastinum may not occur. In this case, an apparently small pneumothorax may cause marked deterioration in the infant's condition.

Investigation. Transillumination of the chest with a fibre-optic light source may show hyperlucency of the affected side. Confirmation of the pneumothorax is made by antero-posterior and lateral chest radiographs. On the antero-posterior view, the lung may be seen collapsed towards the hilum and surrounded by a rim of pleural gas (Fig. 4.8). The lateral view will show the presence of an anterior pneumothorax with the lung pushed back against the posterior chest wall (Fig. 4.9).

When a pneumomediastinum is present, the thymus gland may be lifted clear of the heart giving rise to the characteristic 'sail sign'. With PIE, the gas appears to be distributed in the perivascular and peribronchial spaces. The radiograph shows quite large widespread lucent areas in the interstitium of the lung giving rise to a frothy appearance. When pneumopericardium is present, a rim of translucency is seen around the heart which appears unusually small (Fig. 4.10).

In the acute phase of the pneumothorax, the most characteristic finding is hypercapnia and acidosis, though hypoxaemia is also seen in many cases.

Management. In the acutely ill infant, air should be aspirated from the anterior pleural space using a syringe and needle with a three-way tap. This should be followed by the placement of a pleural drain in the anterior pleural space connected to an underwater seal drainage. When PIE occurs in an infant with severe RDS, the outlook is considerably worsened and more aggressive ventilation is needed in order to improve the infant's condition. Recently, high-rate mechanical ventilation using lower peak pressures has been used with some success. Pneumopericardium is usually a very serious situation as cardiac tamponade readily occurs. The placement of a pericardial catheter is urgently

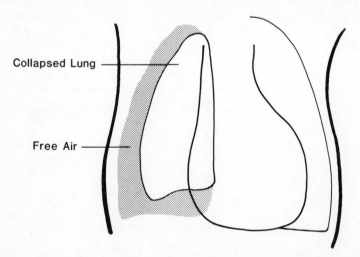

Collapsed Lung

Free Air

Figure 4.8 Schematic representation of chest radiograph of pneumothorax on the antero-posterior view.

Figure 4.9 Schematic representation of chest radiograph of pneumothorax in the lateral view.

required but this should only be done if the infant's condition is critical and even then only by an experienced person.

The onset of pulmonary air leak in an infant with RDS who is having assisted ventilation represents a serious deterioration in his condition. Mortality rates are significantly increased when this occurs. It has been suggested that acute pneumothorax is also associated with the development of intraventricular haemorrhage and that survivors of PIE are more likely to develop broncho-pulmonary dysplasia. Muscle relaxants may reduce the incidence of pulmonary air leak.

Patent Ductus Arteriosus

Patent ductus arteriosus (PDA) occurs in many preterm infants but especially those recovering from RDS who may develop a murmur on the third or fourth day.

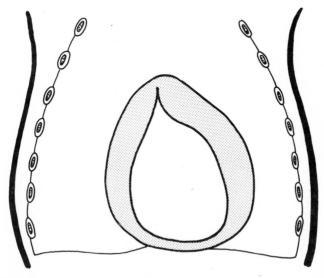

Figure 4.10 Schematic representation of chest radiograph of pneumo-pericardium.

This is often associated with a deterioration of the infant's condition and the need for increased mechanical ventilation.

Incidence

This is determined to some extent by the gestational age of the infant and on the presence or absence of RDS. For the very low-birth-weight infant, it appears that some 20% develop significant PDA but that only half of these require closure either by surgical ligation or indomethacin therapy.

Pathogenesis

The circulatory changes occurring in the newborn infant at birth have already been described in Chapter 2. The ductus of the preterm infant tends to close later and less effectively than the term baby. When a small infant is recovering from RDS, the pulmonary vascular resistance falls below that of the systemic circulation, the ductus may remain open and left-to-right shunting occurs. The pulmonary blood flow will increase considerably and pulmonary oedema may occur.

In addition to low gestational age and the presence of RDS, excessive fluid intake has been suggested as a predisposing factor for PDA.

Clinical Presentation

The usual presentation of PDA is with a murmur which may be systolic or continuous and heard best at the upper left sternal edge with radiation under the left clavicle and into the back. However, PDA may be present in the newborn in the absence of an audible murmur. Additional clinical findings include a hyperactive praecordium and bounding peripheral pulses. When the infant still has significant RDS these findings may be masked so that the first signs may be the need for increased mechanical ventilation, hypercapnia, metabolic acidosis or apnoea.

Investigation

The chest radiograph may show cardiomegaly, increased pulmonary vascularity and pulmonary oedema. The ECG is rarely helpful. Echocardiography is now an essential tool in the investigation of babies with PDA. M-mode echocardiography will show increased left heart dimensions and the left atrial to the aorta ratio, which is normally 1 : 1, will usually be greater than 1.5 : 1 when significant PDA is present. More recently, real-time sector scanners have been used to demonstrate dilatation of the ductus arteriosus itself and Doppler techniques can detect turbulent flow in the pulmonary artery. Confirmation of the diagnosis by cardiac catheterization is now rarely needed. Blood gas analysis will often show the presence of hypercapnia and acidosis.

Management

The first aim is prevention. This may be done by restricting the fluid intake in the first days of life. If PDA occurs, it is initially treated with diuretics to reduce the circulatory overload but if this fails, or the infant's condition worsens, the ductus should be closed. This may be done with indomethacin, which inhibits prostaglandin synthetase, or by surgical ligation. Indomethacin may be given orally or intravenously in a dose of 0.1–0.2 mg/kg given three times at 12-hr intervals.

The presence of a large PDA in the tiny infant recovering from RDS prolongs his acute illness and may increase the risk of death. By prolonging the need for mechanical ventilation, there may be a significantly increased risk of broncho-pulmonary dysplasia and of death from complications such as sepsis or intraventricular haemorrhage.

Once the ductus has closed and the infant has fully recovered, reopening is unlikely. In a few instances however, the ductus may reopen later in the neonatal period in response to a stress such as sepsis or excessive fluid intake. In a very few infants, the ductus appears to constrict significantly but does not close fully and the infant develops signs of chronic persistent ductus arteriosus. Under these circumstances, the baby should be followed up at the cardiac clinic as ligation may be necessary later.

Intraventricular Haemorrhage

Haemorrhage occurs into the subependymal germinal matrix at the edge of the lateral ventricle close to the head of the caudate nucleus. The haemorrhage may extend into the basal ganglia, the lateral ventricles or into the cerebral hemisphere. It is rarely seen in the full-term infant.

Incidence

Significant periventricular and intraventricular haemorrhages are usually seen only in the very low-birth-weight infant. Before the advent of computerized tomography and ultrasound scanning of the brain, the diagnosis could be made only on clinical grounds or with the discovery of blood-stained cerebrospinal fluid (CSF) at lumbar puncture or upon aspiration of ventricular fluid. Using clinical methods to make the diagnosis and including autopsy examination of those infants who die, the incidence of intraventricular haemorrhage was about 3–5% of very low-birth-weight infants. Since the introduction of ultrasound scanning of the brain, it is recognized that 40–50% of all infants less than 1500 g show some evidence of periventricular or intraventricular haemorrhage.

Pathogenesis

The subependymal germinal matrix of the preterm infant is highly vascular and poorly supported. As a result, these blood vessels are rather friable and may rupture in the presence of hypercapnia, hypoxia or hypertension. Hypercapnia and hypoxia cause cerebral vasodilatation and increase cerebral blood flow. In addition, hypoxia and hypotension are associated with venous congestion and disturbance of the vascular endothelium. Hypertension, occurring, for example, in acute asphyxia, will be transmitted directly to the cerebral blood vessels since cerebral autoregulation may be lost in the sick preterm infant. This may predispose to bleeding in the area of the germinal matrix. Further bleeding in this area may cause rupture into one or both lateral ventricles or the cerebral substance which will result in profound clinical deterioration. Periventricular leucomalacia (PVL) may also occur. In this condition, cerebral ischaemia leads to the development of brain softening and liquefaction. It is often seen in association with haemorrhage, hypotension and septicaemia. Babies with PVL are at high risk of neurological impairment and developmental delay.

Clinical Features

From recent ultrasound observations, it is apparent that periventricular and intraventricular haemorrhage may be silent or subclinical. In other infants, there may be sudden deterioration with the onset of extensor spasms, arching of the back, decerebrate posturing of the limbs or frank seizures. Anaemia may rapidly develop. Other infants may present with apathy, apnoea and shock. Occasionally, the first indication that haemorrhage has occurred is the development of post-haemorrhagic hydrocephalus.

Investigation

Infants who are receiving intensive care for RDS should have routine serial ultrasonic scans to look for such haemorrhages. The haemorrhages are initially seen as white areas in the subependymal region near the head of the caudate nuclei and extend into the cerebral substance or into the ventricles. In addition, there may be ventricular dilatation. These haemorrhages are graded according to their ultrasonic appearance (Table 4.8).

Examination of the spinal fluid to confirm the diagnosis is now less frequently performed. Spinal fluid may be frankly bloody and may contain bilirubin formed by the breakdown of haemoglobin. The peripheral blood haematocrit may also fall in an infant with a significant intracranial haemorrhage.

Table 4.8 Grading system of intraventricular haemorrhage (after Papile, 1978)

Grade	Appearance
I	Subependymal haemorrhage
II	Haemorrhage into ventricle
III	Intraventricular haemorrhage with ventricular dilatation
IV	As above with haemorrhage into the cerebral substance

Management

Prevention of significant intraventricular haemorrhage is obviously better than cure. Birth asphyxia is an important predisposing factor. Postnatally, the avoidance of sudden changes in homeostasis, such as may occur with blocking or kinking of endotracheal tubes or the development of tension pneumothorax, should reduce the incidence of this condition. Abnormalities of pH, oxygen tension and blood pressure should be corrected without delay. There should be judicious use of alkaline solutions to correct acidosis and of blood or plasma transfusions to correct hypotension. The use of ethamsylate and vitamin E are currently under investigation in the prevention of this condition.

When haemorrhage occurs and dilatation of the ventricular system has been found and/or the head circumference is increasing, repeated daily lumbar punctures are done to remove as much CSF as possible. Between 10 and 20 ml of CSF are obtained at each lumbar puncture in the hope of lowering CSF protein and removing cellular debris from the fluid. Drugs such as acetazolamide and isosorbide have been used in an attempt to prevent the progression of hydro-cephalus but are of doubtful benefit. If repeated lumbar punctures fail to control progressive hydrocephalus, ventricular shunting is necessary.

Sometimes an infant with a large intraventricular haemorrhage has suffered irreversible brain damage. This is not always easy to determine but there are occasions when a decision to reduce the level of care provided to a tiny baby with a large intraventricular haemorrhage has to be made. This is done after careful consideration of all clinical and ultrasound findings and after discussion with both parents. The decision is one that should be endorsed by two consultant neonatologists.

Sub-clinical intraventricular haemorrhage diagnosed only on ultrasound scan (grades I and II) appears to have a very good prognosis with outcome comparable with that of infants without intraventricular haemorrhage. In those infants who survive following a large intraventricular haemorrhage (grade IV) and whose symptoms include profound neurological disturbance with seizure activity, about 50% will die, and of the survivors 40–50% will have persistent abnormal neurological signs. In approximately 10–20% of survivors, there will be severe neurological disturbance with developmental retardation, spastic diplegia or quadriplegia and microcephaly. Infants who show ultrasonic evidence of PVL have the worst prognosis.

Chronic Complications of RDS

These problems may follow RDS but are also related to many other factors of perinatal or prenatal origin.

Bronchopulmonary Dysplasia

This form of chronic neonatal lung disease occurs in infants who required prolonged mechanical ventilation.
Incidence. About 20% of babies treated with mechanical ventilation show radiological changes of this condition.
Pathogenesis. The pathological picture of bronchopulmonary dysplasia is one

of alveolar and bronchiolar necrosis in the acute stages and repair with bronchial metaplasia and interstitial fibrosis occurring later. There is continuing debate about whether these changes are the result of toxic effects of high oxygen concentrations or the effects of barotrauma during high-pressure mechanical ventilation. Oxygen is known to be toxic to respiratory epithelium causing overproduction of mucus and later metaplasia. However, bronchopulmonary dysplasia is rarely seen in infants who have not been treated with positive pressure mechanical ventilation via an endotracheal tube. It seems likely that both high concentrations of oxygen and positive pressure ventilation and, perhaps, infection are essential for this condition to develop. PIE and PDA are also associated with bronchopulmonary dysplasia.

Clinical Features. Bronchopulmonary dysplasia is characterized by a prolonged chronic respiratory illness which may last for several months. The initial respiratory disorder is usually RDS but other respiratory diseases such as meconium aspiration syndrome can underlie it. Resolution of the underlying respiratory disease does not occur and the clinical condition of the baby remains poor with prolonged respiratory distress, overinflation of the chest, oxygen dependence and wheezing.

Initially, the chest radiographs show signs of severe RDS but, by approximately 10–20 days, small radiolucent cysts can be seen, usually in the perihilar region, and there may be overinflation, particularly of the lower lobes.

As the disease progresses the infant fails to thrive, may develop right heart failure and, radiologically, there is marked overinflation of the lungs with emphysematous change at the bases and a generalized streaky opacification (Fig. 4.11).

Bronchopulmonary dysplasia usually improves spontaneously in the second six months of life as new alveoli are generated.

Management. Treatment of bronchopulmonary dysplasia is largely symptomatic. Oxygen should be administered to keep arterial oxygen tension above 7 kPa (55 mmHg). Levels below this are associated with pulmonary vasoconstriction and right heart failure. There may be marked exudation of fluid and cellular debris into the bronchial tree as the disease progresses, and, at this stage, gentle physiotherapy with suctioning of the airways may prove helpful. Adequate nutrition with provision of vitamins and trace elements is essential for adequate

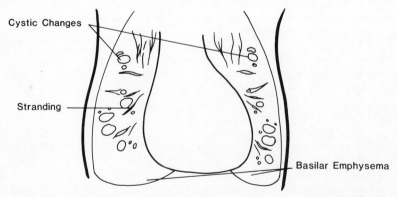

Figure 4.11 Schematic representation of chest radiograph in BPD.

lung growth and repair. Steroid therapy may have a role and diuretics and fluid restriction may prevent the occurrence of cor pulmonale. In order to reduce the fluid intake, one of the newer proprietary milk formulae containing 0.8 cal/ml is recommended. Bacteriological investigation should be performed and the infant treated with antibiotics if any suspicion of infection is found. Recently, vitamin E, which has anti-oxidant properties, has been used in an attempt to prevent and treat bronchopulmonary dysplasia. The evidence of benefit is not clear-cut but these infants should be given 10–15 mg of vitamin E daily.

Most infants who develop chronic bronchopulmonary dysplasia will recover, although some may be chronically oxygen-dependent and may require to go home on supplemental low-flow oxygen therapy. A few, however, show progressive fibrosis with cor pulmonale and die during the first few months of life. Those who survive show clearing of the chest radiograph during the first year of life and are usually clinically and radiologically normal by the age of 6 months–2 years. A number of infants, however, have recurrent attacks of respiratory infection and may require frequent hospital admissions during the first two years of life. There is also an increased risk of sudden infant death syndrome in this group, so home apnoea monitoring may be advisable. Follow-up pulmonary function testing suggests that these infants have some persistent alteration in airway resistance. This does not correlate with clinical findings and the majority appear to be clinically normal.

Retrolental Fibroplasia (Retinopathy of Prematurity)

The term retrolental fibroplasia describes the changes that occur in the retina of the preterm baby in association with high arterial oxygen tensions.

Incidence. The incidence of retrolental fibroplasia varies with birth weight. Lighter babies have a higher incidence and recent American studies suggest an incidence of about 40% in babies less than 1500 g. However, studies from the UK show a much lower incidence of retrolental fibroplasia (about 3% of infants less than 1500 g). This difference may relate to variations in classification.

Pathogenesis. It is known that excessive oxygen administration produces vasoconstriction in the retinal vessels of the preterm baby. This vasoconstriction, which is reversible in its early stages, occurs in the terminal arterioles leading to retinal ischaemia. This may be followed by capillary proliferation, scarring and retinal detachment.

In general, the severity of the vascular changes is directly proportional to the duration and concentration of increased arterial oxygen tension and to the immaturity of the infant. However, some preterm infants have developed retrolental fibroplasia without having received supplemental oxygen and the changes have been described in still births and in infants with cyanotic heart disease. Other factors in addition to oxygen administration and immaturity obviously play a part in the pathogenesis of this condition. The roles of hypocapnia, circulating prostaglandins, vitamin E deficiency and the presence of adult haemoglobin following blood transfusions have still to be determined.

Clinical Features. In mild cases of retrolental fibroplasia, proliferation of vessels occurs only in the periphery of the retina.

In severe cases, the entire retina may undergo neovascularization with early changes often occurring in the temporal region. When gross proliferation occurs, the retina may become detached. The cicatrical phase of retrolental fibroplasia starts at about the age of 3 months with proliferation of retrolental fibrous tissue which usually leads to severe impairment of vision. Vision is impaired in varying degrees from myopia to complete blindness.

Management. In the preterm infant, oxygen must be treated as a dangerous drug and there is no safe level of oxygen concentration in these babies. Retrolental fibroplasia is associated with high arterial oxygen concentrations and not with high environmental oxygen concentrations; the requirements of an individual baby may therefore only be monitored by measuring arterial oxygen tensions. It has been suggested that levels of 13 kPa (100 mmHg) may predispose to retrolental fibroplasia after only 2−4 hr exposure. Arterial oxygen tensions of 6.5−9 kPa (50−70 mmHg) should be maintained in all preterm infants who are receiving supplemental oxygen. In addition, all infants less than 1500 g should receive supplemental vitamin E as this may help to prevent the condition. All newborn babies who have received supplemental oxygen therapy should have an ophthalmological examination before and after discharge from hospital, with 6 weeks as the optimum interval. Using the indirect ophthalmoscope and after pupillary dilatation with cyclopentolate, the retina should be fully ex-amined paying particular attention to the temporal regions. If no abnormalities are noted, the examination should be repeated after 6 weeks. If established retrolental fibroplasia is found, examination of the eye under anaesthesia is justified. In some cases, the ophthalmologist will attempt to limit the progress of retrolental fibroplasia with laser photocoagulation which may prevent subse-quent retinal detachment.

DEVELOPMENTAL ABNORMALITIES IN INFANTS SURVIVING SEVERE RDS

All infants who have suffered from RDS should be carefully and regularly examined in order to detect any neurological problem. Major problems will be found in 5−10% of infants where artificial ventilation has been used. These handicaps include gross neurological problems such as cerebral palsy and mental retardation, visual and hearing disturbances, learning disorders, hyper-activity and recurrent seizures.

Such problems are more frequently seen in infants who have had asphyxia and who have had neurological dysfunction in the neonatal period such as seizure activity or intracranial haemorrhage, especially when hydrocephalus or PVL occur.

OUTCOME OF INFANTS WITH RDS

The overall mortality of RDS throughout the UK is of the order of 25%. However, when this condition is treated in hospitals that can provide intensive care, mortality rates of less than 5−10% are usually found. In the very low-birth-weight infant, the effect of RDS on outcome is profound. The mortality of infants less than 1500 g with RDS is five times higher than those who do not develop this disease.

For infants who survive the neonatal period, long-term follow-up studies suggest that sequelae are uncommon, with about 5–10% of infants who survive mechanical ventilation having significant handicaps as described above. Such problems appear in the first year of life with the obvious exceptions of perceptual and learning problems which become apparent in the early school years. However, the ultimate developmental achievements of the children may be determined more by genetic and socio-economic circumstances than by birth weight or the development of RDS.

Periodic Breathing, Apnoea and Bradycardia

Apnoea in the newborn is cessation of breathing for more than 15 sec and may be associated with bradycardia (heart rate less than 110/min) and cyanosis. When apnoeic spells of 5–15 sec occur frequently and at regular intervals, the respiratory pattern is known as periodic breathing.

Incidence

Periodic breathing occurs in 25–50% of preterm infants. The incidence is related to gestational age; infants of less than 34 weeks have an incidence of significant apnoeic attacks of around 30%.

Pathogenesis

Periodic breathing may be a physiological process in the preterm infant or may be the result of some more serious underlying disorder (Table 4.9).

Apnoea at Birth

When apnoea or severe periodic breathing occurs at or shortly after birth, the cause is most commonly hypoxia or brain immaturity. Usually, in these circumstances, the baby requires assisted ventilation and full intensive care. However, in some cases, especially those of extremely low birth weight, this may be inadvisable as the risk of death or brain damage may be unacceptably high. A decision to withdraw intensive support may then have to be made and this should be done by the consultant.

Table 4.9 Causes of apnoea

1. Handling of baby or alteration of environment (especially temperature)	
2. Hypoxia	RDS, airway obstruction, oversedation
3. Sepsis	Septicaemia, pneumonia, meningitis
4. Metabolic	Hypoglycaemia, hypocalcaemia, hyponatraemia
5. Cerebral	Intraventricular haemorrhage, birth trauma, seizures, kernicterus
6. Apnoea of prematurity	

Apnoea of Prematurity

Apnoea and periodic breathing occurring some time after birth may be seen in the absence of any obvious cause when the term 'apnoea of prematurity' is frequently applied. Periodic breathing disappears after a few weeks as the infant approaches 40 weeks post-conceptional age, suggesting that immaturity, particularly of the central chemoreceptors in the respiratory centre of the brain, may be responsible. It is known that the response of the preterm baby's respiratory centre to hypercapnia and hypoxia is reduced or paradoxical. Normally, these chemical changes would cause stimulation of respiration with an increase in rate and depth of breathing, but in the preterm infant the opposite tends to occur. The onset of apnoea of prematurity is often delayed until the second or third day of life but the reason for this is not clearly understood. It may be that, at this time, lung volumes are at their minimum, perhaps as a result of patchy atelectasis and that this may be associated with hypoxaemia.

Clinical Features

The pattern of periodic breathing is quite characteristic. A period of apnoea of 5–10 sec is followed by hyperventilation lasting 10–15 sec at a rate of 50–60/min. During the period of apnoea, there are usually no changes in heart rate, colour or body temperature, and only minor changes in blood gases have been found. Apnoeic spells that last more than 15–20 sec are often associated with bradycardia and cyanosis. If they occur frequently, profound disturbances in cerebral function with hypotonia and lethargy may occur.

The onset of apnoea of prematurity is usually on the second and third days of life; when it begins earlier or later an underlying pathology is suggested. However, no matter when the attacks occur, the infant should be examined closely for evidence of an underlying cause (Table 4.9).

Investigations

Laboratory investigations of apnoea include a full blood picture, platelet count, C-reactive protein and blood culture to exclude infection. Blood glucose, electrolytes and calcium should be measured. It may be necessary to perform a chest radiograph and blood gas examination. If the baby appears ill, a lumbar puncture should be performed to exclude meningitis and an ultrasonic scan of the brain carried out to exclude cerebral haemorrhage.

Management

All babies of 34 weeks gestation or less should be observed closely and their heart and respiration rates recorded continuously until it has been established that they are not having apnoeic attacks or periodic breathing. Simultaneous recording of the transcutaneous oxygen tension gives additional information. When apnoeic attacks are discovered, any underlying cause should first be corrected.

Apnoea may be reduced by effective control of ambient temperature using either a servo-controlled incubator or a heat shield within an incubator. If this fails, repeated stimulation of the infant by stroking, gentle shaking or rocking may help to prevent or shorten the attacks. These forms of stimulation probably work by increasing the input to the immature respiratory centre via cutaneous, vestibular and proprioceptive pathways.

It may become necessary to use intermittent bag and mask ventilation for apnoeic attacks. It is important that the oxygen concentration used should be the same as that which the baby has been breathing because retrolental fibroplasia may occur if higher concentrations are employed repeatedly. If the infant's condition fails to improve, an aminophylline infusion or assisted ventilation using either CPAP or IPPV may be needed.

The outcome depends upon the underlying cause of the apnoeic attacks and the gestational age of the infant. Infants of 24–25 weeks who have severe apnoeic attacks have high mortality rates and those who survive may have developmental sequelae.

OTHER RESPIRATORY PROBLEMS

Transient Tachypnoea of the Newborn (TTN)

TTN is a common neonatal respiratory problem seen in both term and preterm infants, especially following Caesarean section, birth asphyxia, maternal diabetes, excessive maternal analgesia or fluid intake and neonatal polycythaemia.

It is generally agreed that the aetiology of TTN is a delay in resorption of lung fluid which normally either passes up the trachea or into the pulmonary capillaries or lymphatics. This may lead to a reduction in lung compliance causing tachypnoea. In a few babies, pneumothorax may occur.

Clinical Features

TTN is clinically similar to mild RDS, though tachypnoea is the predominant symptom with respiratory rates up to 120/min. Grunting, flaring and subcostal retraction are much less common. The onset of these symptoms is usually within the first hour but may be delayed until the second and third hours of life. There is often striking overinflation of the chest but there is rarely significant cyanosis. Auscultation of the chest is not helpful and the clinical course rarely extends beyond the first 3–4 days of life. The babies may become oedematous and have reduced urinary output although these features are also transient. Affected babies usually require less than 40% oxygen to maintain normal arterial oxygen tensions. Very occasionally, babies become markedly hypoxaemic and require mechanical ventilation. In such patients, echocardiography reveals right-to-left shunting of blood across the ductus arteriosus, foramen ovale and within the lung. These babies probably suffer from a combination of TTN and persistent fetal circulation.

Investigations

On the chest radiograph, there is usually hyperinflation of the lungs and increased pulmonary vascular markings. There may be mild cardiomegaly and fluid in the horizontal fissure and costophrenic angles resembling the findings of pulmonary oedema (Fig. 4.7).

Blood gas analysis may reveal the presence of a low arterial pH early in the course of the illness, but this acidosis is usually metabolic in origin and arterial carbon dioxide tensions are usually normal or low. Echocardiography is helpful in investigation of the severe form of this disease and to exclude structural congenital heart disease.

Management

It may be possible to prevent TTN by avoiding excessive use of analgesics or hypotonic intravenous fluids during labour. In addition, careful resuscitation and the prevention of cooling may further reduce the incidence. When TTN occurs, oxygen should be supplied to maintain arterial oxygen tensions in a range of 6.5–9 kPa (50–70 mmHg). Metabolic acidosis should be corrected with intravenous sodium bicarbonate and the haematocrit should be measured to detect polycythaemia which may have to be treated by partial exchange transfusion with plasma. Feeding should be withheld until the tachypnoea has settled and fluids should be provided intravenously. Penicillin should be given until streptococcal pneumonia can be excluded.

Outcome

All babies with TTN should survive without sequelae.

Congenital Pneumonia

This condition may be seen in babies of any gestational age although it occurs most frequently in preterm infants. Congenital pneumonia often has a clinical and radiological picture very similar to that of RDS.

Incidence

The true incidence of congenital pneumonia is unknown since the diagnosis is difficult to make unless positive cultures can be obtained from tracheal fluid and blood. Severe bacterial infections in the newborn occur in about 5 per 1000 live births so that it is probable that pneumonia occurs in about 2 per 1000 births.

Pathogenesis

The baby may become infected *in utero* as a result of ascending infection after premature rupture of the membranes, by transplacental infection or following aspiration of infected vaginal contents during birth. Associated factors are prolonged rupture (lasting more than 24 hr) of the membranes, maternal illness with fever, the presence of foul-smelling amniotic fluid and birth asphyxia with aspiration. The organisms most commonly isolated in congenital pneumonia are beta-haemolytic streptococci, coliforms, *Listeria monocytogenes*, bacteroides, staphylococci, pseudomonas and klebsiella.

Infection with group B, beta-haemolytic streptococci is becoming an increasingly common cause of neonatal illness in the UK. Between 7 and 10% of women in pregnancy will carry this organism in their genital or lower gastro-intestinal tracts. Most of the infants born to these colonized mothers will themselves become colonized and at least 1% of them will develop a serious illness. Infection may occur in the absence of prolonged rupture of the membranes and even in babies who have been born after elective Caesarean section.

Clinical Features

Infants with intrauterine pneumonia usually show signs of severe illness from birth. Characteristically, the 1-min Apgar score is good, but by 5 min the infant appears to be markedly distressed with cyanosis, grunting, indrawing and tachypnoea. With some infections, particularly those with coliforms or anaerobic organism such as bacteroides, the infant may have a foul smell from birth. In infants who become infected because of aspiration of infected amniotic fluid, the onset of their illness may be somewhat delayed until after the first few hours of life.

The clinical features of congenital pneumonia may mimic closely those of RDS and it is only after investigation that infection is found and appropriate treatment instituted. However, sepsis and pneumonia should be suspected when an infant is born in the presence of purulent or foul-smelling amniotic fluid or whose mother was febrile before or after delivery.

Investigation

Gastric aspirate, tracheal secretions, swabs from the surface of the infant and blood cultures should be taken. The gastric aspirate and tracheal secretion should be immediately examined by direct microscopy. A full blood picture with white cell count and platelet count may also suggest infection. Serum C-reactive protein is raised in some neonatal infections. The chest radiograph may look precisely like that of RDS, though the presence of coarser infiltrates which may or may not be generalized is suggestive of infection. In addition, there may be signs of aspiration with changes present especially in the right upper lobe. Rarely is there evidence of lobar consolidation.

Management

Antibiotics should be given in labour if there are signs of sepsis in the mother or if she is known to be colonized with group B streptococci; intravenous ampicillin or penicillin should be used. All infants who are suspected of having congenital pneumonia should be treated with antibiotics from birth after cultures have been obtained. In addition, all babies with significant respiratory distress should be treated with penicillin from birth, and, if there are features suggestive of pneumonia, an aminoglycoside such as gentamicin or netilmicin should also be given. If it is suspected that the infant is suffering from streptococcal pneumonia, either because it is known that the mother harboured streptococcus in her vagina, or because the neonatal gastric aspirate reveals the presence of Gram-positive cocci, then high-dose penicillin should be given. The infant should be kept in the neutral thermal environment. Metabolic acidosis should be corrected and transfusions with fresh whole blood may be helpful by providing opsonins which will improve the newborn's white cell function. Disseminated intravascular coagulation may occur and is treated by transfusions of fresh blood and plasma with correction of predisposing disturbances such as acidosis, hypothermia and hypoxia. Respiratory assistance may be necessary.

The overall mortality of infants with congenital pneumonia, particularly those due to beta-haemolytic streptococcus, is about 40–50%. This is despite early and apparently adequate treatment with antibiotics. The reasons for the poor outcome may be intrauterine onset of infection, delay in diagnosis, immaturity of the infected infants or associated immunological deficiencies. Screening of pregnant women for carriage of streptococci and early and aggressive treatment of perinatal infections helps to lower this mortality rate to about 20%. Work is at present under way to develop a vaccine to protect against streptococcal infection.

Aspiration Pneumonia

There are two distinct types of aspiration pneumonia: meconium aspiration which occurs predominantly in the term and post-term infant (Chapter 8), and aspiration of secretions or milk which is more likely to occur in the preterm infant sometime after birth.

Incidence and Pathogenesis

The true incidence of aspiration of milk is not known, but if small preterm infants are given too much milk by tube feed, they may regurgitate and aspirate because of deficient gag and cough reflexes. This type of aspiration pneumonia is also seen after extubation following a period of assisted ventilation when the glottis may not close sufficiently to prevent aspiration. Furthermore, recent studies suggest that up to 70% of preterm infants undergoing mechanical ventilation may aspirate despite the presence of an endotracheal tube.

Clinical Findings

Aspiration may cause acute apnoea due to airway obstruction or by reflex stimulation of the hypopharyngeal area. If sufficient milk passes through the glottis into the lungs, there may be acute respiratory distress and secondary pneumonia. The signs of respiratory distress are tachypnoea and indrawing, and on auscultation there may be reduced air entry with crepitations, usually over the right lung.

Investigations

A chest radiograph will show the presence of some collapse and consolidation, especially in the right-upper lobe.

Management

Adequate suctioning of the infant's hypopharynx after an episode of aspiration is essential. Once milk has been aspirated from the airway, the infant should be manually ventilated with 40% oxygen until spontaneous respiration occurs. After this, the infant should be carefully monitored for a few days in case the episodes recur. It is customary to start antibiotics because of the high risk of superimposed infection and this should be done after a full sepsis work-up.

Infants usually recover with gradual improvement over 3–4 days. However, in some infants, there may be overwhelming aspiration of milk resulting in a fatal outcome. Some infants who aspirate may develop intraventricular haemorrhage or patent ductus arteriosus. The presence of these complications prolong the period of recovery and increase the mortality rate.

Wilson–Mikity Syndrome

Wilson–Mikity syndrome is a form of chronic respiratory distress of the very preterm infant. Clinically and radiologically, it resembles bronchopulmonary dysplasia but may be differentiated by the fact that the baby has not inspired oxygen in high concentrations nor received mechanical ventilation.

Incidence

The incidence of Wilson–Mikity syndrome is less than that of bronchopulmonary dysplasia. It occurs in about 2% of very low-birth-weight survivors.

Pathogenesis

The aetiology of Wilson–Mikity syndrome is unknown, although there have been many theories. Perhaps it results from a disturbance in ventilation/perfusion ratios secondary to abnormal air distribution in the immature lung. The syndrome may be associated with fluid retention from either excessive administration or persistent patent ductus arteriosus. Trace element and vitamin deficiencies have also been postulated as possible causes. Another suggestion is that a chronic underproduction of surfactant causes alveolar instability with patchy collapse and overinflation. It seems unlikely that oxygen toxicity is a cause of Wilson–Mikity syndrome. Pathologically there is no evidence of pulmonary necrosis, repair or fibrosis in infants who die.

Clinical Features

The syndrome usually occurs in infants of less than 1500 g birth weight and most often there is no preceding history of severe RDS. At about 7–10 days of age, the infant develops progressive respiratory distress with tachypnoea and indrawing and increasing oxygen requirements. Oxygen requirements of up to 30% are usual and apnoea may occur during the course of the illness. The pattern is one of increasing respiratory distress for 2–3 weeks, followed by gradual improvement over the next 6 weeks, although some infants may require oxygen supplementation for the first 6 months of life.

Investigations

The chest radiograph usually shows streaky infiltrates which may be generalized at first with later cystic changes occurring in the lung bases. There is often overinflation of the chest. Blood gas analysis usually shows the presence of hypercapnia, and there may be moderate acidosis at first. Later, renal retention of bicarbonate compensates for this acidosis.

Management

Treatment is aimed at maintaining normal blood gases by providing added oxygen. If the infant is ill, oral feeding may have to be stopped and fluids and calories provided intravenously. It is useful to restrict fluid intake and diuretic therapy may be beneficial. It is important to supply the infant with an adequate intake of protein, trace elements and vitamins. Assisted ventilation is rarely needed.

In most cases the disease is self-limiting and there is gradual recovery over 6–8 weeks. The mortality rate is generally low but some series report rates of 15–30%.

Fluid and Electrolyte Balance

Fluid and electrolyte balance is often difficult to achieve, especially in the smallest infants. This is because there is a very high insensible water loss through the skin, which may be of the order of 50 ml/kg/day, and poor development of renal function.

Requirements

The fluid and electrolyte requirements depend upon gestational age, birth weight and postnatal age of the infant. Infants in incubators require 50–80 ml/kg of fluid a day and 40–50 cal/kg/day on day 1 rising to 150 ml/kg/day of fluid and 110 cal/kg/day on day 5. Infants treated under radiant warmers or who need phototherapy require more because of their increased insensible water loss.

Infants who need intensive care are usually given 5 or 10% dextrose infusions and electrolytes are added after 24 hr. Thereafter, if the infant still requires intensive care, full intravenous nutrition becomes necessary.

In order to achieve fluid and electrolyte balance, it is important to measure regularly the blood and urinary electrolytes and osmolality, and to weigh the infant at least once every day.

Hypoglycaemia

Hypoglycaemia is an important problem in preterm infants since it may cause apnoea and seizures and lead to irreversible brain damage.

Prior to birth, the fetus relies on the transplacental passage of maternal glucose. After birth, this ceases and the preterm infant may have an inadequate exogenous source of glucose because of delayed feeding and therefore the blood glucose falls (to less than 1.5 mmol/l). The neonatal brain is given some protection from hypoglycaemia as it appears that ketone bodies and fatty acids may also be utilized as energy sources for brain growth and metabolism.

Hypoglycaemia is generally preventable by ensuring that sufficient glucose is given and by regularly measuring the blood sugar. If hypoglycaemia does occur, it is corrected by an infusion of 10% dextrose or by promptly feeding the infant. The blood sugar should then be regularly measured to ensure that it does not fall again.

Hyperglycaemia is defined as a blood sugar greater than 8 mmol/l and may occur in the preterm infant who is having 10% dextrose or parenteral nutrition. Glucose intolerance in the preterm infant is quite common and may be an early sign of sepsis. The problem is usually corrected by changing the infusion fluid from 10 to 5% dextrose and only very occasionally is insulin required.

Hypocalcaemia

Hypocalcaemia is fairly common in the preterm infant because of inadequate calcium intake, poor parathyroid response to hypocalcaemia and reduced renal excretion of phosphate. A calcium level below 1.8 mmol/l or ionized calcium below 0.7 mmol/l is taken as indicating hypocalcaemia. Infants with hypocalcaemia may be irritable or lethargic, and develop seizures or apnoea. If seizures are present, hypocalcaemia should be corrected by slow intravenous infusion of 10% calcium gluconate. Otherwise, treatment is by oral or intravenous calcium supplementation.

Other Common Electrolyte Upsets

Alteration in the serum sodium level is fairly common in ill, preterm infants. Hyponatraemia may occur in a variety of conditions where there is either an increase in the loss of sodium as in vomiting and diarrhoea, bowel obstruction or from the kidney. Hyponatraemia may also occur because of inappropriate secretion of ADH following cerebral disturbance and may occur in adrenal insufficiency. It may also occur with inappropriate intravenous fluid therapy and in heart failure.

Hyperkalaemia may occur in sick newborn infants often as a complication of renal failure or where there has been gross tissue underperfusion.

FEEDING THE NORMAL PRETERM INFANT

The preterm infant differs in many respects from a term infant, especially since he may have inadequately developed sucking and swallowing reflexes. Before 34 weeks gestation, infants will require tube feeding with small, frequent feeds. In general, the healthy preterm infant should be fed within 2 hr of birth. If the baby is unable to suckle at the breast, the milk should be expressed and given to the infant via an orogastric tube. If mother's own breast milk is not available, the infant may either be fed with donor breast milk or one of the newer proprietary milks which contain 75–80 cal/100 ml. For infants over 1500 g, it is usual to start with feeds every 2 hr and as these are tolerated to extend the feeding interval to 3 hr. Many infants less than 1500 g birth weight will require intravenous nutrition for some days; oral feeding, once begun, should be increased cautiously. Feeds should be started at a rate of 1 ml/kg/hr and gradually increased, but care should be taken that the tube does not become displaced leading to aspiration. Continuous orogastric feeding may be replaced by intermittent orogastric feeding as the infant gets bigger or becomes more active. Occasionally, orojejunal feeding is used when the risk of aspiration is particularly high, as for example, infants on ventilators or those with chronic lung disease.

Energy requirements for growth are about 90–110 cal/kg/day. It is usually not possible to provide this amount of energy either orally, intravenously or by combination for the first 4 or 5 days of life. For this reason, and because of excessive fluid losses, the preterm infant may lose up to 10% of his birth weight in the first week of life. Weight loss greater than this should give rise to concern and probably indicates excessive dehydration and the need to increase fluid intake. Some infants fail to lose weight after birth and they develop oedema. This may occur in the ill infant when fluid leaks from the capillaries into the interstitial tissues, or may occur as a result of excessive fluid intake or congestive heart failure.

It is customary to provide preterm infants with routine vitamin supplements using one of the proprietary multivitamin preparations (Abidec or Children's Vitamin Drops). Folic acid is usually given and iron is commenced at 6 weeks.

Necrotizing Enterocolitis (NEC)

NEC is an inflammatory condition of both large and small bowel characterized by the presence of gas in the bowel wall and, sometimes, in the portal tract. It is more common in the preterm than term infant and more likely to occur in the infant who has been ill with RDS or infection. Recently, there has been increased interest in this condition, which is becoming more common. This may be because, with improved intensive care techniques, more small infants are surviving and so the population of babies at risk has increased. At present, the incidence of necrotizing enterocolitis in very low-birth-weight infants is about 10%.

Pathogenesis

The aetiology and pathogenesis of NEC remain unclear. NEC is probably the result of an ischaemic insult to the bowel wall which may follow birth asphyxia, haemodynamic changes during exchange transfusion or arterial embolism and thrombosis associated with umbilical vessel catheterization. Certainly most infants who develop NEC are either ill or very low birth weight. Term infants who have suffered from asphyxia or have undergone cardiac catheterization may also develop NEC, and somewhat paradoxically these babies present earlier and have a higher mortality than preterm babies. Ischaemic damage to the bowel may encourage bacterial invasion from the lumen with release of gas into the bowel wall. NEC rarely occurs before feeding has been started and it may be that colonization of the intestine with Gram-negative organisms is a prerequisite for this disorder. A totally breast-fed baby is less likely to develop NEC, perhaps because his intestine is colonized primarily with lactobacilli or because of the other antibacterial properties of breast milk (Chapter 2).

Pathological examination may show diffuse involvement of the gastro-intestinal tract or the lesion may be restricted to a short segment of the small intestine near the terminal ileum. Where the bowel is very necrotic, there may be perforation leading to peritonitis.

Clinical Features

The earliest sign of NEC may be abdominal distension with increasing gastric aspirates. Other symptoms include vomiting, bloody stools and erythema of the anterior abdominal wall. In addition, there may be non-specific findings such as apnoeic attacks and lethargy, temperature instability and thrombocytopenia. This may occur as part of a disseminated intravascular coagulation or may be the result of platelet consumption within the necrotic bowel. The degree of thrombocytopenia correlates quite well with the severity of the inflammatory process. Tenderness suggests peritonism. Signs of perforation occur late.

Investigations

Abdominal radiographs may show dilated bowel loops with thickened oedema-tous walls. Later, linear or circular streaks of intramural gas appear and perforation may occur (Fig. 4.12). With perforation, free peritoneal gas may be

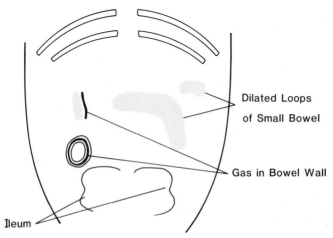

Dilated Loops
of Small Bowel

Gas in Bowel Wall

Ileum

Figure 4.12 Schematic representation of abdominal radiograph showing NEC.

seen under the diaphragm or under the umbilicus. Gas may also be seen in the portal venous system or within the hepatic veins which is often an ominous sign signifying marked bowel ischaemia. Blood cultures may be positive as septicaemia commonly occurs in this condition. The white cell count and platelet count may be low. Stools should be sent for culture and tested for occult blood.

Once the presence of intramural air has been documented, lateral radiographs of the abdomen should be repeated at 8-hr intervals to look for bowel perforation which may occur without immediate clinical deterioration.

Management

NEC may be preventable by careful placement of umbilical catheters, delay in feeding the very low-birth-weight and asphyxiated infant and more liberal use of expressed breast milk. Once signs are present, oral feeding must be stopped and parenteral feeding started. As septicaemia is common, parenteral antibiotics should be given. If perforation has occurred, surgery must be carried out. At operation, minimal resection of non-viable bowel and double-barrelled enterostomies are usually performed. Extensive resection will lead to later problems of the short-bowel syndrome so surgery should be conservative. In infants who recover, gradual refeeding should be undertaken when the clinical and radiological findings have cleared. This usually is not possible for about 10 days.

Outcome

The mortality of this condition is about 10%. Death may result from perforation and peritonitis, renal and hepatic failure, septicaemia and bleeding. Later complications of this syndrome include stricture formation which may require surgery, and malabsorption syndrome from damage to the intestinal villi or short bowel syndrome as a result of extensive surgery.

Jaundice

The preterm infant is more likely to develop jaundice than the term infant because of immaturity at many different points in the pathway of bilirubin metabolism. Jaundice may be detected clinically in the newborn at bilirubin levels greater than 70 μmol/l.

Incidence

About 20–50% of all normal newborn infants and a considerably higher percentage of preterm infants will demonstrate clinical jaundice during the first week of life. In the very low-birth-weight infant, significant jaundice requiring phototherapy occurs in about 30% of infants.

Pathogenesis

Jaundice in the preterm infant is really an exaggeration of the physiological jaundice of the normal full-term infant. An outline of bilirubin metabolism is given in Fig. 4.13 and the possible mechanisms involved in jaundice of prematurity are shown in Table 4.10.

Jaundice in the preterm infant may also occur for the same reasons (for example blood group incompatibility) as in the term baby (Chapter 10).

The major significance of jaundice is that it may lead to kernicterus. This is an acute neurological syndrome caused by free bilirubin which damages certain parts of the brain, notably the basal ganglia and VIIIth cranial nerve. Bilirubin is normally bound to albumin and is thus rendered harmless, but the preterm infant has a reduced serum albumin and is unable to bind as much. In addition, certain drugs including digoxin, gentamicin, indomethacin and frusemide, which may be used in the newborn, displace bilirubin from albumin.

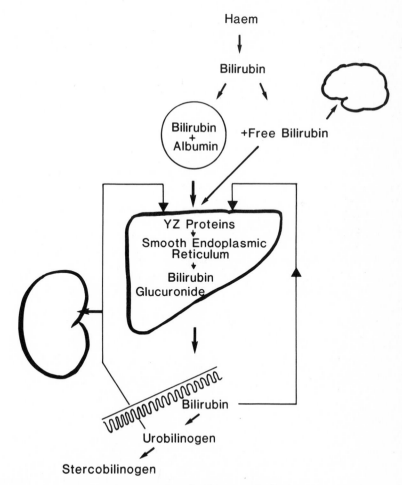

Figure 4.13 Bilirubin metabolism.

Table 4.10 Jaundice of prematurity

1. Increased production of bilirubin
   - Increased red cell mass
   - Reduced red cell survival
   - Increased entero-hepatic circulation of bilirubin
2. Defective hepatic uptake of bilirubin from the plasma
   - Decreased Y proteins
   - Binding of Y and Z proteins by other amines
   - Inadequate calorie intake
3. Defective bilirubin conjugation
   - Reduced glucuronyl transferase
4. Defective bilirubin excretion
5. Changes in hepatic circulation
   - Reduced oxygen supply to the liver when umbilical cord clamped

The development of kernicterus is enhanced when there is or has been acidosis, hypoxia or hypoglycaemia. For these reasons, exchange transfusion is carried out at much lower levels in preterm infants.

Clinical Features

The onset of jaundice in the preterm infant is usually after the first 24 hr of life and tends to reach a peak at 4–5 days of age, although in very immature infants it may last considerably longer than this. Jaundice that is apparent within the first 24 hr of life suggests the presence of haemolysis or intrauterine infection and requires urgent investigation. Jaundice may be associated with increasing lethargy in the preterm infant.

Kernicterus may present with hypotonia or hypertonia and there may be opisthotonus and convulsions. In the very immature infant, apnoea may be the presenting sign. The presence of neurological signs in a preterm infant who is jaundiced is ominous.

Persistent jaundice (more than 2 weeks) is seen in a few very preterm infants and is usually due to the effects of sepsis or parenteral nutrition solutions, although it may occasionally be due to other conditions such as hypothyroidism, galactosaemia, hepatitis and biliary atresia.

Investigation

Serum bilirubin levels should be measured once or twice a day in the preterm infant when jaundice is clinically apparent. If the infant is ill, other investigations may be indicated to exclude co-existing causes of jaundice such as infection.

Management

Phototherapy is used prophylactically in very immature infants, especially those who have marked bruising. In larger infants, it is started when the bilirubin is seen to be rising. During phototherapy, the infant is exposed to a white or blue light source which reduces the serum bilirubin, probably by converting it in the skin into water-soluble compounds which are then excreted in the urine. Exchange transfusion is usually carried out in the healthy term infant at the bilirubin level of 350 μmol/l but in the preterm infant may be carried out at bilirubin levels as low as 150 μmol/l.

Most preterm infants with jaundice recover spontaneously or following a period of phototherapy but about 5% require exchange transfusion. Infusion of albumin prior to exchange transfusion increases bilirubin binding and allows more bilirubin to be removed by the procedure.

Infection

Discussion here will be confined to bacterial infections of the preterm infant. Intrauterine viral infections of the TORCH complex will be discussed in Chapter 13 and congenital pneumonia has been discussed earlier in this chapter. The other bacterial infections likely to involve the preterm infant are superficial skin infections, conjunctivitis, septicaemia, meningitis, urinary tract infection, osteomyelitis and gastroenteritis.

Incidence

Severe bacterial infections occur in the newborn at the rate of about 5 per 1000 births. For full-term infants, the incidence is about 1 per 1000 births but for preterm babies it is much higher (4–30%) depending upon gestational age.

Pathogenesis

Bacterial infection may be acquired *in utero* or nosocomially. There are basically three routes of infection: ascending through the cervical canal after rupture of the membranes, across the placenta or by aspiration of infected vaginal contents during birth. Infection that is acquired postnatally from the environment is known as nosocomial infection and originates from nursery personnel, mechanical ventilators and incubators, sinks and blood gas analysers. Transmission of organisms from one infected infant to another most commonly occurs on the hands of nursery personnel and so strict hand-washing before and after touching an infant is essential.

Apart from immaturity, there are other factors that predispose to infection in the newborn. These include prolonged rupture of the membranes, operative deliveries, perinatal asphyxia, congenital malformations, the male sex, invasive procedures such as umbilical catheterization and the use of humidified gases. The commonest pathogens are *Escherichia coli*, staphylococci, group B beta-haemolytic streptococci, pseudomonas, listeria, klebsiella, enterococci, anaerobes, haemophilus, serratia and pneumococci.

There are immunological reasons why the newborn infant and especially the preterm infant is at increased risk of infection. These are summarized in Table 4.11.

Table 4.11 Impairment of neonatal defences against infection

1. Decreased humoral immunity: only IgG crosses the placenta (IgM contains specific bacterial antibodies to Gram-negative organisms)
2. Decreased cellular immunity: still debated but the preterm infant probably has impaired cell-mediated immunity
3. Decreased white cell activity: phagocytosis reduced due to deficient opsonizing antibody. Newborn white cells function well in adult serum
4. Deficient complement system

Clinical Features

The signs of sepsis in the newborn are protean and some of these are shown in Table 4.12. Systemic symptoms and signs of sepsis are more common than specific ones; lethargy, poor feeding and apnoea being particularly common. It is important that medical staff pay careful attention to comments from individual nurses who are looking after preterm babies. Any report of an infant apparently doing less well than previously should be taken seriously, the infant should be examined and appropriate investigations carried out. The clinical features of specific infections will be discussed later in this chapter and in Chapter 14.

Investigation

The laboratory investigations of suspected neonatal infection are shown in Table 4.13. Before starting antibiotic therapy, it is important to perform cultures of blood, spinal fluid and urine. Microscopy of these fluids may be helpful giving early indications of the type of infection, Gram stain of gastric aspirate and cerebrospinal fluid being particularly useful in this respect. An abnormal full blood picture with leucopenia, leucocytosis or thrombocytopenia may also

Table 4.12 Signs of neonatal sepsis

1. Pallor or mottling, shock
2. Hypotonia or poor Moro reflex
3. Lethargy
4. Poor feeding
5. Vomiting
6. Hypothermia or fever
7. Jaundice
8. Apnoea or tachypnoea
9. Tachycardia or bradycardia
10. Abdominal distension
11. Splenomegaly, hepatomegaly
12. Enlarged kidneys
13. Bloody stools or diarrhoea
14. Seizures
15. Omphalitis
16. Sclerema
17. Abnormal bleeding, petechiae

Table 4.13 Laboratory investigation of suspected neonatal infection

1. Cultures: blood, cerebrospinal fluid, urine, skin, external ear, throat, rectum, cord, amniotic fluid, gastric aspirate, catheter tips
2. Microscopy: cerebrospinal fluid, urine and gastric aspirate (Gram stain)
3. Full blood picture, ESR, C-reactive protein
4. Chest radiograph (especially if respiratory distress)
5. Others (if indicated): immunoglobulins, blood gases, calcium, electrolytes, coagulation studies
6. Histopathology – umbilical cord or placenta

be an early clue to the presence of infection. Pathological examination of the placenta and cord will detect the presence of amnionitis and may help the paediatrician in deciding which infants to treat in the early neonatal period.

Specific Infections

Superficial Infection

Septic spots are often seen on the skin of infants and are treated by local cleansing. Omphalitis is seen as a serous or purulent ooze from the umbilicus with an area of redness or induration around it.

Local infections are generally not dangerous but the infant should be observed closely because the infection may spread, in which case systemic antibiotics should be given.

Conjunctivitis

Conjunctivitis may be caused by chemicals, bacteria or viruses. Bacteria causing conjunctivitis include staphylococcus, chlamydia and gonococcus. This last infection should be treated with local penicillin eye-drops and systemic penicillin, whereas chlamydial infection responds to treatment with systemic erythromycin and tetracycline eye ointment.

Septicaemia

This may be caused by coliforms, streptococci or staphylococci, including *Staphylococcus albus*. The symptoms and signs are as described in Table 4.12. Babies with this condition may be seriously ill and in 30% there will be associated meningitis. The portal of entry may be the umbilicus or infection may be secondary to infection anywhere in the body. Many very preterm babies become ill when infected with *S. albus* from colonized intravenous catheters, especially when these are used for parenteral nutrition. Respiratory support, blood transfusion and antibiotics are urgently needed. Culture-proven septicaemia requires antibiotic therapy for 2 weeks.

Meningitis

The initial symptoms are usually non-specific such as vomiting or lethargy. More specific symptoms of seizures, high-pitched cry and a tense anterior fontanelle do not occur until meningitis is well established. The most common causative bacteria are coliforms and haemolytic streptococci. Antibiotics should be given systemically; there is little evidence that intrathecal antibiotics are of any value.

Urinary Tract Infection

The presentation is often non-specific with poor feeding, vomiting and jaundice. Urine culture is done either by obtaining several voided samples or one specimen by suprapubic aspiration. All voided specimens should reveal the same organisms at a concentration of greater than 100 000/ml and the sample should contain pus cells. Parenteral antibiotics are given for 10 days. Renal ultrasonography and micturating cystogram should be carried out as renal anomalies will be found in 10–20% of cases. The recurrence rate of urinary infection is high.

Osteomyelitis

This may occur up to 6 weeks after a staphylococcal or streptococcal septicaemia. The bones most commonly affected are the long bones, notably the tibia although on occasion the vertebrae and maxilla are involved. Local infections have been reported in the skull bones after application of fetal scalp electrodes and in the os calcis after heel stabs for blood sampling. The infant may show systemic symptoms with lethargy, pyrexia and poor feeding, and local signs may appear late. These include redness, tenderness, local oedema and loss of movement in the affected limb. Radiographic changes may take some weeks to appear. The diagnosis may be confirmed by aspiration of the infected area to obtain fluid for culture. The duration of antibiotic therapy is 6 weeks.

Gastroenteritis

This condition is now much less common in the normal newborn but may cause problems in the preterm baby. Most infections are caused by viruses such as rotavirus or astrovirus but a bacterial pathogen may be found in 20–40% with pathogenic *E. coli*, shigella and salmonella being the commonest. Mild cases usually respond to discontinuation of milk feeds and replacement with oral clear fluids. In severe cases, the infant may be dehydrated or develop hypernatraemia, in which case intravenous fluids are required. Infected infants should be isolated by placing them in incubators and scrupulous hand-washing is essential as nosocomial infection is common.

Management of Neonatal Infection

Prevention of infection in neonatal nurseries is extremely important and the importance of good hand-washing has already been stressed. Infants suspected of being infected should be isolated in incubators but there is probably no need for strict barrier nursing in isolation units. A policy of selective admission of babies born outside hospital and of closure of a nursery when infection rates become excessive should be adopted. Local treatment to the umbilical cord may be helpful in reducing colonization rates with staphylococci. Hexachlorophane in a concentration of 0.3% has not been shown to be harmful after a single application. A new compound, pseudomonic acid (muprocin) is showing promise in the control of outbreaks of methicillin-resistant *Staphylococcus aureus* infection.

Once infection has been established, antibiotics form the mainstay of the therapy. Other supportive care is important and includes the provision of adequate fluids and nutrition, maintenance of the neutral thermal environment and prevention of complications such as hypoxaemia and acidosis.

Antibiotic therapy will depend upon the type of infection, the age of the infant and the organisms isolated. As a rule, a single antibiotic should be used to treat specific infections such as group B streptococcal infection and listeriosis, but for other non-specific infections it is common to use a combination of a penicillin and an aminoglycoside. In general, antibiotics should be given by slow intravenous infusion or intramuscularly. Serum levels of aminoglycoside should be measured to ensure adequate concentrations of antibiotic and to prevent damage to the auditory nerves and kidneys from excessive doses. In addition to penicillin and aminoglycosides, the newer cephalosporin antibiotics and chloramphenicol have a place in the treatment of serious neonatal infection. Chloramphenicol in the correct dose is not toxic to the newborn and has the advantage of achieving adequate levels in the cerebrospinal fluid even after oral administration. In the past, the 'grey baby syndrome' occurred when chloramphenicol was given in inappropriately large doses. In this condition, the infant developed diarrhoea and vomiting, abdominal distension and peripheral circulatory collapse.

Outcome

The outcome of infection in the preterm infant depends upon the gestational age of the infant, the type of infection and its severity. Infants who suffer from bacterial meningitis have a high mortality of about 30–40% and up to half of survivors will show developmental sequelae which include intellectual and physical handicaps, deafness, blindness and hydrocephalus. Proven septicaemia in the newborn has a mortality rate of about 20%, although this may be even higher in the very low-birth-weight infant. Early onset infection with the group B streptococcus is fatal in 30–50% of cases. In the past, gastroenteritis had a high mortality in the newborn although this problem seems to have lessened considerably in recent times.

Haematological Problems

Anaemia

Anaemia in the preterm infant may occur at birth, or may develop during the first 3 months of life or after the sixth month. These are sometimes referred to as immediate, early and late anaemia of prematurity. Immediate anaemia is defined as a haemoglobin level less than 13 g/dl and early and late anaemias as haemoglobin values of less than 9 g/dl.

Pathogenesis

Immediate anaemia is usually due to blood loss as in feto-maternal transfusion or fetal haemorrhage from vasa praevia, or may be due to haemolysis as in rhesus incompatibility or haemoglobinopathy. Immediate anaemia may also be exacerbated by early cord clamping.

Early anaemia of prematurity is due to deficient erythropoiesis combined with reduced red cell survival times. The anaemia may be made worse by excessive blood sampling and chronic haemolysis as occurs with rhesus and ABO incompatibility or vitamin E deficiency.

Late anaemia is often due to a deficiency of iron, or less frequently, of vitamin E and folic acid.

Clinical Findings

When anaemia is present at birth because of blood loss, the infant may be pale and shocked, have tachypnoea and tachycardia and the blood pressure may be low. If chronic haemolysis has occurred *in utero*, the infant may not be so acutely distressed but will be pale with hepatosplenomegaly. There may be signs of hydrops with generalized oedema and ascites.

Early and late anaemia present with increasing pallor which of itself is not significant, but if associated with tachypnoea and tachycardia, suggests inadequate delivery of oxygen to the tissues. However, infants may tolerate anaemia particularly well and may have no symptoms with haemoglobin levels as low as 7 g/dl.

Investigation

If a baby is found to be anaemic at birth, it is important to determine whether this has been caused by a feto-maternal transfusion by performing the Kleihauer test on maternal blood. Blood group incompatibility can be confirmed by measuring the haemoglobin, indirect bilirubin and Coombs test on the baby's blood, and by determining the baby's and mother's blood groups (Chapter 10). Intrauterine infection can be confirmed by measuring TORCH titres (Chapter 14). Other investigations include coagulation screen to exclude a bleeding disorder, red cell enzyme assays and haemoglobin electrophoresis to look for congenital haemolytic anaemia.

Physiological anaemia of prematurity (early anaemia) is due to delayed onset of erythropoiesis and is a normochromic, normocytic anaemia, whereas late anaemia of prematurity is often hypochromic and microcytic.

Vitamin E deficiency sometimes occurs in infants less than 1500 g. Vitamin E has anti-oxidant properties and protects the red cell membrane from the adverse affects of oxidants such as oxygen or iron. These may cause breakdown of the red cell and give rise to haemolytic anaemia which usually presents after the first 6 weeks of life. This anaemia is characterized by the presence of a high reticulocyte count and low serum vitamin E.

Management

If the baby shows signs of acute blood loss or severe anaemia immediately after birth, it may be necessary to give an immediate transfusion of blood in the labour ward (Chapter 11). In some infants with chronic intrauterine haemolysis, exchange transfusion with blood is used to increase haemoglobin concentrations and to remove bilirubin; alternatively, small transfusions of packed cells may be used if hyperbilirubinaemia is not a problem (Chapter 10). Preterm infants with physiological anaemia are not transfused unless they have symptoms suggesting hypoxaemia such as tachypnoea, tachycardia or poor feeding or have a haemoglobin less than 7 g/dl.

Outcome

Anaemia of itself is rarely a life-threatening disorder in the newborn, except when acute blood loss occurs in the immediate neonatal period. Otherwise, the prognosis depends upon the cause.

Polycythaemia

This condition is uncommon in the preterm infant but is more likely if the infant is small for gestational age. Polycythaemia is arbitrarily defined as a venous packed cell volume greater than 65% which corresponds to a haemoglobin greater than 22 g/dl.

Incidence

Polycythaemia occurs in less than 5% of preterm infants but in about 20–25% of small-for-dates infants.

Pathogenesis

The causes of polycythaemia are listed in Table 4.14. The importance of polycythaemia is that the blood viscosity increases linearly with increasing packed cell volume until the latter reaches 65%, whereupon viscosity increases in a logarithmic fashion. Hyperviscosity is associated with a decreased flow both in the microcirculation and in the large veins, and is associated with cerebral, renal or inferior vena caval thrombosis. There is decreased oxygen delivery to the tissues and, later, significant jaundice may develop because of the breakdown of the excess red cells.

Table 4.14 Causes of polycythaemia

1. Delayed cord clamping and milking of umbilical cord
2. Intrauterine growth retardation
3. Diabetic mother
4. Twin-to-twin transfusion
5. Materno-fetal transfusion
6. Thyrotoxicosis

Clinical Features

The most ominous signs are cerebral hyperexcitability with irritability and, occasionally, seizures. There may be apathy, vomiting, abdominal distension, congestive heart failure, central cyanosis, hypoglycaemia, jaundice and persistent fetal circulation.

Management

The packed cell volume should be checked routinely in ill infants, those of diabetic mothers and small-for-dates babies. If the venous haematocrit is greater than 65% and the infant has any symptoms attributable to polycythaemia, a partial exchange transfusion with the albumin or plasma should be carried out (20 ml/kg). If the packed cell volume is greater than 70%, corresponding to haemoglobin greater than 25 g/dl, a partial exchange should also be carried out even if symptoms are absent. The aim is to lower packed cell volume to about 55%.

Outcome

The prognosis for babies who are polycythaemic largely depends upon the underlying cause. In a few, particularly those whose mothers are diabetic, renal vein thrombosis may occur. One study has shown that polycythaemic infants have lower developmental scores than babies who had normal haemoglobin levels at birth.

Bleeding Disorders

Incidence

Haemorrhagic disease of the newborn is extremely uncommon and occurs in less than 1 per 5000 births but is more common in preterm babies. It is preventable by giving vitamin K routinely to all newborn infants at birth (Chapter 2). Disseminated intravascular coagulation may occur in any ill preterm infant who is suffering from sepsis, hypoxia or acidosis. No true incidence of this condition is known.

Pathogenesis

Haemorrhagic disease of the newborn is caused by a reduction in hepatic production of vitamin K-dependent coagulation factors. These include factors II (Prothrombin), VII, IX and X. Since cow's milk contains four times as much vitamin K as breast milk, haemorrhagic disease is normally seen only in breast-fed infants. Vitamin K deficiency may also occur in chronic diarrhoeal states or in preterm babies who are treated with prolonged broad-spectrum antibiotic therapy and parenteral nutrition. Some of the anticonvulsant drugs such as phenytoin also inhibit vitamin K and, if given to the mother during pregnancy, may affect the baby.

In disseminated intravascular coagulation (DIC) nearly all clotting factors are reduced including I, V and platelets.

Clinical Features

The baby with haemorrhagic disease of the newborn may present with bruising, bleeding from the umbilical cord or more severe internal bleeding involving the gastrointestinal tract. Intracerebral haemorrhage can occur but is extremely rare. The usual onset is the third to seventh day of life, though in the preterm infant who is having parenteral nutrition, this may be delayed into the second and third week of life.

The infant with DIC is usually extremely ill and may have severe RDS, septicaemia or necrotizing enterocolitis. The clinical presentation may be of persistent oozing from the umbilical cord, from venepuncture sites or of major haemorrhage into any organ. The platelet count of all ill babies should be regularly estimated as the development of thrombocytopenia may be the first indication of DIC. Fibrin degradation products are increased in blood and urine.

Management

Haemorrhagic disease of the newborn is treated by giving intravenous or intramuscular vitamin K. For continued or life-threatening bleeding, fresh frozen plasma or fresh whole blood may be transfused and local bleeding from the umbilical cord may stop after pressure or application of topical thrombin.

The corner-stone of treatment of DIC is the correction of underlying abnormalities such as hypoxia, acidosis and infection.

Outcome

In general, infants with haemorrhagic disease do well unless there has been intracerebral bleeding. The prognosis for DIC is largely dependent on the underlying cause.

MOTHER–INFANT BONDING

The mother of a preterm baby often expects that her baby will die. This is especially so if she does not see her baby after birth or if the baby requires transfer to another hospital for care. The mother will then grieve in anticipation of her baby's death and so be unable to develop the natural mother–infant bond that occurs soon after birth. It is especially important that the mother of a preterm baby sees her infant after birth if only for a brief moment. This situation may, of course, be difficult if the mother requires Caesarean section, though, with more liberal use of epidural and spinal anaesthesia, it is often possible. If babies require transfer for intensive or special care, a Polaroid photograph should always be provided for the mother.

Mother and father should be encouraged to visit the baby early and regularly, and frequent contact with the infant is recommended. Gentle touching of the baby, with fondling and stroking is good for the parents and appears to reduce the number of apnoeic attacks and to increase weight gain in a tiny preterm baby. Visits by siblings should also be encouraged once the initial intensive-care period has ended.

It is helpful to ask the mother to make some tangible contribution to her infant's care such as providing expressed breast milk. If the baby cannot be fed soon after birth, the mother should be reassured that her milk will be given to another deserving baby in the unit until her own baby is ready to take feeds.

It is important that parents are talked to frequently by the medical and nursing staff. Their fear may lessen and they will certainly benefit from the feeling that others are concerned about their baby. Explanations should be clear, gentle and

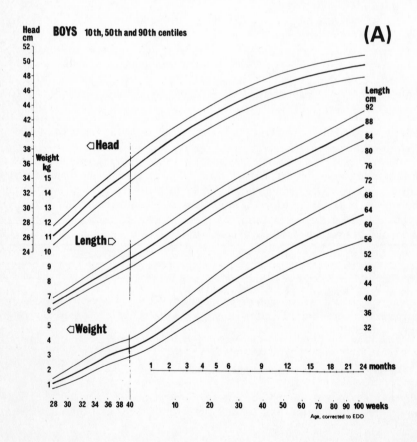

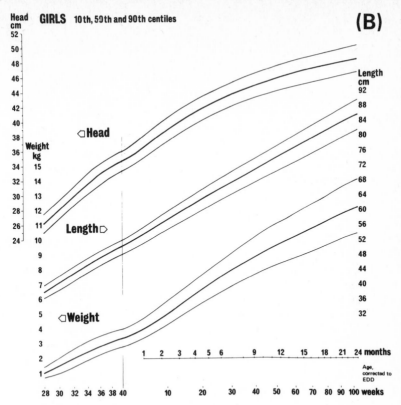

Figure 4.14 Growth charts for the first 2 years of life: (A) boys, (B) girls. (After Gairdner and Pearson, 1971.)

consistent, and pessimistic remarks should be avoided unless the situation is absolutely hopeless.

Once the preterm baby is over the acute early stages and is beginning to grow he should be dressed in attractive clothing. The more attractive the tiny preterm baby is to his parents, the easier it is for them to grow attached. The parents should be encouraged to suggest a name for the baby early and this should be used by medical and nursing staff instead of 'he' or 'she' or, worse still, 'it'.

Despite these attempts to foster the mother–infant bond, a few mothers will find difficulty in relating to their babies. These babies may fail to thrive, have frequent hospital admission, may show delayed developmental milestones or show signs of frank neglect or baby battering.

Follow-up of the Preterm Infant

The preterm infant is followed up at the hospital baby clinic so that his growth and development may be assessed; this should continue at least to the age of 3 years. This clinic also serves to reassure parents and give them continuing advice on rearing their baby. At each visit, the baby should have his weight, length and head circumference measured and plotted on an appropriate growth chart (Fig. 4.14). It is important to correct for gestational age at least until the baby is 18 months–2 years old. This means that the baby of 32 weeks gestation who has reached a postnatal age of 10 weeks should be considered as a baby of 2 weeks corrected age. Developmental screening of the infant is best carried out at the age of 6 weeks, 6 months, 10 months, 18 months and 2 years. The follow-up of these tiny, at-risk babies is really a team effort and should involve the neonatal paediatrician, ophthalmologist, audiologist, physiotherapist and hospital liaison health visitor. Feedback to the community is especially important so that the community health visitor and the general practitioner can be kept adequately informed of the infant's progress.

Current follow-up results suggest that between 5 and 10% of very low-birth-weight infants who have needed intensive care with life support have some development sequelae. In two-thirds of these infants (about 7% overall) the developmental handicap is mild and includes slight visual disturbances such as squint or myopia, slight hearing loss or evidence of increased tone and reflexes in the legs which may be transient. In one-third of these infants (about 3% overall) the handicaps are severe with significant impairment of vision and hearing, hydrocephalus or microcephaly and signs of cerebral palsy, usually of the diplegic type. These infants and their families require intensive and continuing help.

FURTHER READING

Anderson, A., Beard, R. W., Brudenell, J. M. and Dunn, P. M. (1977) *Preterm Labour*. Royal College of Obstetrics and Gynaecology, London.

Beard, R. W. and Sharp, F. (1985) *Preterm Labour and its Consequences*. Royal College of Obstetrics and Gynaecology, London.

Boyer, K. M. and Gotoff, S. P. (1986) Prevention of early-onset neonatal group B streptococcal disease with selective intrapartum chemoprophylaxis. *N. Engl. J. Med.* **314**: 1665.

Dubowitz, L. M., Dubowitz, V. and Goldberg, C. (1970) Clinical assessment of gestational age in the newborn infant. *J. Pediatr.* 77: 1.

Gairdner, D. and Pearson, J. (1971) A growth chart for premature and other infants. *Arch. Dis. Child.* **46**: 783.

Halliday, H. L., McClure, G., Reid, M. (1985) *Handbook of Neonatal Intensive Care*, 2nd edn. Baillière Tindall, London.

Hey, E. N. and Katz, G. (1970) The optimal thermal environment for naked babies. *Arch. Dis. Child.* **45**: 328.

Kelnar, C. J. H. and Harvey, D. (1986) *The Sick Newborn Baby*, 2nd edn. Baillière Tindall, London.

Klaus, M. H. and Fanaroff, A. A. (1986) *Care of the High Risk Neonate*, 3rd edn. W. B. Saunders, Philadelphia, PA.

Klaus, M. H. and Kennell, J. H. (1982) *Parent–Infant Bonding*, 2nd edn. C. V. Mosby, St Louis, MO.

McClure, B. G. (1979) Delivery room care of the preterm infant. *J. Mat. Child Health.* 4: 466.

Papile, L. A., Burstein, J., Burstein, R. and Koffler, H. (1978) Incidence and evolution of subependymal and intraventricular hemorrhage. *J. Pediatr.* **92**: 529.

Robertson, B. (1985) Overview of surfactant replacement therapy. In Clinch, J. and Matthews, T. (eds), *Perinatal Medicine* MTP Press, London, pp. 285–292.

Whittle, J. J., Wilson, A. I., Whitfield, C. R., Paton, R. D. and Logan, R. W. (1982) Amniotic fluid phosphatidyl glycerol and the lecithin/sphingomyelin ratio in the assessment of fetal lung maturity. *Br. J. Obstet. Gynaecol.* **89**: 727.

5

Intrauterine Growth Retardation

INTRODUCTION

During the antenatal period poor fetal growth is commonly referred to as intrauterine growth retardation (IUGR) and the resulting infants are described as being 'small for gestational age' (SGA) or 'small for dates' (SFD).

For several reasons, it is important to detect IUGR and to recognize those babies who are SGA. Brain growth is maximal in the second half of pregnancy and the first year of extrauterine life, a time called the 'period of critical brain growth'. It is suggested that impairment of brain growth at this time may be irrecoverable. Further, infants who are growth retarded *in utero* because of some pathological process are at risk, and any deterioration in the primary disease or additional insult may lead to intrauterine death. Additionally, some infants who are SGA have a chromosomal abnormality or have infection while others may be vulnerable to a variety of problems such as hypoglycaemia, hypoxia and polycythaemia.

DEFINITION

Traditionally, an infant weighing less than the 10th centile for gestational age at birth has been defined as SGA (see Figs. 2.9 and 5.1). This includes the majority of infants in whom clinical problems occur, though two difficulties arise from this definition. Firstly, this group will include many infants who are small but otherwise perfectly normal, merely underlining the biological variation in birth weight. Secondly, some babies weighing more than the 10th centile will be growth retarded because they have failed to achieve their own growth potential, i.e. without growth retardation, their birth weights would have been significantly greater.

The distribution of birth weights at a given gestational age is derived from measurements made on large numbers of infants from a given population. These are cross-sectional data and have the major disadvantage of not allowing for individual growth variation. Also, many infants who were born at less than 37 weeks and whose birth weights were used in the compilation of these graphs were born early because of some complication of pregnancy which may have altered fetal growth. In spite of these limitations, charts derived from cross-sectional data are used, since it is difficult to obtain accurate sequential estimates of fetal weights and no chart based on such information is available.

The majority of babies who are born 'small' are preterm. Most of these babies are appropriately grown but about one-third are growth retarded as well as being preterm. The clinician must determine whether a particular infant is preterm, SGA or a combination of both, since each is associated with different clinical problems and recurrence rates in future pregnancies vary.

INCIDENCE

Nine per cent of all babies are SGA in that they have birth weights below the 10th centile. One-third of babies whose birth weights are less than 2.5 kg are SGA. The most serious problems usually occur in infants whose birth weights are below the 3rd centile.

AETIOLOGY

The most important determinant of fetal size is gestational age, but other factors influence fetal growth: environmental, maternal, placental and fetal – disturbance of any of these may lead to IUGR. Table 5.1 shows an estimated distribution of causes in the UK.

Environmental Factors

A protein- and calorie-deficient diet is the commonest cause of mild IUGR, particularly in developing countries where poverty and infection often co-exist. Pre-conceptional maternal weight and weight gain during pregnancy are both related to birth weight. Malnutrition can affect growth at any stage in pregnancy but has most effect during the third trimester. The exact mechanism is not known, but mean birth weight has been improved in a deprived community by calorie and protein supplementation of the maternal diet.

The influence of altitude on fetal growth is slight but may cause asymmetrical retardation because of preferential distribution of better oxygenated blood to the fetal brain.

Maternal Factors

Maternal vascular disease is the most common cause of IUGR in developed countries and includes chronic essential hypertension, pre-eclampsia and chronic renal disease. Other diseases causing vascular damage, such as diabetes mellitus and disseminated lupus erythematosus, may occasionally be associated with IUGR.

A reduction in the oxygen-carrying capacity of maternal blood may limit fetal growth. This may occur in the haemoglobinopathies, particularly sickle-cell disease and in cyanotic heart disease.

Table 5.1 Distribution of causes of intrauterine growth retardation in the UK

Normal variation	10%
Chromosome and other congenital abnormality	10%
Congenital infection	5%
Maternal vascular disease	35%
Uterine abnormality	1%
Placental and cord problems	2%
Drugs and smoking	5%
Others	32%

From Dawes (1974).

Heavy cigarette smoking during pregnancy is associated with a decrease in birth weight. A number of mechanisms are thought to be involved: smoking causes an increase in maternal blood carbon monoxide levels with a consequent decrease in oxygen-carrying capacity of haemoglobin, leading to a reduction in available oxygen for fetal consumption; carbon monoxide may interfere with placental enzyme activity; and nicotine reduces the utero-placental blood flow. Smoking is also associated with poor maternal food intake and increased alcohol intake.

The fetal alcohol syndrome is now well recognized and the physical characteristics include a short upturned nose with a broad nasal bridge and small eyes with narrow palpebral fissures. Growth is usually retarded and intelligence is affected. Although normally the result of considerable alcohol intake, the syndrome may be associated with frequent intake of small amounts of alcohol, and in its mildest form may go unrecognized. Addiction to other drugs such as heroin can have a similar effect on growth.

Environmental factors such as altitude, nutrition and climate are partly responsible for the differences observed in birth weight between races, but true genetic racial differences are also important. The size of the parents, particularly the mother, will also affect the size at birth. Maternal weight has a more positive correlation with birth weight than maternal height.

First-born babies are generally lighter than subsequent siblings. Birth weight increases with parity until the third pregnancy and usually decreases subsequently.

Placental Factors

There is a fairly close correlation between placental weight and fetal size. Placental size is usually determined by maternal or fetal influences rather than by a primary placental problem. Infarction is associated with a reduction in the area of placental exchange especially when the infarction is extensive or multiple. Infarctions are commonly associated with maternal disease but may occur independently. Haemangioma is a rare condition of the placenta or cord, causing mechanical interference with the placental circulation. A single umbilical artery, abnormal insertion of the cord or thrombosis of fetal vessels may be associated with growth retardation. Growth retardation may occur with placenta praevia. It may also occur with circumvallate placenta, especially if associated with repeated haemorrhage. Malformations of the uterus are common (1–2%) and can cause preterm birth, deformities of the fetus and may restrict growth.

Fetal Factors

Growth failure in a baby with a chromosomal abnormality is due to an intrinsic defect in the fetus; the placental weight and morphology may be normal. The mean birth weight of babies with some common chromosomal disorders are shown in Table 5.2.

The mechanism of growth retardation resulting from intrauterine infection is complex and in part is due to villous placentitis with damage to vascular endothelium. Fetal viraemia has a direct effect on fetal cells causing an arrest of metabolic activity. In general, the earlier in pregnancy an infection occurs the

Table 5.2 Mean birth weight (g) of babies with some common chromosomal disorders

Down's syndrome	2900
Trisomy 18	2340
Trisomy 13	2480
Cri-du-chat syndrome	2600
Turner's syndrome	2750

greater the risk of damage to the fetus and the more pronounced the growth retardation. This is particularly so of rubella but also occurs with infections with cytomegalovirus (CMV), toxoplasmosis, herpes simplex, HIV and syphilis (Chapter 14).

Non-chromosomal fetal abnormalities such as neural tube defects may lead to low birth weight, and skeletal malformations to dwarfism.

The weight of the fetus is related to the number of fetuses and the birth order. The second twin is often lighter than the first and may suffer from growth retardation. In other mammals this effect may be due to deficient utero-placental blood flow, but in humans a placental 'steal' of blood between fetuses is more likely to be responsible, particularly in monozygotic twins.

The influence of fetal sex on birth weight becomes apparent after 24 weeks gestation. By term, the male baby weighs 150–200 g more than the female; whether this effect is due to sex hormones or to the Y-chromosome is unknown.

DIAGNOSIS

Antenatal diagnosis of IUGR is difficult and 50–70% of affected fetuses remain unrecognized before birth. Specific clues in the patient's past or present history should alert the obstetrician to the possibility of growth retardation (Table 5.3): in 50–60% of cases of IUGR one or more antenatal factors known to be associated with an increased risk of this condition are present.

Estimation of the date of confinement (EDC) is of prime importance in the management of pregnancies where IUGR is suspected; the subsequent inter-pretation of clinical and laboratory findings during pregnancy depends upon an accurate knowledge of the length of gestation (Chapter 2).

Table 5.3 Risk factors for intrauterine growth retardation

Poor obstetric history
Previous SGA baby
Multiple pregnancy
Pre-eclampsia, hypertension, chronic renal disease
Malnutrition and poor weight gain
Small maternal stature
Heavy smoking
Alcohol abuse
Long-standing diabetes or collagen disease

Having decided the gestational age of the fetus it is then feasible to attempt to decide whether or not fetal growth is appropriate in later pregnancy by clinical measures (Chapter 3). In particular an impression of the amount of amniotic fluid is important, as in IUGR the uterus 'hugs' the fetus and parts cannot be balotted easily.

INVESTIGATION OF SUSPECTED IUGR

The two objectives in the investigation of a patient with suspected IUGR are to confirm that growth retardation has occurred and to decide whether the fetus is at serious risk. Two types of growth retardation may be seen on ultrasound scan (see p. 47).

Biochemical Investigations

Plasma oestriol, urinary oestriol/creatinine ratio and serum HPL estimation are the most commonly used tests. They are easy to carry out but are of limited value because of their wide normal range, gross overlap between normal and abnormal fetuses and delay in obtaining results (Chapter 3).

The lecithin/sphingomyelin area ratio is also useful when the timing of delivery is under consideration.

Biophysical Investigation (see Chapter 3)

Ultrasonic examination may be used to estimate fetal size and to exclude abnormality, especially where there is oligohydramnios (Chapter 6). The major problem is that the gestational age must be known accurately before interpreting such information. Symmetrically growth-retarded fetuses cannot be distinguished ultrasonically from normal babies of shorter gestational ages. If there is doubt about the gestational age, other features that suggest IUGR should be sought and Table 5.4 shows how they may be differentiated.

The amount of liquor can be estimated and the appearance of the placental architecture determined. The liquor volume may be low in IUGR and the placental architecture may be more mature than expected for the length of pregnancy (Chapter 3).

Regular slower fetal breathing movements (FBM) usually appear at 35–36 weeks, but in IUGR this pattern appears earlier. Additionally, recent studies performed on umbilical blood flow waveforms using Doppler ultrasound are showing encouraging results, and suggest that the compromised IUGR fetus may be recognized by absence of a diastolic component to the umbilical artery waveform.

Antepartum Heart Rate Monitoring (Chapter 3)

Antepartum cardiotocography (non-stress test) is of value in managing the pregnancy once a diagnosis of IUGR has been established. This test may be especially sensitive in IUGR since the amniotic fluid volume is diminished and decelerations of the fetal heart rate due to cord compression are common. It should be repeated twice weekly. Negative results provide reassuring information that the fetus is unlikely to be in immediate danger. Positive tests warrant very careful surveillance in hospital and delivery if the test remains abnormal.

Table 5.4 Differentiation of suspected intrauterine growth retardation (IUGR) and preterm

Investigation	Preterm	Symmetrical IUGR	Asymmetrical IUGR
BPD – rate of growth	Normal	Slow for many weeks	Normal then abrupt slowing down
Abdominal circumference	Normal for gestation	Small reduction for gestation	Large reduction for gestation
Abdominal trunk diameter (ATD)	Appropriate	Appropriate	Smaller than BPD
BPD:ATD	Normal	Normal	More than 1 : 1 after 36 weeks
Placental architecture	Usually early changes only	Often early changes only	Often advanced changes for gestation
Fetal breathing movements	Rapid and irregular	Rapid and irregular changing to slow and regular by 35–36 weeks	Often slow and regular before 35–36 weeks
Amniotic fluid volume	Normal	Sometimes reduced	Often reduced

Fetal Activity Charts (Chapter 3)

These should be recorded daily in all patients with IUGR.

MANAGEMENT OF IUGR

Hospital admission for bed rest is essential as improvement in utero-placental blood flow can be expected and clinical improvement may occur. The tests described above should be performed serially and used as a basis to time the delivery of the fetus. Vasodilating drugs such as isoxsuprine and betamimetics like ritodrine have no place in the management of IUGR. Underlying disease such as hypertension should be managed as in Chapter 9.

Timing of Delivery

If poor or static fetal growth is positively established the pregnancy should be terminated, particularly after 34 weeks gestation. Delivery may be necessary before this time if there is additional evidence of fetal compromise such as abnormalities of the CTG or alteration in umbilical artery blood flow wave-forms.

In recent years, most patients have had a booking scan to establish accurately the gestational age of the fetus. Knowing this, there is less need to estimate fetal lung maturity by amniocentesis. Further, the amount of amniotic fluid is decreased in IUGR which increases the risk of this procedure. New information such as fetal breathing patterns and placental architecture compatible with late gestation correlate with fetal lung maturity. However, amniocentesis may be necessary where little or no information of early pregnancy is available and where there are pressing indications for delivery. The colour of the amniotic fluid should be noted and the LSAR and PG estimated.

Route of Delivery

Each case must be decided on its own merits. The growth-retarded fetus has a poor response to hypoxic stress during labour due to inadequate glycogen stores in the liver, heart and muscles, so this must be avoided. Vaginal delivery is considered when the cervix is favourable for induction and when delivery can be expected within 6 to 8 hr. Induction by artificial rupture of the membranes (ARM) and immediate intravenous oxytocin with continuous fetal heart rate monitoring using a scalp electrode is performed. If, at ARM, amniotic fluid is absent or stained with meconium, Caesarean section is indicated unless there are doubts about fetal normality. If labour is allowed to progress, scalp pH sampling should be performed.

If the cervix is unfavourable, Caesarean section is the route of choice since it avoids the hazards of prolonged labour and reduces the likelihood of intra-partum hypoxia. The operation should be carried out with the patient in left lateral tilt and with as short an interval as possible between anaesthetic induction and delivery.

123

NEONATAL CARE

The birth of a suspected SGA infant should be attended by a paediatrician since these infants may become acutely distressed during the second stage.

After delivery the airway should be cleared of any meconium present and the cord clamped promptly. These infants frequently have an increase in red cell mass because of hypoxia due to placental insufficiency and a placental transfusion would increase the haematocrit further, leading to hyperviscosity.

If necessary, the infant should be resuscitated (Chapter 2) but special care should be taken to avoid hypothermia to which they are unusually prone because of reduced amounts of brown fat and the large surface area to body weight ratio.

The next stage is to assess whether the infant is indeed SGA. This decision can be made clinically by estimating the gestational age (Chapter 4) and determining whether the birth weight is appropriate using standard growth charts (Figs 2.9 and 5.1).

SGA infants fall into the major categories which can be recognized before birth (p. 47) – those who are small but proportionate and those in whom growth of the head is relatively normal while body growth is poor. These two groups can be readily distinguished by measurement of head circumference, weight, length, mid-arm circumference and skin-fold thickness.

Symmetrical Growth Retardation

This heterogeneous group of babies includes a wide range of infants, from those who are small but are otherwise perfectly normal, to those with gross chromosomal abnormalities. In this group, congenital malformations must be sought and appropriate laboratory investigations performed since the result may influence management.

Down's syndrome is described more fully in Chapter 6. This syndrome is usually fairly easy to recognize with the characteristic facies, hands, feet, heart defects and muscle hypotonia, but occasionally the clinical diagnosis is much less clear especially in the mosaic forms. Trisomies 13 and 18 are usually easy to recognize, as are other syndromes such as Patau's syndrome (Chapter 6).

The same cannot be said of congenital infection, especially with CMV. The classical signs (Chapter 13) of hepatosplenomegaly, microcephaly, retinitis, purpura and abnormal head growth are absent in the majority of cases, so, in those babies who are SGA for no obvious reason, evidence of congenital infection by TORCH screening should be sought. This is important not only for investigation of the present baby but also because these infections may adversely affect future pregnancies.

Asymmetrical Growth Retardation

These babies have been subjected to a hostile intrauterine environment, usually because of placental problems. Typically, they have small bodies with disproportionately large heads. They look thin and wasted and frequently have loose folds of skin. Such babies tend to be active, feed hungrily and are unlikely to develop the respiratory distress syndrome probably because of increased production of surfactant secondary to intrauterine stress.

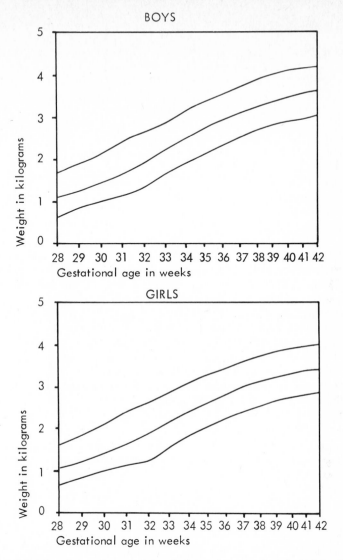

Figure 5.1 Weight charts for newborn babies, boys and girls (10th, 50th and 90th centiles).

These babies face several imminent dangers. At birth, asphyxia and meconium aspiration are not uncommon. After birth, hypoglycaemia is common, occurring as a consequence of intrauterine malnutrition resulting in deficient hepatic reserves of glycogen, so that monitoring of blood glucose is mandatory. Oral feeds should be started early unless the baby has suffered from severe asphyxia or is otherwise ill when intravenous dextrose solutions should be used.

Haematological problems may also occur. Hyperviscosity syndromes occur since the haematocrit may be elevated to dangerous levels as a result of intrauterine hypoxia. The haematocrit should be measured and a dilutional exchange transfusion performed when indicated (Chapter 4). Blood clotting problems are also more common due to reduced hepatic synthesis of vitamin K-dependent clotting factors. Clotting defects, hypothermia and hypoglycaemia are associated with massive pulmonary haemorrhage which is always of serious import. Very small babies (less than the 3rd centile) should have coagulation studies performed and a transfusion of 10–15 ml/kg of fresh frozen plasma given if a major coagulation defect is detected. Vitamin K is given at birth. In addition to being small, many of these infants are also immature because of early delivery and may suffer from the additional problems posed by immaturity (Chapter 4).

Another feature of these infants is their behaviour; they are active, irritable and jittery. They are often difficult to rear and their small size and difficult behaviour may engender fear and worry in the parents which can in turn lead to further deprivation.

Long-term Prognosis

SGA babies have a variable outlook but the symmetrically small babies have much poorer prognoses. This is not surprising since many have malformations or congenital infections. The outlook for the disproportionately grown baby is much less certain. The incidence of handicap is higher than for appropriately grown babies but may be minimized by detection and treatment of events which cause cerebral damage such as hypoglycaemia. The IQ of moderately SGA infants does not significantly differ from appropriately grown infants and the incidence of severe handicaps can certainly be reduced by good perinatal care. Other problems such as minimal cerebral dysfunction which occurs in about 25%, are possibly predetermined by the relative failure of brain growth before birth. Where there is a combination of prematurity and poor fetal growth, there is an increased risk of handicap and up to 25% of such infants may have developmental problems.

Somatic growth tends to be impaired. These children tend to be shorter and lighter than usual but there may be an accelerated pattern of head growth in the first 4 years of life.

CONCLUSION

Retarded fetal growth is a major problem in obstetrical and neonatal care. Great difficulties remain in early antenatal diagnosis and appropriate obstetrical management. Once severe growth retardation has occurred there is often significant mortality and both short-term and long-term morbidity. Meticulous attention to detail, identification of the high-risk patient and the use of a 'perinatal team' approach will help reduce some of these problems. The early detection of IUGR and the prevention of birth asphyxia has a major influence on long-term outcome.

FURTHER READING

Campbell, S. (1976) Fetal Growth. In Beard, R. W. and Nathanielsz, P. W. (eds), *Fetal Physiology and Medicine*. W. B. Saunders, London.
Davies, D. P. (1981) Growth of small-for-dates babies. *Early Hum. Dev.* 5: 95.

Dawes, G. S. (1974) General discussion. In: Eliot, K. and Knight, J. (eds), *Size at Birth, Ciba Foundation Symposium*, no. 27. Associated Scientific Publications, Amsterdam.

Dobbing, J. and Sands, J. (1973) Quantitative growth and development of human brain. *Arch. Dis. Child* **48**: 757.

Dornan, J. C., Ritchie, J. W. K. and Ruff, S. (1984) The rate and regularity of breathing movements in the normal and growth-retarded fetus. *Br. J. Obstet. Gynaecol.* **91**: 31–36.

Halliday, H. L., Reid, M. and McClure, G. (1982) Results of heavy drinking in pregnancy. *Br. J. Obstet. Gynaecol.* **89**: 892.

Halliday, H. L., McClure, G. and Reid, M. (1985) *Handbook of Neonatal Intensive Care*, 2nd edn. Baillière Tindall, London.

Hutchins, C. J. (1980) Delivery of the growth retarded infant. *Obstet. Gynaecol.* **58**: 683.

Jones, M. D. and Battaglia, F. E. (1977) Intrauterine growth retardation. *Am. J. Obstet. Gynaecol.* **127**: 540.

Kelnar, C. J. H. and Harvey, D. (1986) *The Sick Newborn Baby*, 2nd edn. Baillière Tindall, London.

Usher, R. H. and McLean, F. (1969) Intrauterine growth of liveborn Caucasian infants at sea level. *J. Pediatr.* **74**: 901.

Widdowson, E. M. and McCance, R. A. (1975) A review: new thoughts on growth *Pediatr. Res.* **9**: 154.

6

Genetic Problems and Congenital Malformations

INTRODUCTION

Congenital malformations are major causes of perinatal and infant death and are now responsible for approximately one-third of them. They are also major causes of long-term handicap of varying degrees and contribute greatly to childhood illness. The Medical Research Council (1978) stressed in a review of clinical genetics that 'handicaps due to a genetic disorder or congenital malformations are the major child health problem today'.

Recently, it has become possible to diagnose many congenital abnormalities prior to birth because of advances such as amniocentesis and ultrasonography. Unfortunately, these techniques cannot be applied to the whole population so obstetricians must be selective in their application. This can only be done with knowledge of the aetiology of the malformation and of the risk of recurrence. Prepregnancy counselling and antenatal genetic clinics have been developed to meet this need, where the expertise of the obstetrician and geneticist combine to provide counselling, diagnosis and treatment of disease. In some cases prevention may be possible.

AETIOLOGY OF ABNORMALITIES

Abnormalities may be due to chromosomal defects, genetic disorders, multi-factorial conditions or because of adverse environmental factors.

Chromosomal Abnormalities

Incidence

One in 160 live births has a recognizable chromosomal abnormality. There is a wide range of these anomalies and they vary considerably in their effects.

1. Spontaneous abortion and stillbirth, for example Trisomy 16 (50% of 1st trimester spontaneous abortions are associated with chromosomal anomalies).
2. Severely abnormal fetus often dying shortly after birth, for example trisomies 13 and 18.
3. Mentally retarded infant, for example Trisomy 21 (Down's syndrome).
4. Infants who are relatively normal physically but who have latent problems such as Turner's or Klinefelter's syndrome.

Down's syndrome is the most important accounting for 1 in 650 live births. The incidence rises progressively with maternal age and by the age of 40 is 1 in 100 live births. If amniocentesis is carried out at 16–18 weeks in women aged

40, the incidence of Down's syndrome is 2%, indicating that there is a high spontaneous abortion rate in this condition.

Other trisomies include trisomy 18 (Edward's syndrome) and trisomy 13 (Patau's syndrome).

Sex chromosomal anomalies occur in about 4–5 per 1000 births and include 45XO (Turner's syndrome) and XXX who are female, and XXY (Klinefelter's syndrome) who have a male phenotype.

Genetic Disorders

In autosomal disease, the abnormal gene is located on a chromosome other than the sex chromosome. The inheritance may be 'dominant' when only one of a gene pair need be abnormal for the disease to occur, or 'recessive' when both genes of a gene pair must be abnormal.

In sex-linked disease, the abnormal gene is on the X-chromosome. Again, the condition may be dominant or recessive.

Autosomal Dominant

People who possess the abnormal gene on only one member of a chromosome pair (heterozygotes) are usually clinically affected. The gene must pass from one parent only for the child to develop the condition and the risk is 1:2.

These disorders include tuberous sclerosis, neurofibromatosis, craniofacial dysostosis, polycystic disease of the kidneys (adult type), achondroplasia and dystrophia myotonica.

Some disorders can arise spontaneously as a mutation, for example achondroplasia and acrocephalysyndactyly (Apert's syndrome). Where such diseases occur as a result of a mutation, the recurrence rate is very low.

Autosomal Recessive

In such disorders, the abnormal gene is present on both chromosomes. The parents are clinically normal but both must carry the gene for the child to be affected and the risk of recurrence is 1:4. These conditions are more common where parents are consanguinous. Examples of such disorders are cystic fibrosis, phenylketonuria, infantile polycystic kidneys and galactosaemia.

X-linked Diseases

The classic examples are those where heterozygous (carrier) females transmit the gene to their male children.

These disorders include haemophilia, Duchenne muscular dystrophy and some types of mental handicap. Half of the male children will be affected and half of the females will be carriers.

Multifactorial Disorders

Many disorders exist in which there is no simple inheritance and no obvious chromosome anomaly.

Major disorders of this type include anencephaly, spina bifida and congenital heart defects.

Environmental Disorders

Table 6.1 lists some environmental factors known to have teratogenic effects on the fetus. Many more remain to be discovered.

RISKS OF RECURRENCE OF BIRTH DEFECTS

At genetic counselling clinics, the majority of individuals requesting counselling are healthy couples who have had a child with a serious defect or who have a family history of congenital malformations.

These couples ask about the risks of having an abnormal baby, the methods available for diagnosis and treatment and the prognosis for an affected child. Clearly the answers depend on the disease and its mode of inheritance taken against a background of social and environmental factors. These risks will be discussed later in relation to specific diseases.

DEVELOPMENTS IN PRENATAL DIAGNOSIS

In recent years, it has become possible to diagnose early in pregnancy many diseases affecting the fetus. The objectives of early diagnosis are to allow termination of pregnancy, to permit treatment of the fetus prior to birth or to arrange for the birth of the baby in a hospital where appropriate treatment is readily available. Methods of early diagnosis include maternal blood tests,

Table 6.1 Environmental teratogens

Factors	*Birth defect*
Maternal infections	
Toxoplasmosis	Chorioretinitis, central nervous system involvement, microcephaly
Rubella	Cataracts, congenital heart disease, deafness, osteitis, hepatosplenomegaly
Cytomegalovirus	Chorioretinitis, deafness, microcephaly
Syphilis	Facial, skeletal and eye anomalies
Drugs	
Thalidomide	Phocomelia, cardiac, intestinal genitourinary defects
Phenytoin	Cleft palate, congenital heart disease, hypertelorism, hypoplastic digits
Warfarin	Chondrodysplasia punctata, nasal hypoplasia
Alcohol	Abnormal facies, mental retardation and congenital heart defects
Sex hormones	Vertebral, anal and oesophageal anomalies
Lithium	Congenital heart disease

Table 6.2 Some conditions which may be diagnosed from examination of amniotic fluid

Cause	Effect
Chromosomal disorders	Trisomies
	X-linked disease, for example haemophilia
Neural tube defects	
Metabolic disorders	Lipid metabolism, for example Fabry's disease
	Carbohydrate metabolism, for example galactosaemia
	Mucopolysaccharide metabolism, for example Hurler's syndrome
	Amino acid metabolism, for example homocystinuria
Blood disorders	Rhesus haemolytic disease
Others	
Cystic fibrosis	

amniocentesis, ultrasonic scanning, chorionic villus biopsy and cordocentesis to allow fetal blood sampling.

Maternal Blood Tests

The most useful investigation is the measurement of serum alpha-fetoprotein (AFP) which is widely available throughout the UK. This is a useful screening test for neural tube defects and allows the selection of a high-risk group in whom more definitive tests may be carried out. The major disadvantage of this test is that there is a high false positive rate at 16 weeks. It is also important to know accurately the gestational age of the fetus as the normal blood levels of AFP change rapidly from week to week in early pregnancy. Multiple pregnancy may increase the serum AFP level and for these reasons an accurate ultrasound assessment of gestational age and of fetal number is necessary before interpretation of the result.

Amniocentesis

The examination of the liquor and its contents remains a widely used, reliable and relatively safe method of antenatal diagnosis. Some conditions which can be diagnosed from the examination of amniotic fluid are given in Table 6.2.

Method (Fig. 6.1)

Prior to amniocentesis, all patients are informed about the risk – which is about 1% – of spontaneous abortion associated with the procedure. Following counselling at 15–16 weeks gestation, an ultrasonic scan is performed to determine placental position and the largest 'pools' of liquor.

An appropriate site is selected and a 22-gauge spinal needle with stylet is inserted to the predetermined depth, endeavouring to avoid the placenta. This must be done under ultrasonic control. On removal of the stylet, the first 1 ml of liquor is allowed to leak out and is discarded to avoid contamination of fluid

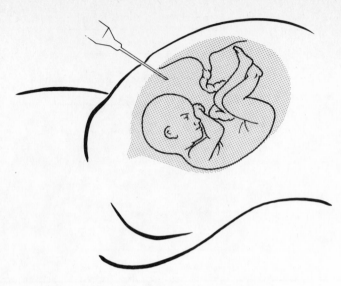

Figure 6.1 Amniocentesis for prenatal diagnosis.

with maternal cells. The next 15–25 ml of liquor is then withdrawn slowly using a 10-ml syringe to prevent sudden decompression. Following amniocentesis, the needle is removed and the patient rescanned to ensure that the fetus has come to no harm.

During the procedure, fetal blood cells may escape into the maternal circulation and for this reason anti-D immunoglobulin should be given to rhesus-negative women.

It should be recognized that measurement of amniotic fluid AFP is not always diagnostic of a neural tube defect. A raised AFP may be found in omphalocele and in liver disease.

The combined use of AFP, acetyl-cholinesterase measurement and of rapidly adherent cells has significantly improved the diagnosis of central nervous system anomalies.

Cystic fibrosis may be diagnosed prenatally by an immunoassay based on monoclonal antibodies with specificity for the three major isoenzymes of alkaline phosphatase (ALP). In cystic fibrosis, the level of intestinal ALP is low. The sensitivity of the test is 90% and the false positive rate is 6%. This technique is still under investigation.

Approximately 70 of the 200 known inborn errors of metabolism can be diagnosed prenatally. Cells obtained at amniocentesis are cultured and then appropriate enzyme assays are performed. Unfortunately, it may take 2–3 weeks to grow the cells leading to delays in diagnosis.

Ultrasound

The advent of high-resolution ultrasound has made it possible to diagnose prenatally many structural abnormalities.

Good ultrasonic equipment and experienced ultrasonographers are obligatory to a successful genetic clinic.

Table 6.3 Abnormalities diagnosed by ultrasound

System affected	Abnormality
Central nervous	Anencephaly
	Spina bifida
	Hydrocephaly
	Encephalocele
	Microcephaly
	Porencephalic cysts
	Hydranencephaly
Gastrointestinal	Omphalocele
	Gastroschisis
	Diaphragmatic Hernia
	Atresia
	Oesophageal
	Duodenal
	Jejunal
	Anal
	Enterogenous cysts
	Cystic fibrosis
Renal	Obstructive uropathy
	Renal cysts
	Renal agenesis
	Megaureter
Respiratory	Pulmonary hypoplasia
	Tracheal stenosis/agenesis
	Bronchogenic cysts
Locomotor	Achondroplasia
	Phocomelia
	Absent long bones
	Short-limbed dwarfism
Cardiovascular	Septal defects
	Valve stenosis
	Major chamber deficiencies
	Transposition of the great vessels
Miscellaneous	Hydrops
	Cystic hygroma

Table 6.3 lists abnormalities which can reasonably be expected to be diagnosed by an experienced ultrasonographer, the vast majority being diagnosed before 20 weeks gestation.

Central Nervous System

Anencephaly is normally easy to diagnose by ultrasound. However, in early pregnancy (8–12 weeks) the diagnosis may be missed if the fetus is lying well down in the pelvis and therefore cannot be easily seen.

Spina bifida may be diagnosed by longitudinal and transverse views of the fetal spine. A V-shaped defect on a transverse view is pathognomonic. 'Normal' limb movements and full bladder do not exclude a spinal lesion. After 18 weeks, a suboccipito-bregmatic view of the fetal head may reveal an abnormal shape to the skull known as the 'lemon sign' and a curved shape to the cerebellum known as the 'banana sign'.

Hydrocephalus is easily diagnosed in the second trimester. A biventricular diameter of more than half the biparietal diameter denotes hydrocephaly.

Microcephaly requires serial scans and may not be confirmed until after 24 weeks when a reduced pattern of head growth will be seen.

Gastrointestinal System

Gastrointestinal anomalies are often associated with polyhydramnios, making the diagnosis easier (Table 3.2, p. 46).

The stomach is normally seen at 16 weeks and may be identified as early as 12 weeks as a small, echo-free area on the left side of the upper abdomen. In duodenal atresia, two such areas are seen – the 'double-bubble' appearance. In gastroschisis and omphalocele, bowel is seen lying outside the peritoneal cavity. The cord insertion in gastroschisis is normal which helps to distinguish it from an omphalocele where the cord insertion is into the herniated sac. This is of great importance because of the higher incidence of chromosomal abnormalities and congenital heart defects associated with an omphalocele.

Recently, it has been suggested that cystic fibrosis may be diagnosed at about 20 weeks of pregnancy when an appearance suggestive of meconium ileus with loops of obstructed bowel are seen on ultrasound. This finding remains to be verified.

Renal System

Renal problems are often associated with oligohydramnios. The bladder is easily recognized as a central almost circular, echo-free structure lying anteriorly within the fetal pelvis and dilatation of the bladder and ureters or renal cysts are usually easily visualized.

It is more difficult to be as certain of absence or hypoplasia of the genito-urinary system. When the kidneys and bladder cannot be visualized, the mother is sometimes given an intravenous diuretic in an attempt to induce a fetal diuresis which may possibly help to outline the fetal genito-urinary tract.

Cardiovascular System

A four-chamber view of the heart is best observed between 18 and 24 weeks. All four chambers, atrioventricular valves, intraventricular septum, foramen ovale and pulmonary and aortic valves are all identifiable with careful scanning. The fetal heart should be scanned in those with a strong family history of congenital heart disease or where the fetus has developed a cardiac arrhythmia.

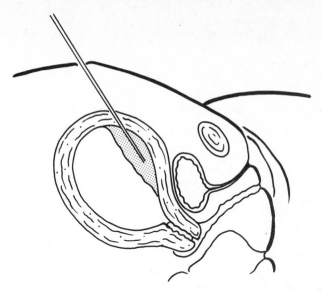

Figure 6.2 Chorionic villus biopsy.

Chorionic Villus Biopsy (Fig. 6.2)

Chorionic villus biopsy is a relatively new technique whereby mesenchymal cells of the chorionic villi are obtained for chromosomal and DNA analysis. This technique has immense potential for diagnosis of many disorders.

Under ultrasonic guidance, a needle is advanced through the mother's anterior abdominal wall to the chorionic plate and a sample of chorionic villi obtained. This method is considered to be safer than the transcervical approach because of a reduced risk of introducing infection.

Cordocentesis

This technique is described in Chapter 3 and is particularly useful when a rapid diagnosis is required after 18 weeks gestation. Fetal blood cells obtained from the umbilical vein or artery may be karotyped within 24 hr. The sample may also be used in the diagnosis of blood disorders such as haemoglobinopathies, immunodeficiencies, viral infections and metabolic disorders.

Cordocentesis has replaced fetoscopy as it has fewer complications. However, cord haematoma and vagal stimulation of the fetus may occur.

MALFORMATIONS DIAGNOSED IN THE NEONATAL PERIOD

The majority of babies with a malformation or a chromosomal defect are diagnosed in the neonatal period despite the best efforts of the obstetrician and geneticist to make an antenatal diagnosis. This is because in the majority of cases there is no significant family history of disease and therefore nothing to alert the antenatal team. It rests with the paediatrician to diagnose the defect, institute treatment, discuss the problem with the parents and to inform his obstetrician and geneticist colleagues.

The range of congenital malformations is vast so only selected major or common malformations will be discussed here.

Chromosomal Disorders

Trisomy 21 (Down's Syndrome) (Fig. 6.3)

Trisomy 21 is the commonest chromosomal disorder. The problem may have been detected antenatally by chromosomal analysis of amniotic fluid, but much more usually the first suspicion of the disease occurs when the baby is born.

The majority of children (95%) with the condition have 47 chromosomes with three 21 chromosomes which is the result of a non-dysjunction during the meiotic process. Other affected children (3%) have 46 chromosomes but have a chromosomal translocation. This may be inherited from a parent who is phenotypically normal but who carries the translocation (balanced translocation) or may occur *de novo* as the result of a mutation. A small group of children with Down's syndrome have a normal cell line as well as a cell line with an extra 21 chromosome. These 'mosaic' forms are seen in about 2% of children with Down's syndrome who are often less severely mentally retarded and who may be fertile.

Generally, Down's syndrome is easy to recognize. The most consistent sign is profound hypotonia with hyperflexibility of the joints. The infant's head and facies are also characteristic (Fig. 6.3). The head is brachycephalic, looking abnormally round, and there is typical clustering of the eyes, nose and mouth towards the centre of the face. The ears are small and the eyes have epicanthic folds and appear slanted. The iris may show Brushfield spots and the tongue protrudes. The hands appear square with short stubby fingers and the little finger is short and curved (clinodactyly). There is also a single transverse palmar crease (the simian crease) (Fig. 6.3). The great toe is widely separated from the next and a deep skin crease runs posteriorly from between these toes. About

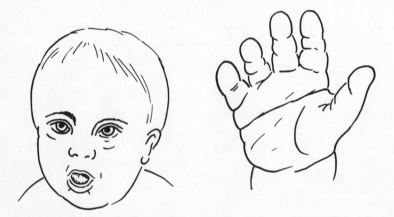

Figure 6.3 Down's syndrome: facial features and Simian crease.

40% of these infants suffer from a congenital heart defect such as endocardial cushion defect, atrial septal defect, ventricular septal defect or patent ductus arteriosus; duodenal atresia is also common. Chromosomal analysis should be performed to confirm the diagnosis and to assist in counselling. If the condition has been caused by a balanced translocation, the recurrence rate varies from 100% to 3% depending on the chromosomes involved. The risk of recurrence in the non-dysjunction and mosaic forms is low.

Trisomy 18 (Edward's Syndrome)

The incidence of trisomy 18 is 0.5 per 1000 births. These babies are SGA (Chapter 5) and are often born preterm. They have low-set abnormal ears, microstomia, a long, narrow skull with a prominent occiput and there is often ptosis of one or both eyelids. The hands show characteristically flexed fingers with the index finger overlapping the middle fingers and the little finger overlapping the third. There is often a congenital heart defect and the children who survive are mentally retarded. The prognosis is poor and the majority die in the first few months of life.

Trisomy 13 (Patau's Syndrome)

Trisomy 13 condition occurs in 0.2 per 1000 live births. These babies have marked bifrontal narrowing of their foreheads with microcephaly. There is cleft lip and palate with low-set abnormal ears. They also have flexion deformities of wrists, hand and fingers and there may be extra digits. There is often congenital heart disease, and the majority of babies with this die in early infancy. At autopsy, the brain is grossly malformed.

Spina Bifida (Myelomeningocele)

The incidence of spina bifida at birth has diminished over the past decade from 6 per 1000 births to 1.5 per 1000. This decline has been due mainly to unknown factors but antenatal detection with pregnancy termination and preventive measures have had a considerable effect (see below). The malformation is due to a failure of closure of the neural tube in the first 3–4 weeks of fetal life, due to a combination of genetic and environmental factors.

The condition may recur in a family. If a mother has a previously affected child, the recurrence rate is 3–5%. A further affected pregnancy increases the risk to 10–12%.

The condition may be manifest by the presence of a small pink naevus or patch of hair along the line of the spine (spina bifida occulta). However, the majority of children have a cystic lesion usually in the thoraco-lumbar region but which may occur anywhere along the line of the spine. The myelomeningocele may be covered with a thin membrane through which flattened neural tissue may be visible.

There may be paralysis of the lower limbs with a paucity of movements, hypotonia and absent reflexes. If the bladder and bowel are affected, the bladder may be palpable and urine will dribble from the urethra; anal tone will be poor and the anal reflex absent. There may be hydrocephaly, marked spinal deformity and other malformations of the lower limbs such as talipes.

The aim of operative treatment is to reduce the likelihood of infection. In general, immediate surgery is not performed if there is hydrocephaly, bladder, bowel and severe lower limb paralysis, or if there is a marked spinal deformity making closure technically difficult. Surgery will not improve any neurological deficit; indeed hydrocephaly may develop after closure of the defect which may require some form of ventricular fluid shunt operation at a later date.

Myelomeningoceles may also be seen in other conditions such as Meckel's syndrome and trisomy 13 and 18. Since these conditions have differing recurrence rates and prognoses, it is important that definitive diagnosis be made in order that the parents may be appropriately counselled.

Congenital Heart Disease

Congenital heart disease occurs in approximately 7–8 per 1000 births; in most cases the cause of the defect is unknown. Some cases are associated with other malformations such as Down's syndrome or congenital rubella syndrome. Patent ductus arteriosus is particularly associated with low-birth-weight infants. Occasionally, cardiac defects are detected on ultrasonic scanning of the fetus.

Usually the first evidence of congenital heart disease is when a murmur is detected at routine neonatal examination. However, some present in other ways.

Cyanosis

Central cyanosis is always serious and may indicate severe underlying congenital heart disease. In cardiac disease, the cyanosis will usually worsen during feeding or crying. Cyanosis caused by a cardiac malformation indicates that the defect is major such as transposition of the great vessels, truncus arteriosus or single ventricle. Cyanosis is not improved by the administration of oxygen.

Pallor

Some infants present with pallor and a poor peripheral circulation. This occurs when the cardiac output is poor as in hypoplastic left-heart syndrome, severe heart block or tachyarrhythmia.

Cardiac Failure

The cardinal signs of cardiac failure in a baby are tachycardia (heart rate greater than 160/min), tachypnoea and hepatomegaly. Other signs of cardiac failure seen in adults and older children – such as oedema and raised jugular venous pressure – are inconsistent features in babies.

Occasionally, infants present in cardiac failure having been previously examined and deemed to have normal hearts since no murmur had been heard. The reason for this is that in the first few days of life, shunts may be balanced because of a high pulmonary vascular pressure so no murmur can be heard. Later, as the pulmonary vascular pressure falls, a shunt develops. The murmur can be heard and the baby develops cardiac failure about 3–6 weeks after birth.

Some Specific Cardiac Defects

The incidence of the commoner cardiac problems seen in the neonatal period is shown in Table 6.4.

Patent Ductus Arteriosus. This is a particularly common defect in the low-birth-weight infant, especially those with respiratory distress. The condition is discussed in Chapter 4.

Ventricular Septal Defect. This is the second most common cardiac malformation. Most often, these defects are detected at routine examination when an otherwise healthy infant is noted to have a harsh pan-systolic murmur at the left edge of the sternum and the pulses are full. Occasionally, the infants present in cardiac failure after 3–6 weeks. Chest radiograph may show cardiac enlargement and pulmonary vascular congestion. Ultrasound examination confirms the diagnosis and treatment is initially conservative since many of these defects close spontaneously in the first 2 years of life.

Transposition of the Great Vessels. This condition occurs in about 1 in 2500 live births. The pulmonary artery arises from the left ventricle and the aorta from the right ventricle. There must be shunting of blood either through a ventricular septal defect or through a patent ductus arteriosus, otherwise there would be two totally independent circulations and the systemic blood would be totally anoxic.

The babies present with cyanosis in the first days of life and progressive cardiac failure. Thrills are uncommon and murmurs of the associated shunts may be heard. Chest radiograph shows cardiac enlargement with a narrow cardiac base ('egg on edge' appearance) and there is pulmonary vascular congestion. The diagnosis is confirmed by ultrasound and treatment is either by balloon septostomy or total surgical correction.

Complex Heart Defects Including Single Ventricle. These infants may present

Table 6.4 Frequency of clinical presentation of neonates with congenital heart disease at the Hospital for Sick Children, Toronto 1975

Patent ductus arteriosus	31%
D-transposition great arteries	12%
Ventricular septal defect	11%
Hypoplastic left heart syndrome	9%
Coarctation of aorta	7%
Tetralogy of Fallot	4%
Hypoplastic right heart syndrome	4%
Pulmonary valve stenosis	3%
Dextrocardia	3%
Aortic valve stenosis	2%
Other	14%

Rowe *et al.* (1981).

with cyanosis or with cardiac failure. In many, there is no murmur audible and in such cases it is often difficult to decide whether the infant is suffering from a cardiac or respiratory problem. In such cases, the response to the inhalation of 100% oxygen may be of help. If the problem is cardiac in origin, the arterial oxygen concentration will not change; whereas in those with respiratory disease, it will rise. In babies with persistent fetal circulation, there will be no change.

In many cases, the precise nature of the defect is unclear until the infant is seen by a paediatric cardiologist and echocardiography and cardiac catheterization are performed.

Hypoplastic Left Heart Syndrome. These infants present in the first few days of life when they develop shock and severe congestive failure. The pulses are poor and the blood pressure is low. The pathophysiology of this problem is that while the ductus arteriosus remains open, the body is perfused with blood from the right ventricle via the ductus. When the ductus closes, the systemic circulation becomes extremely poor. Chest radiograph shows cardiomegaly and pulmonary congestion and an echocardiogram may reveal a very small left ventricle, aortic atresia, mitral atresia and interrupted aortic arch.

Coarctation of the Aorta. These infants usually present with cardiac failure and absent or weakened femoral pulses, although these may be palpable if the ductus arteriosus is patent. The blood pressure in the legs is lower than expected and the arm blood pressure may be raised. A systolic murmur may be heard between the scapulae and the chest radiograph shows cardiomegaly and pulmonary congestion. Cardiac catheterization and echocardiogram are needed to confirm the diagnosis.

Tetralogy of Fallot. This tetrad comprises pulmonary stenosis, ventricular septal defect, overriding of the aorta and right ventricular hypertrophy. These infants are usually not markedly cyanosed in the neonatal period and present with a systolic murmur at the mid-left sternal border which is heard at routine examination.

The second heart sound in the pulmonary area is soft. Signs of congestive heart failure are uncommon in the neonatal period. The characteristic radiographic appearance of a 'boot-shaped' heart is also uncommon at this time. Diagnosis may be confirmed by ultrasonic examination and cardiac catheterization.

Gastrointestinal Malformation

Oesophageal Atresia

Oesophageal atresia may be suspected prior to birth by the presence of poly-hydramnios. The condition should be diagnosed at birth by the routine passage of a catheter from the mouth down towards the stomach. If the infant has an oesophageal atresia, the tube will come to a halt at approximately 5–7 cm from the gingival margin. This test will avoid delay in diagnosis and may prevent the development of aspiration pneumonia from overflow of mucus or milk into the infant's respiratory tract. The diagnosis may be confirmed radiologically using a radio-opaque catheter which will be seen to curl up in the upper oesophageal pouch.

The condition is a neonatal emergency. Prior to operation the infant's head should be slightly elevated and the upper pouch should be continuously aspirated. The infant should be examined for the presence of congenital heart disease and other gastrointestinal defects which are commonly associated. At operation, either a gastrostomy or an end-to-end anastomosis is performed depending on the severity of the lesion.

Exomphalos/Gastroschisis

In an exomphalos, abdominal contents herniate into the umbilical cord, whereas in gastroschisis there is an abdominal wall defect near the umbilicus. In either case, if the herniation is large then delivery of the infant may be difficult.

The sac or abdominal contents should be immediately covered with warm saline dressings to reduce heat and fluid loss. A gastric tube should be placed in position to empty the stomach and avoid aspiration of gastric contents before surgery. Exomphalos can occur in Beckwith's syndrome – macroglossia, visceromegaly and hypoglycaemia.

Duodenal Atresia

Duodenal atresia may be suspected prior to birth by the detection of polyhydramnios and may be confirmed by ultrasound. It is common in babies with Down's syndrome who account for 30% of all cases. The condition should be suspected in these children if they vomit persistently soon after birth. Abdominal radiograph shows the classical 'double bubble' appearance of air in the stomach and pylorus. The treatment is surgical and at operation, further atresias of the gastrointestinal tract may be found.

Renal Malformations

Renal malformations are important since they are not uncommon, are sometimes inherited and may be lethal. The defects affecting the kidney are complex and of great variety.

Some of the common problems are described briefly.

Renal Agenesis (Potter's Syndrome)

These infants are of low birth weight and may suffer acute birth asphyxia following a pregnancy complicated by oligohydramnios.

The infants have low-set ears, receding chins, flattened noses and spade-like hands. Many are stillborn and the remainder die in the first hours of life because of pulmonary hypoplasia.

Polycystic Disease

This condition may be of the infantile or adult types. In the infantile variety, the baby presents with large bilateral masses in the flanks, associated occasionally with hypertension. Ultrasonic examination is used to confirm the diagnosis. An intravenous pyelogram (IVP) shows contrast media in the dilated collecting tubules with a nephrogram effect. This condition is inherited on an autosomal recessive basis.

The adult type is rarely seen in the neonatal period and is more commonly detected in adulthood. The presentation in the neonatal period is with bilateral masses and hypertension. The IVP reveals very thin elongated calyces. The condition is inherited as an autosomal dominant.

Hydronephrosis

This may be caused by an obstructive lesion in the genito-urinary tract, for example the posterior urethral valve, or may be due to a neurogenic lesion as in meningomyelococle. The obstruction may be anywhere between the pelviureteric junction and the bladder neck or urethra.

The condition may present as abdominal masses or as a urinary tract infection. A full urological investigation is required to delineate the exact nature of the problem.

FETAL ALCOHOL SYNDROME (FAS)

This syndrome occurs in 1 per 750–1000 live births. The syndrome may be difficult to recognize but some infants are small-for-dates and present with microcephaly and have abnormal facies with short palpebral fissures, epicanthic folds, short upturned noses and thin upper lips.

The amount of alcohol required to produce this effect is unknown. There is no treatment other than special schooling for retarded children. Pre-pregnancy counselling and health education in schools provide the only means of prevention.

Screening Tests in the Neonatal Period

Screening tests are now widely used to detect diseases before the onset of symptoms so that treatment may be employed early either to prevent the disease or to limit its effects. The mainstay of screening is the Guthrie test. In this procedure, drops of blood are placed on filter paper and the dried blood used for screening. For diseases such as phenylketonuria the spot is incubated with bacilli which grow well in the presence of the abnormal metabolite. Such testing can be used for phenylketonuria, homocystinuria and maple syrup urine disease, among others. Blood spots obtained at the same time are used to screen for hypothyroidism and cystic fibrosis.

Phenylketonuria

This condition leads to severe brain damage if undetected and untreated. The disease incidence varies but is of the order of 1 per 10 000 live births.

There are no symptoms in the neonatal period. The Guthrie test is performed on the fifth day of life when the infant is established on milk feeds. If the screening test is positive, the blood phenylalanine level is measured. If the infant is proven to have phenylketonuria, immediate dietary restriction of phenylalanine is necessary to avoid mental retardation. This diet is not totally phenylalanine-free since this is an essential amino acid. The diet is continued until late childhood when it may be stopped.

A newly emerging problem is that of phenylketonuria in women of repro- ductive age. Evidence is accruing that high maternal phenylalanine levels in early pregnancy lead to malformation – notably microcephaly – in the fetus. It is advisable for these women to go on a low phenylalanine diet before pregnancy and continue with it throughout.

Hypothyroidism

Hypothyroidism condition occurs in approximately 1 per 3500 births. Only about one-tenth of the babies are recognizable in the neonatal period with coarse facies and hair, protruding tongue and prolonged jaundice. If this condition is undiagnosed, mental retardation develops.

Thyroid-stimulating hormone (TSH) is assayed on the Guthrie test paper. If the TSH is high, T_4 is estimated and if this is low, treatment with thyroxine is started. Evidence to date suggests that early treatment improves the intelligence of affected babies.

Cystic fibrosis

Cystic fibrosis affects the exocrine glands of the body and leads to multisystem disease with repeated attacks of respiratory infections, malabsorption and failure to thrive. Ten per cent present in the newborn period with meconium ileus and intestinal obstruction. It is inherited as an autosomal recessive pattern and the incidence is about 1 per 2000 births.

Children with cystic fibrosis are not usually diagnosed until irreversible damage has occurred. It is hoped that screening and early treatment will improve the prognosis.

The assay of immunoreactive trypsin (IRT) on a blood spot provides the basis of screening and is currently under investigation in some centres. Raised levels of IRT are seen in cystic fibrosis but there are also false positive results. If the IRT level is raised, the test is repeated and if again elevated, the diagnosis must be confirmed or excluded by measurement of the sweat electrolytes at about 2 months.

Dislocation of the Hips

This condition is covered in Chapter 2.

Prevention

In the majority of cases, malformations occur sporadically and the cause is often unknown. Prevention is therefore not possible. However, an advance has been made with neural tube defects. Supplementation of the maternal diet with multivitamins and iron for 1 month prior to conception and for 2 months after has been associated with a reduction in the recurrence rate of neural tube defects from an expected rate of 1 in 20 to an actual rate of 1 in 200 in a group of mothers with a previously affected infant. Randomized controlled studies have not yet been reported, but this advance is already being hailed as a major breakthrough.

Counselling Parents of Malformed Children

This is an extremely difficult area of perinatal medicine and there are extremely complex problems to be faced.

The parents should be spoken to, holding their baby, by a senior member of the staff. Most people should be told the truth as simply and gently as possible in a language that they understand. They should be encouraged to express their fears and grief and to ask as many questions as they wish. This is time consuming but the clinician should never hurry or appear to minimize their anxieties. Often parents find the least important clinical detail the most distressing, for example the child's appearance. Only by careful listening and encouragement will the facts emerge and help can be given.

Discussion may need to take place over many months or years and it is important that the parents see the same clinician each time. This avoids conflict of information and disruption of good doctor–patient relationships. Often these parents become somewhat dependent on the clinician as the one person who can be trusted and who understands. This is one of the privileges of practising medicine.

FURTHER READING

Blyth, H. and Carter, C. (1969) *A Guide to Genetic Prognosis in Paediatrics*. Heinemann Medical, London.

Clayton, B. (1976) Screening and management of infants with amino acid disorders. In Hull, D. (ed.), *Recent Advances in Paediatrics*, no. 5. Churchill Livingstone, Edinburgh.

Halliday, H. L., Reid, M. and McClure, G. (1982) Results of heavy drinking in pregnancy. *Br. J. Obstet. Gynaecol.* 89: 892.

Loeffler, F. E. (1984) Prenatal diagnosis: chorionic villus biopsy. *Br. J. Hosp. Med.* 6: 418.

McNay, M. B. and Whitfield, C. R. (1984) Prenatal diagnosis: amniocentesis *Br. J. Hosp. Med.* 6: 406.

MRC (1978) Working party on amniocentesis: an assessment of the hazards of amniocentesis. *Br. J. Obstet. Gynaecol.* 85 (Suppl. 2): 1.

Nicolaides, K. and Rodeck, C. H. (1984) Prenatal diagnosis: Fetoscopy. *Br. J. Hosp. Med.* 6: 396.

Rickham, I. P., Lister, J. and Irving, I. M. (1978) *Neonatal Surgery*, 2nd edn. Butterworths, London.

Rowe, R. D., Freedom, R. M., Mehrizi, A. and Bloom, K. R. (1981) *The Neonate with Congenital Heart Disease*. W. B. Saunders, Philadelphia, pp. 101–109.

Smith, D. W. (1982) *Recognizable Patterns of Human Malformation*, 3rd edn. W. B. Saunders, Philadelphia.

Smith, P. A., Chudleigh, P. and Campbell, S. (1984) Prenatal diagnosis: ultrasound. *Br. J. Hosp. Med.* June: 421.

7

Malpresentation and Multiple Pregnancy

INTRODUCTION

A malpresentation occurs when some part of the fetus other than the vertex is presenting, i.e. lies in the lower uterine segment closest to the internal cervical os. The most common type is breech presentation which occurs in approximately 3% of all patients at term. Other types are shoulder, face, brow and compound presentations. Malpresentations are of particular importance since they lead to difficult labour, birth trauma and asphyxia and increase the need for operative intervention.

BREECH PRESENTATION

The perinatal mortality rate associated with breech presentation is 3–5 times higher than with vertex presentation. This is due to the higher incidence of congenital abnormalities, prematurity, birth asphyxia and trauma.

There are three types of breech presentation: those with flexed legs, those with extended legs and the hips flexed, or the 'footling breech' where the hips are extended (Fig. 7.1). This last type is associated with a high risk (one in four) of cord presentation and of cord prolapse.

The incidence of breech presentation in normal pregnancy falls from 30% at 30 weeks to 3% at term. In early pregnancy, the fetus can move around freely, but later the larger pole, i.e. the breech and legs, tend to occupy the roomier upper segment of the uterus. In breech presentation, this does not occur and, in the majority of cases, no reason is found. Various factors are associated with breech presentation such as polyhydramnios, oligohydramnios, uterine

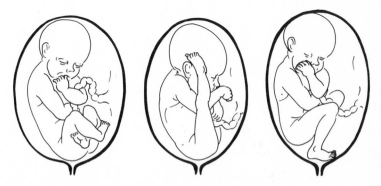

Figure 7.1 The three types of breech presentation. Left – with flexed legs, the complete breech. Centre – with extended legs, frank breech. Right – 'footling breech', incomplete.

abnormality, multiple pregnancy, placenta praevia, prematurity and fetal abnormality, for example hydrocephalus.

The diagnosis is made on palpation, the presenting part being soft and irregular with the firm, round, ballottable head palpable in the fundus of the uterus.

Management

No action is necessary until 32 completed weeks, in view of the frequency of spontaneous version to cephalic presentation. At this time, an ultrasound examination should be performed to confirm the diagnosis and to exclude an obvious fetal abnormality or placenta praevia. External cephalic version may then be attempted. This technique corrects the presentation of the fetus by external abdominal manipulation and is usually carried out between 32 and 34 weeks. The procedure should not be attempted where there is any risk to the fetus or mother such as in antepartum haemorrhage, intrauterine growth retardation, hypertension or if there is a history of Caesarean section or premature labour. The operator's hands are warmed and an attempt is made to rotate the fetus by gently moving the head forwards and the breech backwards (Fig. 7.2). It is only carried out if force is unnecessary and without a general anaesthetic. After the procedure is completed, the fetal heart is auscultated.

The risks of this procedure are placental separation, cord entanglement and feto-maternal transfusion. Because of this last risk, anti-D is given to rhesus-

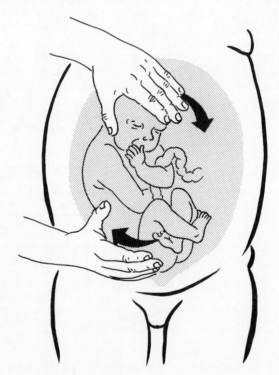

Figure 7.2 External cephalic version.

negative patients, although the use of external cephalic version in such cases is controversial. If unsuccessful, further attempts may be made each week, but after 36 weeks the procedure rarely succeeds.

Delivery of Breech Presentation at Term

In general, there is a tendency towards delivery by elective Caesarean section in primigravid patients, particularly if the fetus is thought to be large, or if there is extension of the hips.

The decision on the mode of delivery should be made by an experienced obstetrician. The parity of the mother and weights of previous infants influence this decision. The weight of the fetus should be assessed clinically and ultrasonically and a radiograph may reveal an unrecognized malformation or extension of the hips or neck. The shape and size of the maternal pelvis should also be assessed clinically. If the baby is large and the pelvis is small, delivery should be by elective Caesarean section. If the baby is of average size and the pelvis seems adequate, vaginal delivery should be allowed.

Labour

If vaginal delivery is anticipated, close supervision in labour is essential. A fetal heart electrode should be attached to the fetal buttock and the intrauterine pressure recorded. Vaginal examination at 2-hr intervals will allow early detection of slow progress, a useful indication of borderline disproportion. The use of oxytocin where progress is slow is contraindicated. Meconium staining with a breech presentation can be due to pressure on the fetal abdomen in advanced labour, but, in early labour, it must be considered to be a sign of fetal distress.

Epidural analgesia is recommended because it provides optimal pain relief and allows manipulation during the second stage of labour. This avoids the necessity for rapid induction of general anaesthesia which delays the delivery and puts the mother and fetus at risk.

Second Stage of Labour

This is the most difficult phase of breech delivery because of the risks of hypoxia and trauma. Problems arise at three periods. The first is when the second stage has commenced and the breech is not on the perineum after 30 min. It is generally safer to proceed to Caesarean section because of the dangers of disproportion and asphyxia. There is no longer a place for 'breech extraction', except in delivery of a second twin, since this may be extremely traumatic.

The second problem is with the delivery of the arms. If they are folded across the chest, they are usually easy to deliver. If they are extended above the head or more rarely extended at the shoulder but flexed at the elbow with the forearm behind the fetal head – 'nuchal displacement' – Lovset's manoeuvre is used to deliver them. In this technique, the infant's trunk is rotated and gentle downwards traction is applied (Fig. 7.3). This allows a shoulder to appear just below the symphysis pubis. The operator's finger then crooks into the infant's elbow and pulls the arm down. The infant is then rotated in the opposite direction until the second shoulder appears and the second arm is brought down.

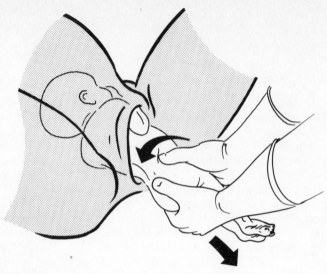

Figure 7.3 Lovset's manoeuvre to deliver the arms in breech presentation.

The third problem may arise with the delivery of the head. The commonest cause for delay in delivering the head is a tense perineum, and for this reason an episiotomy is always performed when the fetal buttocks are distending the perineum. Other causes of delay are more sinister and are associated with significant trauma and asphyxia. The cervix may not be fully dilated and treatment of this usually requires stretching or incision of the cervix. There may be disproportion possibly due to undiagnosed hydrocephalus, or the head may have inadvertently been allowed to rotate to the occipito-posterior position. Hydrocephalus can be detected prior to the onset of labour by means of an ultrasonic scan. If the head has been allowed to rotate to the occipito-posterior position, an attempt may be made to rotate it to the occipito-anterior position, but this may be extremely difficult and the morbidity is high.

Preterm Breech (Chapter 4)

The low-birth-weight fetus presenting by the breech is exposed to several potential hazards. There is an increased risk of footling breech presentation and thus of cord prolapse. The small breech may pass through an incompletely dilated cervix with subsequent entrapment of the head. The small fetal head may deliver too rapidly and there is a lower tolerance of asphyxia and trauma during delivery. Caesarean section lowers the neonatal morbidity and mortality in very low-birth-weight infants, between 1000 and 1500 g, but may be difficult if the lower segment is not well formed.

FACE PRESENTATION (Fig. 7.4)

The incidence of face presentation is 1 per 600 deliveries. In this situation, the fetal neck is hyperextended and the face presents at the internal cervical os. In

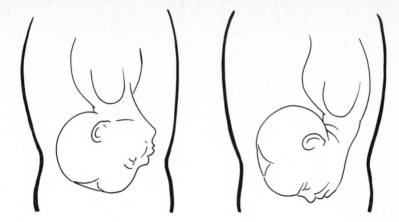

Figure 7.4 Brow and face presentations.

many cases a specific cause is not identified although increased tone of the extensor muscles of the neck has been suggested. Recognized causes are fetal abnormality (for example anencephaly), tumours of the fetal neck (for example large goitre), cystic hygroma, loops of cord around the neck, intrauterine death, prematurity, cephalopelvic disproportion and multiparity.

The diagnosis may be made on abdominal palpation when the cephalic prominence is felt on the same side as the back. An ultrasonic scan is essential to confirm the presentation and exclude obvious abnormalities. Spontaneous onset of labour should be allowed, recognizing that the position of the fetus presenting by the face interferes with the normal mechanism of labour. Unless the chin rotates to the anterior position when the sinciput reaches the pelvic floor, further descent and delivery cannot occur, so that Caesarean section is necessary. If the chin does rotate anteriorly, vaginal delivery is possible but labour tends to be prolonged because the facial bones do not mould.

Oedema of the face can be so marked as to lead to confusion with a breech on vaginal examination, so the face and eyes may be traumatized during labour due to clumsy technique or the application of a scalp electrode. Whatever the mode of delivery, the face and mouth of the neonate may be markedly oedematous, leading to partial obstruction of the airway.

BROW PRESENTATION (Fig. 7.4)

The incidence of brow presentation is 1 per 2000 deliveries. The fetal neck is less hyperextended than with a face presentation so that the brow, the area between the orbital ridges and the anterior fontanelle, is presenting. This is the most unfavourable of the malpresentations as this position presents the widest diameter of the fetal skull. But, as the neck is not completely extended, many cases of brow presentation in the antenatal period revert spontaneously to vertex presentation or there is further extension to a face presentation. The aetiological factors are the same as for face presentation.

The diagnosis is rarely made by abdominal palpation; vaginal examination and an ultrasonic scan are necessary for diagnosis.

In labour, unless the fetus is very small, vaginal delivery cannot occur because the large presenting diameter will not enter the pelvic brim. Caesarean section is the safest method of delivery although on occasion one may observe progress in labour closely for a short while, hoping for spontaneous reversion to a face or vertex presentation. There is the added risk of uterine rupture in cases of undiagnosed brow presentation in multiparous patients.

SHOULDER PRESENTATION (Fig. 7.5)

In shoulder presentation the lie of the fetus is usually transverse, but is sometimes oblique, with the fetal shoulder close to the internal os and the head in one or other iliac fossa.

This presentation is associated with grande multiparity, due to laxity of the uterus and abdominal wall, placenta praevia, polyhydramnios, prematurity, uterine abnormality, contracted pelvis, pelvic tumour or an abnormal or dead fetus. The diagnosis is made on palpation, and ultrasonic scan is required to exclude abnormality of the fetus or pelvic tumour, to assess the amount of amniotic fluid and to localize the placenta.

The management before 36 weeks includes correcting the lie at each antenatal visit and advising the patient about the risk of cord prolapse after rupture of the membranes and of the necessity for early hospital admission at the onset of labour. After 36 weeks it is best to admit the patient to hospital, correct the lie daily and await spontaneous onset of labour.

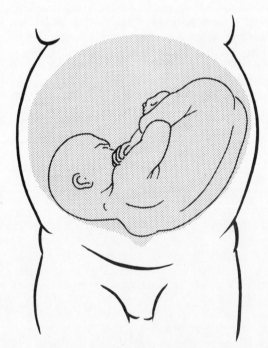

Figure 7.5 Shoulder presentation.

In general, Caesarean section should be performed in patients with a transverse lie but difficulties may arise because of the increased incidence of placenta praevia and increased maternal age. External cephalic version may be attempted if it is felt that this is likely to be easy and there is no evidence of a contracted pelvis or placenta praevia. The risks to the fetus of transverse lie are cord prolapse, severe asphyxia and trauma.

COMPOUND PRESENTATION

In cases of compound presentation a fetal limb enters the pelvis alongside the presenting part, usually the forearm beside the fetal head, a situation which is more common in preterm labour and polyhydramnios. During labour, progress must be assessed carefully to decide whether the limb is preventing the descent of the presenting part. If this is the case, delivery should be by Caesarean section unless the limb can be pushed above the head.

MALPOSITION

In 15% of all pregnancies, the occiput is in a posterior position at the onset of labour. In 80%, the occiput rotates anteriorly, but the remainder stay in the occipito-posterior position, or start to rotate anteriorly and arrest in the transverse position ('deep transverse arrest'). When this happens, the progress of labour stops and the head must be rotated to allow vaginal delivery.

The diagnosis may be suspected prior to the onset of labour by palpating the back of the fetus more laterally than usual and the fetal limbs more anteriorly. The fetal heart sounds may be loudest laterally or in the midline. On vaginal examination, the posterior fontanelle is palpable posteriorly.

If the diagnosis is made prior to the onset of labour, no action is necessary. When labour commences, regular vaginal examinations should be performed to determine the position of the head, as labour may be prolonged and the risk of fetal distress is high. If the occiput rotates posteriorly, the baby will be born spontaneously face-to-pubes. If deep transverse arrest occurs, rotation of the fetal head by Kielland's forceps or ventouse is necessary to allow delivery.

NEONATAL ASPECTS OF MALPRESENTATION

The three major neonatal problems associated with malpresentation are asphyxia, trauma and congenital malformation. The presentation and consequences of asphyxia have been described elsewhere (Chapter 4).

Trauma

Trauma may be neurological, visceral, soft tissue or bony, and may occur as a result of difficulties experienced in manipulation to correct the malpresentation. In this situation, there may be pre-existing vascular distension of the traumatized part which predisposes to and may exacerbate the effects of trauma. Today, traumatic injuries are much less frequent than previously, largely as a result of more frequent and earlier recourse to Caesarean section.

Neurological Damage

Trauma may occur to the brain, skull, spinal cord or peripheral nerves.

Subdural Haemorrhage. This is caused by laceration of the tentorium cerebelli with rupture of the straight sinus, the vein of Galen or the lateral sinus. Alternatively, the falx cerebri is lacerated with rupture of the inferior sagittal sinus. These injuries are usually the result of difficult delivery and the infant may show obvious manifestations of birth asphyxia. There may be alteration of tone, progressive distension of the anterior fontanelle, increasing irritability and convulsions. Occasionally, a subdural haematoma may present more covertly with a rapid increase in skull circumference and anaemia. In addition to these gross manifestations of neurological damage, there may be the more subtle features of persistent or rotatory nystagmus, impaired feeding and an abnormal cry.

The diagnosis of a subdural haematoma is sometimes confirmed by cranial ultrasound, although a CAT scan is usually necessary to reveal the presence of a haematoma and the associated distortion of the underlying brain substance. Aspiration of the subdural space with a subdural needle confirms the diagnosis and reduces cerebral compression. This procedure may have to be repeated if the fluid reaccumulates.

Treatment should be directed to the prevention of further bleeding, by correcting any underlying coagulation problem, and the reduction of cerebral oedema. Phenobarbitone should be given to treat convulsions. Any significant blood loss is replaced and appropriate respiratory and nutritional support given. The long-term prognosis of this rare condition depends largely on the degree of associated cerebral contusion and of asphyxia. Long-term follow-up is essential.

Occipital Osteodiastasis. This injury is caused by separation of the squamous part of the occipital bone and is particularly predisposed to by breech delivery. The injury may cause subdural haematoma or frank brain injury due to laceration of the cerebellum or, alternatively, posterior fossa compression. There may be alteration of muscle tone and consciousness, seizures and signs of blood loss. The condition is extremely difficult to diagnose but a lateral skull radiograph may show overlapping of the squamous and occipital bones. The treatment is supportive but most infants with this condition will die. In the majority of cases the diagnosis is first made at autopsy.

Spinal Cord Injury. Spinal cord injury most commonly affects the cervical cord following breech delivery. It is caused by difficulty in delivery of the aftercoming head with excessive stretching of the cervical cord. In addition to direct tearing of the cord, injury may also be secondary to ischaemia following compression of the vertebral arteries. More frequent delivery by Caesarean section has reduced the incidence of this injury.

The infant presents with flaccid quadriplegia, diminished respiratory effort and the absence of all limb reflexes. The treatment is supportive and prognosis is poor. Any recovery that is likely to occur should take place in the first few days after birth. Persistent flaccid quadriplegia is associated with a very poor outcome.

Peripheral Nerve Injuries. Peripheral nerve injuries usually involve the brachial plexus or the facial nerve. Brachial plexus injury may result in Erb's palsy or Klumpke's palsy due to involvement of cervical roots 5 and 6 or cervical 8 and thoracic 1, respectively. The infant presents with an asymmetrical Moro reflex

Figure 7.6 Infant with Erb's palsy showing 'waiter's tip position'.

or diminished movement of the arm during activity which may be noted prior to feeding or during nappy changing. In Erb's palsy the arm is held adducted, internally rotated with the forearm pronated (waiter's tip position) (Fig. 7.6). In Klumpke's palsy, the hand is limp, immobile, and there is an absent grasp reflex. There may be an associated Horner's syndrome. Erb's palsy is treated by physiotherapy and splinting, but up to 50% of the infants may have a mild residual palsy.

Facial nerve injury is a relatively common condition occurring at the rate of approximately 4 per 1000 live births. Sometimes facial nerve palsy is congenital in origin, but more often the injury to the nerve is acquired during delivery by forceps or by compression of the nerve against the maternal sacral spine. The infants present with facial asymmetry while crying and the majority resolve spontaneously over the subsequent few months so that no specific treatment is required.

Visceral Injury

Visceral injury is uncommon. Such injuries may present as an abdominal mass, shock due to blood loss or bruising of the abdominal wall with associated abdominal distension. In males, the blood from a haemoperitoneum may drain into the scrotum. The injury often follows difficult birth but is also associated with malformations, such as polycystic kidneys or gross ascites, which cause marked abdominal distension. The diagnosis is confirmed by abdominal paracentesis and blood transfusion may be needed. The bleeding is often self-limiting but if the baby's condition indicates that bleeding is severe or prolonged, laparotomy is necessary.

Injury to Bone

Skull fractures may occur spontaneously or following forceps delivery. The fractures may be linear and be associated with a cephalohaematoma – a subperiosteal collection of blood presenting as a scalp swelling limited by the suture lines. The fractures do not require treatment unless there is depression with a neurological deficit. In such cases elevation should be performed.

The most common fracture seen in the newborn period is of the clavicle. Infants born by breech delivery or following shoulder dystocia are at greatest risk but it may also follow an apparently atraumatic delivery. The infant may cry excessively during changing of clothes or, alternatively, be reluctant to move the affected arm. The fracture may be an incidental finding on a chest radiograph performed for some other reason. If there is lateral displacement of the fracture, a figure-of-eight bandage should be used. No long-term complications have been noted.

Fracture of the humerus or femur is associated with breech delivery, prematurity and multiple pregnancy. It may also occur in fetal growth retardation and osteogenesis imperfecta. The fracture may be noted by the obstetrician at delivery when the bone is felt or heard to crack. After birth, the affected limb is immobile (pseudopalsy) or there is excessive crying on movement of the limb. Treatment is by stabilization or traction if the femur is fractured. The long-term results are excellent.

Malformation of the Fetus Predisposing to Malpresentation

A malformation of the fetus increases the risk of malpresentation. Infants born following malpresentation should be carefully examined to exclude such conditions.

The most common neurological problem leading to malpresentation is a neural tube defect. These infants often present by the breech and problems in labour may occur, especially if there is associated hydrocephalus.

MULTIPLE PREGNANCY

Although twin pregnancy occurs in only 1 in 80 births in the UK, the contribution made to perinatal mortality and morbidity is considerable, being approximately five times that for the singleton pregnancy. The incidence of triplets is 1 in 7000 and of quadruplets 1 in 350 000. The incidence of multiple pregnancy may be mainly due to the increasing use of gonadotrophin therapy to induce ovulation, and more recently to development of *in vitro* fertilization programmes (Table 7.1).

Table 7.1 Rates of multiple births per 1000 maternities from 1961 to 1984

Years	Twins	Triplets	All multiple births
1961–65	11.5	0.110	11.6
1966–70	10.6	0.110	10.7
1971–75	9.9	0.110	10.0
1976–80	9.6	0.112	9.8
1982–84	10.0	0.113	10.2

Twin pregnancy is more common in older and multiparous patients and there is a great variation between ethnic groups, being three times more common among blacks than in the Japanese.

Aetiology

Twins may occur from fertilization of one ova (monozygotic) or two ova (dizygotic) – the latter accounting for 80% of all cases. There is often a family history of multiple pregnancy in dizygotic twins.

Dizygotic twins have their own membranes with placentae which have separate circulations. In monozygotic twins, there is some degree of anastomosis between the two fetal circulations if the placenta is monochorionic, leading to an increased risk of twin-to-twin transfusion.

Diagnosis

The diagnosis of multiple pregnancy may be suspected by finding that the uterus is larger than expected for the period of amenorrhoea; the diagnosis is confirmed by ultrasound. In the first trimester, two amniotic sacs and fetuses may be seen although it is not unusual for one of these to disappear later.

Later in pregnancy, the diagnosis may be suspected by palpation of more than two fetal poles in a uterus which is large-for-dates.

Maternal Complications

All women with multiple pregnancy should attend a consultant unit for ante-natal care where they will be seen at each visit by an experienced obstetrician.

In early pregnancy, morning sickness occurs more often and is more severe than with singleton pregnancies. Similarly, in the third trimester, the usual pressure effects, including shortness of breath, lower limb oedema, varicose veins and haemorrhoids, may be exaggerated.

The following complications are particularly common in multiple pregnancy.
Premature Labour. This is the most important contributor to the high perinatal mortality and morbidity. Mothers are managed as outpatients and are strongly advised to stop work, avoid heavy housework and rest as much as possible. At each 2-weekly visit from 20 weeks, the cervix is assessed for effacement or dilatation and the woman admitted to hospital if there has been any significant change. If there are other factors, such as a previous premature labour,

admission to hospital is advisable and oral beta-sympathomimetics may be of value. Many would advocate their prophylactic use for all cases of multiple pregnancy from 20 weeks but there is little evidence of their efficacy.

Pre-eclampsia. The incidence is significantly increased and it is likely to occur earlier, i.e. before 28 weeks, and to be more severe, particularly in primigravidae.

Polyhydramnios. This complication occurs in 10% of twin pregnancies and contributes to the risk of premature labour. Acute polyhydramnios is particularly associated with uniovular twins. The condition usually presents towards the end of the second trimester with severe abdominal pain, distension and shortness of breath.

Antepartum Haemorrhage. Antepartum haemorrhage is more likely to occur from a placenta praevia since the large placenta is liable to encroach on the lower uterine segment. Placental abruption may occur because of the associated higher incidence of pre-eclampsia and polyhydramnios. Vasa praevia also occurs more commonly.

Cord Problems. Umbilical cord prolapse is more common in multiple pregnancy, particularly of the second cord after delivery of the first twin.

Anaemia. Maternal iron deficiency and megaloblastic anaemia are both more common because of the increased fetal requirements.

Fetal Complications

The major risks to the fetus are those associated with premature labour and cord prolapse, particularly if there is a malpresentation or polyhydramnios. There is also a significant increase in fetal malformations and growth retardation. This latter complication may occur with or without co-existing pre-eclampsia and is very difficult to detect antenatally. The second twin is also at an increased risk of asphyxia during labour.

Labour

Labour presents a major hazard to the fetus in cases of multiple pregnancy. The majority of twins are delivered vaginally but there is an old dictum which states that 'twins plus another complication warrants Caesarean section', in particular if there is polyhydramnios, antepartum haemorrhage or malpresentation.

During labour, the problems that may be encountered are malpresentation, cord presentation and cord prolapse. Epidural analgesia is recommended in labour as the most effective way of providing pain relief and permits manipulation in the second stage of labour without recourse to general anaesthesia. A scalp electrode should be applied to the presenting part of the first twin, but monitoring the heart rate of the second twin is notoriously difficult and ultrasonic scanning provides the only reliable means.

Usually the first twin presents by the vertex (Table 7.2) and is delivered normally. After this has been achieved, the cord is divided between two clamps and the time noted. The second twin should be delivered within 15 min of the first, an oxytocin infusion and instrumental delivery often being necessary. It is during this time that the fetus is at greatest risk from prolonged hypoxia due to contraction of the placental bed or prolapse of the umbilical cord. The lie of the second twin is ascertained by abdominal palpation and, if necessary, corrected

Table 7.2 Presentation of twins at birth

Twin 1	Twin 2	%
Vertex	Vertex	45
Vertex	Breech	35
Breech	Vertex	10
Breech	Breech	8
Other combinations		2

by external cephalic version to ensure that it is longitudinal. If the presentation is cephalic, a normal delivery usually occurs, but in cases of breech presentation or transverse lie, a breech extraction may be necessary. Caesarean section is sometimes used to deliver the second twin.

Postpartum haemorrhage is particularly common in multiple pregnancy because the overdistended uterus may not contract well. This risk is greatly reduced by the routine use of ergometrine with delivery of the second twin and an intravenous infusion of Syntocinon for the following 4–6 hr.

Triplets

The risks with triplets are similar to those for a twin pregnancy but the incidence of premature labour is considerably increased. Admission to hospital from 20 weeks is advised rather than regular outpatient assessment of the cervix.

In labour, the risks to the second and third fetuses are similar to those for twins but there is the added problem of increased length of time necessary to complete three deliveries. This considerable risk is avoided by delivery of such patients by elective Caesarean section at 38 weeks; a similar argument applies to quadruplets and quintuplets.

Neonatal Aspects

Birth Asphyxia

Birth asphyxia is particularly common in the second twin for reasons given above. Additionally, the second twin may have been undiagnosed so an oxytocic may be given inappropriately with the delivery of the first twin.

Preterm Birth

The incidence of prematurity is higher in twins than singletons, with between 20% and 30% of twins being born before the 37th week. This may be due to poor placental function which occurs in the last weeks of pregnancy, to the large intrauterine volume or to premature cervical dilatation.

Additionally, the birth weights of twins are lower than average and the optimal birth weights for twins are less than for singletons (Fig. 7.7). Twins grow at the same rate as singletons until 34 weeks when growth retardation usually occurs. Triplets and quadruplets grow normally until 30 weeks and 25 weeks, respectively. Occasionally there is a significant weight discrepancy between the twins as one may be small for gestational age, therefore being liable to develop problems associated with this condition, especially hypoglycaemia (Chapter 5).

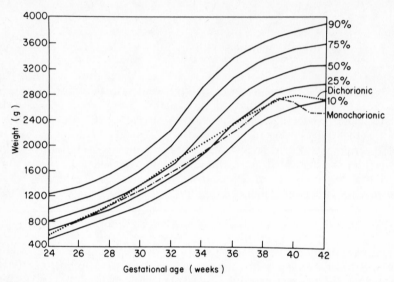

Figure 7.7 Growth of monochorionic and dichorionic twins plotted as weight centiles.

Respiratory Distress Syndrome (Chapter 4)

This syndrome is particularly common in twins because of the frequency of prematurity. It is especially common in the second twin; when both twins develop the disease, it is more severe in the second twin.

This may be explained partially by the increased likelihood of fetal hypoxia in the second twin. A second explanation may be that the first twin sac is more liable to premature rupture than the second and this stress may enhance the production of surfactant. A further explanation is that the lungs of the twins mature at different rates, with the second twin's lagging behind by 1–2 weeks.

Feto-fetal (Twin-to-Twin) Transfusion

Twin-to-twin transfusion may occur either acutely or chronically. For feto-fetal transfusion to occur, there must be some fetal vascular communication so that the condition is seen in monozygotic, monochorionic twins.

In the acute form, the transfusion occurs in labour. The infants are of similar size yet one is pale and shocked while the other is plethoric and may be in cardiac failure. The cord haemoglobin values may be similar, but, if the babies are not treated, repeat haemoglobin levels performed after several hours reveal a marked difference between the two babies.

Immediate treatment of twin-to-twin transfusion is vital. The pale, shocked twin requires a transfusion of blood or plasma to expand its circulating blood volume, while the second plethoric twin may require venesection and plasma exchange transfusion to treat cardiac failure. Jaundice may also occur as a result of polycythaemia, and intravascular thrombosis may occur because of the increase in blood viscosity (see Chapter 5).

Chronic feto-fetal transfusion is usually easy to diagnose. The donor twin is paler than the recipient and shows signs of intrauterine growth retardation since his supply of nutrients has been poor for some time. The donor twin is particularly prone to birth asphyxia because of growth retardation and chronic hypoxia.

After birth, the donor twin may need a blood transfusion although this is seldom needed immediately. Complications of growth retardation, for example hypoglycaemia, may need correction. The recipient twin is heavier and plethoric, and may suffer from the problems of polycythaemia requiring a partial plasma exchange transfusion.

Disseminated Intravascular Coagulation (DIC)

DIC may arise in monozygotic twins when one dies *in utero*. Thromboplastins are released into the circulation of the surviving twin causing DIC and consumption of clotting factors. Porencephalic cysts have been reported in surviving twins who develop this complication.

Congenital Malformations

These are more common in twins of the same sex than in singletons and include congenital heart disease and neural tube defects, particularly anencephaly. Conjoined twins occur rarely and may be suspected prior to birth by observing fetuses lying face to face on radiographic or ultrasonic examination. Referral to a regional centre where paediatric surgical expertise is available is necessary.

Mother–Infant Bonding

The birth of twins is always exciting and the mother becomes the ward celebrity. However, when things settle down, there are often problems to be solved and realities to be faced.

Many mothers are frightened by the responsibilities of twins and this is especially so if either or both are unwell. Additionally, the work involved, with the consequent lack of sleep, leads to increasing tiredness and emotional upset. Most of these problems can be overcome with the caring co-operation of the nurses, general practitioners and paediatricians. The husband assumes an even more important role than usual by sharing in the work and becoming more intimately involved.

Feeding of twins often presents some problems. Breast feeding should be advised as for singleton infants but this occasionally is unsuccessful because of the stress involved in rearing two infants and active discouragement from relatives.

Many problems have to be faced in the first few years because of the huge physical and emotional demands that twins make. These women and their babies require careful attention, gentle help and constant encouragement.

FURTHER READING

Baskett, T. F. (1985) *Essential Management of Obstetric Emergencies*. John Wiley, London.

Beard, R. W. and Paintin, D. B. (1981) Outcomes of Obstetric Intervention in Britain. Proc. RCOG Scientific Meeting, London.

Bryan, E. M. (1983) *The Nature and Nurture of Twins*. Baillière Tindall, London.

Chamberlain, R., Chamberlain, G., Howlett, B. and Claireaux, A. (1975) *British Births 1970*. Vol. 1: *The First Week of Life*. Heinemann Medical, London.

Crowley, P. and Hawkins, D. F. (1980) Premature breech delivery – the Caesarean section debate. *J. Obstet. Gynaec.* **1**: 2.

Dewhurst, J. and Whitfield, C. R. (1986) In Whitfield, C. R. (ed.), *Dewhurst's Textbook of Obstetrics and Gynaecology for Postgraduates*. Blackwell Scientific Publications, Oxford.

Myerscough, P. (1982) *Munro Kerr's Operative Obstetrics*, 10th edn. Baillière Tindall, London.

Saunders, M. C., Dick, J. S., Brown, I. McL, McPherson, K. and Chalmers, I. (1985) The effects of hospital admission for bed rest on the duration of twin pregnancy: a randomised trial. *Lancet* ii: 793.

Schenker, J. G., Yarkoni, S. and Granat, M. (1981) Multiple pregnancies following induction of ovulation. *Fertil. Steril.* **35**: 105.

Volpe, J. J. (1981) *Neurology of the Newborn*. W. B. Saunders, Philadelphia, pp. 575–598.

Wigglesworth, J. S. (1984) *Perinatal Pathology*. W. B. Saunders, Philadelphia, pp. 92–112.

Wood, C., Downing, B., Trounson, A. and Rogers, P. (1984) Clinical implications of development of *in vitro* fertilisation. *Br. Med. J.* **289**: 978.

8

Post-term Pregnancy

INTRODUCTION

A post-term (or prolonged) pregnancy is one which has exceeded 42 completed weeks from the last menstrual period (LMP). The term 'post-mature' applies to the appearance of the newborn.

Incidence

The incidence depends on which method is used to determine the duration of pregnancy. Based solely on the LMP, 10% of pregnancies are prolonged. If the estimate is determined from the date of conception, menstrual history and early ultrasonic assessment, the frequency of prolonged pregnancy falls to 4%.

Pathogenesis

Post-term pregnancy may be considered to occur at one end of the spectrum of normal pregnancy or may be the result of a defect in the normal initiation of labour. If the latter is the cause, the pathogenesis will not be fully understood until the factors controlling the onset of labour at term have been clearly elucidated. Further discussion of the initiation of labour may be found in Chapter 2.

In about one-third of post-term pregnancies, there is evidence of fetal growth impairment and the infant is described as being of a 'post-mature' appearance. The placenta has a finite life and may fail at any time in pregnancy. Failure is especially likely to occur after 42 weeks when it is attributed to placental age. Intrauterine death and birth asphyxia are associated with placental failure; it is therefore important that obstetricians observe prolonged pregnancies closely.

Prolonged pregnancy is also associated with fetal abnormalities such as neural tube defects, hydrocephalus and osteogenesis imperfecta.

Management of Post-term Pregnancy

The British Perinatal Surveys of 1958 and 1970 showed a three- to four-fold increase in perinatal mortality in post-term pregnancies (Fig. 8.1). For this reason, a policy of non-selective induction of labour at about 42 weeks gestation has been practised in many obstetric units. This can have some hidden pitfalls; incorrect assessment of dates may lead to the birth of a preterm infant, and, occasionally, failed induction of labour may increase the rate of Caesarean section. On the other hand, failure to diagnose fetal growth retardation and fetal compromise past term increases the perinatal mortality rate and produces significant neonatal morbidity. American experience, however, has shown that in certain circumstances it is quite safe to allow pregnancies to proceed to 43 and perhaps even 44 weeks provided there is no evidence of fetal compromise.

The corner-stone of successful management of all pregnancies is accurate determination of the true expected date of delivery (EDD) (Chapter 3). If pregnancy is prolonged, labour is induced if the cervix is favourable. If the cervix is unfavourable, spontaneous onset of labour may be awaited in the absence of evidence of impending fetal compromise. This evidence should be sought by twice-weekly biophysical assessment of the fetus using ultrasound scanning (Chapter 3). Liquor volume, fetal movement and growth are most important. Cardiotocography is frequently used as part of fetal assessment but rarely shows

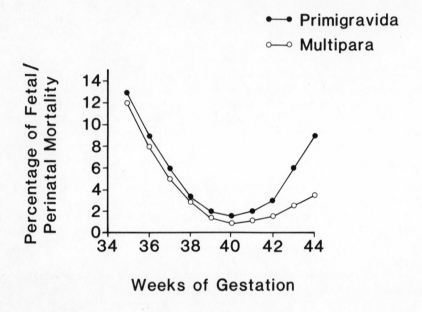

Figure 8.1 Perinatal mortality by gestational age for primigravida and multipara. (After Chamberlain *et al.*, 1975.)

significant change when ultrasonic features are normal. It is important to exclude fetal abnormality by careful ultrasound scanning.

If a full assessment reveals that the fetus and its environment are healthy, no action is necessary; spontaneous onset of labour should be awaited and a reassessment carried out every 3 or 4 days. If there is evidence of fetal risk, the patient should be delivered. The mode of delivery chosen will depend on many variables. If there is severe fetal compromise, for example oligohydramnios with thick meconium, or if the patient has an unfavourable cervix with meconium-stained liquor, Caesarean section is the method of choice. When such factors do not pertain, labour may be induced by ARM and oxytocin infusion. The fetal heart should be monitored using a scalp electrode and the scalp pH measured if there is any sign of fetal distress.

A flow chart of the management of prolonged pregnancy is given in Fig. 8.2.

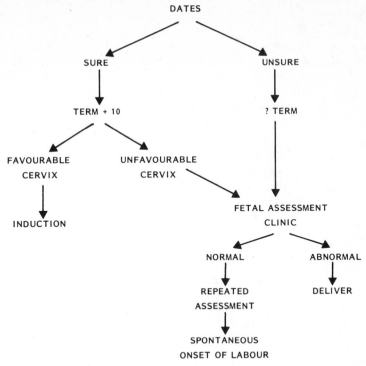

Figure 8.2 Flow chart for the management of post-term pregnancy.

PROBLEMS OF THE NEONATE

In the 1950s, Clifford gave a classical description of the post-mature infant and suggested three stages. In stage 1 there is loss of subcutaneous tissue, desquamation, long fingernails, abundant hair, alert facies and no evidence of meconium staining. In stage 2, the appearance is as in stage 1 with the addition of green meconium staining of the liquor and umbilical cord. Stage 3 is similar to stage 2 though meconium staining of liquor and umbilical cord is yellow, suggesting prolonged intrauterine stress. Such infants are rarely seen in current clinical practice.

The post-mature infant (i.e. post-term plus fetal distress) may suffer from any of the complications listed in Table 8.1.

Meconium Aspiration Syndrome (see also Chapter 3)

Meconium aspiration syndrome is one of the most frequent causes of respiratory failure in the term and post-term infant. Passage of meconium *in utero* is due to a reflex produced by hypoxic stress. This usually occurs in labour and the baby is born with meconium in his mouth and nose which may be inhaled. However, hypoxia prior to the onset of labour may also stimulate fetal respiratory movements so that aspiration can occur *in utero*, before or during labour.

Incidence

In 20% of these deliveries, there is meconium staining of the amniotic fluid, but in less than half of these is any meconium found below the vocal cords before the infant takes his first breath.

Pathogenesis and Pathophysiology

Meconium is aspirated into the airways as a consequence of fetal distress in labour. If the large airways are obstructed, there is immediate respiratory distress and if the blockage is complete the infant may die. The meconium may pass down into the smaller airways which become partially obstructed so that air trapping occurs leading to gross overinflation of the lungs. This, in association with hypoxia and acidosis, may cause pulmonary hypertension with right-to-left shunting of blood.

The presence of meconium in the lung may also produce a chemical pneumonitis with the development of secondary bacterial infection, as meconium

Table 8.1 Complications seen in the post-mature infant

1. Asphyxia
2. Meconium aspiration
3. Hypoglycaemia
4. Polycythaemia
5. Coagulation defects
6. Obstetrical trauma
      Torn falx cerebri
      Shoulder dystocia
      Fractures
      Nerve palsies
7. Increased incidence of anomalies

provides a culture medium for organisms that have been aspirated with the amniotic fluid.

Another complication of the gross pulmonary hyperinflation is dissection of air from the alveolar space leading to pneumothorax and pneumomediastinum. These complications may occur before or after initiation of mechanical ventilation.

Clinical Presentation

In some infants, the presentation is very acute with major airway obstruction at birth; these babies may die unless they are actively resuscitated. In many, respiratory signs may be present from birth and include tachypnoea, subcostal indrawing and cyanosis. The chest may appear overdistended and barrel-shaped as result of air trapping. Bronchial breathing is often present on auscultation and expiration is prolonged, indicating small airway involvement.

In infants with milder degrees of aspiration, there may be a gradual deterioration of respiratory function as meconium passes distally in the bronchial tree finally causing small airway obstruction with progressive overinflation of alveoli. As a result, it is not uncommon for infants who have aspirated meconium to appear reasonably well at birth but then to gradually deteriorate, require increasing concentrations of oxygen and to develop marked respiratory acidosis. At any time, there may be sudden deterioration because of pneumothorax or right-to-left shunting of blood.

Other complications of meconium aspiration syndrome include pulmonary and cerebral haemorrhage, and secondary bacterial infection. In infants who have required mechanical ventilation, bronchopulmonary dysplasia may occur and cases of subglottic stenosis have also been reported.

It is also important to remember that infants with meconium aspiration have often suffered from birth asphyxia with its attendant problems (Chapter 3).

Investigation

Chest radiographs frequently show patchy areas of consolidation which may have a streaky appearance. These are often interspersed with areas where the lung appears to be hyperlucent from overinflation. Pneumomediastinum and pneumothorax may also be present. Arterial blood gas sampling frequently shows a mixed metabolic and respiratory acidosis and hypoxia. The severity of the hypoxaemia depends upon the amount of meconium aspirated and the degree of persistent pulmonary hypertension with right-to-left shunting.

Prevention and Management

Several studies have indicated that efficient tracheal suctioning at birth in infants who have been born through thick meconium will ameliorate or prevent severe meconium aspiration syndrome. Anticipation and prevention of this condition are obviously of great importance. It is essential that a doctor who is experienced in neonatal resuscitation is present at the birth of all infants where labour has been complicated by thick meconium staining. This is especially so if there has been any other evidence of fetal asphyxia, such as fetal heart rate abnormalities or fetal acidosis.

The obstetrician should gently suction the oropharynx and the nasopharynx when the head emerges from the vagina, in an attempt to clear the upper airway before respiration begins. Immediately after birth, the paediatrician should examine the vocal cords under direct vision and suction any meconium present in the hypopharynx and glottic area before intubating to remove any meconium that is present below the cords. Tracheal suction is best performed directly through an endotracheal tube rather than attempting to pass a suction catheter. Endotracheal suction should be continued until all the meconium has been removed from the larger airways, but should not mean undue delay before starting positive pressure ventilation to establish normal respiration. It is best *not* to carry out pulmonary lavage as this may liquefy the meconium and allow it to be carried down to obstruct the smaller airways. All babies in whom meconium has been found below the cords should be admitted to the neonatal intensive-care unit for observation.

In the nursery, the infant may be given chest physiotherapy and postural drainage to clear any meconium that remains in the airways. If the infant has any respiratory symptoms, arterial blood gas sampling and chest radiograph should be performed and oxygen given as necessary to keep the arterial oxygen tension normal. In babies who remain hypoxaemic in high concentrations of oxygen, it may be necessary to use mechanical ventilation. This may also be required for babies who develop respiratory acidosis and for those in whom spontaneous respiration has not started. It may also be used to reduce the effects of cerebral oedema by reducing the arterial carbon dioxide tension thus lowering the cerebral blood flow.

Continuous positive airways pressure should not be used as it frequently leads to deterioration by increasing the hyperinflation of the lungs. This will decrease the lung compliance leading to further hypoventilation and also may impede venous return with a consequent reduction of the cardiac output. Tolazoline may be needed to correct right-to-left shunting. Infants should also be given broad spectrum antibiotic therapy after taking cultures of blood and tracheal secretions. Steroids have not been shown to be helpful in suppression of the chemical pneumonitis that is thought to occur in this syndrome. One controlled trial has shown that they may be harmful.

Further lines of management aim to correct the other effects of severe asphyxia (Chapter 3).

Outcome

Massive meconium aspiration syndrome may cause significant mortality and morbidity. It is a condition, however, that should be seen less and less often as a result of good perinatal management. Once it has developed, even with aggress-ive neonatal management, the mortality rate is around 30%. Pneumothorax occurs in about 15% of infants and bronchopulmonary dysplasia is not uncommon in those who require mechanical ventilation.

Hypoglycaemia

In the post-mature infant, glycogen stores are often reduced and if, in addition, asphyxia occurs, severe hypoglycaemia may result.

It is important to check blood sugar levels on all post-term infants, especially those with signs of post-maturity. If the infant is well, early feeding should be instituted. Ill infants may require glucose infusions to maintain normal blood glucose levels (Chapter 5).

Polycythaemia

Polycythaemia occurs because chronic fetal hypoxia induces erythropoietin production with a consequent increase in red cell production. Hyperviscosity of the blood may result with spontaneous intravascular thrombosis. The venous haematocrit level should be measured and partial exchange transfusion may be necessary (Chapter 5).

Coagulation Defects

Asphyxiated post-term infants may develop signs of disseminated intravascular coagulation (DIC). This may present with bleeding from venepuncture sites or oozing from the umbilicus. Occasionally, more severe haemorrhage may occur into the lung or brain (Chapter 5).

DIC may be confirmed by demonstrating a low platelet count, increased fibrin degradation products and prolonged clotting time. These clotting abnormalities are probably associated with vascular damage from hypoxia and attempts to correct them with fresh blood or plasma transfusions should be energetically made. In addition, babies with pulmonary haemorrhage may benefit from mechanical ventilation with high end-expiratory pressures to reduce bleeding by capillary compression.

Some post-term infants, especially those with growth retardation, though not necessarily with acute asphyxia, may also have coagulation defects as a result of decreased hepatic synthesis of clotting factors. These babies may also show bleeding from venepuncture sites and oozing from the umbilicus. In addition there may also be bruising. These babies have prolonged prothrombin and partial thromboplastin times and should be given vitamin K.

Obstetric Trauma

Birth injuries are sustained during labour and delivery. They may be avoidable or may occur despite skilled obstetrical care. Birth injuries are more common in the post-term pregnancy. This is probably because of increased fetal size as pregnancy progresses beyond term with a consequent risk of shoulder dystocia. Another factor that may be involved is increasing ossification of the fetal skull so that it is less able to mould during passage through the birth canal with a resultant increase in shearing forces (Chapter 7).

CONCLUSION

Post-term pregnancy has traditionally been avoided by routine induction of labour at 10–14 days past 40 weeks gestation. It is important to stress that should pregnancies be allowed to continue post-term, every effort must be made to regularly observe both fetal growth and well-being. This will mean admitting mothers to hospital for observation or having them visit antenatal clinics or special fetal assessment clinics as often as twice weekly. Good perinatal care will reduce the mortality and morbidity associated with post-term pregnancy so that asphyxia, trauma and meconium aspiration syndrome should become rare events.

FURTHER READING

Beischer, N. A., Evans, J. H. and Townsend, C. (1969) Studies in prolonged pregnancy. *Am. J. Obstet. Gynecol.* **103**: 477.

Cardazo, L., Fysh, J. and Pearce, J. M. (1986) Prolonged pregnancy: the management debate. *Br. Med. J.* **239**: 1059.

Chamberlain, R., Chamberlain, G., Howlett, B. and Claireaux, A. (1975) *British Births: The First Week of Life.* Heinemann Medical, London.

Clifford, S. H. (1954) Postmaturity – with placental dysfunction: clinical syndrome and pathologic findings. *J. Pediatr.* **44**: 1.

Vorheer, H. (1975) Placental insufficiency in relation to post-term pregnancy and fetal post-maturity. *Am. J. Obstet. Gynecol.* **123**: 67.

9

Hypertension in Pregnancy

INTRODUCTION

Hypertension may occur during pregnancy either as a result of pre-existing pathology or because of disease specific to pregnancy itself. It is the commonest reason for admission to hospital during the antenatal period and for more frequent attendance at antenatal clinics.

DEFINITION

The indirect measurement of blood pressure is frequently inaccurate with marked diurnal variations making interpretation difficult. The most acceptable definition of hypertension is a blood pressure of 140/90 mmHg or greater recorded on two occasions at an interval of more than 6 hr. The Committee on Terminology of the American College of Obstetrics and Gynecologists suggest that a rise of 30 mmHg in the systolic pressure or 15 mmHg in the diastolic pressure over the 'baseline' pressure recorded either before pregnancy or during the first trimester indicates significant hypertension.

Many attempts have been made to achieve a satisfactory classification of hypertension in pregnancy but none is universally acceptable, although that of Chesley (1978) is commonly used. The proposed four major categories are: pregnancy-induced hypertension (pre-eclampsia and eclampsia), chronic hypertension complicating pregnancy, chronic hypertension with superimposed pregnancy-induced hypertension and late or transient hypertension.

PREGNANCY-INDUCED HYPERTENSION (PRE-ECLAMPSIA AND ECLAMPSIA)

Pre-eclampsia is a disorder of unknown aetiology which affects most systems of the body during the second half of pregnancy. It is more common in the first pregnancy. It may recur in second or subsequent pregnancies, particularly if specific risk factors such as chronic renal disease, pre-existing hypertension or diabetes mellitus are also present. Other predisposing factors include a family history of hypertension and poor social circumstances. It is also more common and may present earlier in multiple pregnancy and in molar pregnancy.

Incidence

Estimates of the incidence of pregnancy-induced hypertension range from 5 to 15% of all pregnancies. Pre-eclampsia accounts for three-quarters of all hypertension seen in pregnancy.

Aetiology and Pathogenesis

In pre-eclampsia, there is a characteristic vasoconstriction of the arteriolar bed especially in the uterus and kidneys. This may be due to overactivity of the renin–angiotensin II system or may be due to an altered response of the arteriolar bed to angiotensin II. Normally in pregnancy, there is a diminution in the vascular response to this hormone due to the vasodilator effects of some prostaglandins, notably prostaglandin E_2. It is possible that prostaglandin levels are reduced in the uterus and blood vessels in pre-eclampsia.

There is fibrin deposition within small blood vessels, possibly as a result of immunological intolerance. This utilization of fibrin may initiate the development of disseminated intravascular coagulation, particularly in the more severe forms of the disease.

Clinical Features

In the early stages, pre-eclampsia is a disease of signs and not of symptoms. This is important to recognize as it may prove necessary to persuade a woman who may feel well that regular observation and assessment are required.

There are four main stages in the progression of the disease. The earliest sign is elevation of the blood pressure sometimes with generalized oedema which may be associated with a falling platelet count and rising blood urate level. This is followed by the development of proteinuria usually accompanied by controllable hypertension and impairment of renal and placental function. A fulminating stage follows with headache, visual disturbances, abdominal pain and tenderness over the liver caused by stretching of the liver capsule. The blood pressure becomes more elevated and difficult to control and renal failure and disseminated intravascular coagulation may occur. There may be ocular fundal changes of hypertensive encephalopathy such as papilloedema, and signs of neurological hyperexcitability with increased deep tendon reflexes. There may be gross fluid retention.

The final stage is eclampsia, with major seizures, when maternal cerebral haemorrhage and fetal death may occur. One additional complication of pre-eclampsia is placental abruption. This association has recently been questioned but for many obstetricians the link remains real (Chapter 11).

Management

Antenatal Care

The first objective is to identify those women who develop hypertension as early as possible and to arrange close observation of their clinical condition in a special weekly antenatal clinic. Usually all that is necessary is regular review, but if there is any evidence of deterioration, such as the development of proteinuria, the patient should be admitted to hospital for further assessment.

In hospital, the condition of the mother and fetus is assessed regularly. The blood pressure is measured every 4 hr, and the urine analysed daily for protein. In addition, a 24-hr urine collection for protein content is performed twice weekly. The glomerular filtration rate is measured if there is proteinuria in the absence of infection. The plasma urea, uric acid, creatinine and platelet count are measured twice weekly. Urinary oestriols may also be performed but these are of little value and have been largely abandoned in most hospitals. Fetal activity should be recorded on a daily 'kick chart'. Cardiotocography, ultrasonic assessment of fetal growth, amniotic fluid volume and umbilical blood flow should be performed regularly (Chapter 3).

A short period of hospitalization may improve the condition of the woman. If the mother's blood pressure falls and the fetus is healthy, she may be allowed home to be reviewed regularly in the fetal assessment clinic and pregnancy should be allowed to continue until 38 weeks when labour should be induced.

If the patient's condition deteriorates either at the time of initial hospitalization or later with the blood pressure rising to more than 105 mmHg with proteinuria or symptoms developing, more active treatment is necessary. Control of the maternal blood pressure is essential for the mother's safety and may help to postpone the need for urgent and possible untimely delivery but will not directly help the fetus.

Hypertension is treated when the diastolic pressure exceeds 110 mmHg. The immediate goal is to reduce the diastolic blood pressure to between 90 and 100 mmHg and maintain it at this level by continuing anti-hypertensive therapy. The commonly used drugs are methyldopa or labetalol. Methyldopa can safely be given in doses up to 4.0 g/day and should be started with a loading dose of 750 mg followed by 500 mg every 6 hr. Labetalol is given in 200-mg doses every 4 hr and may be used intravenously. If the patient develops symptoms, control of the blood pressure is urgent: either intravenous hydrallazine or labetalol should be used since they act rapidly.

Anticonvulsants should be prescribed if neurological signs are present: diazepam and chlormethiazole being the most commonly used. These drugs have both anticonvulsant and sedative effects and readily cross the placenta. Magnesium sulphate is widely used in the USA but has found little favour in Europe. It has much to recommend it because it is safer for the fetus, causing less respiratory depression.

Generalized oedema and oliguria are signs of hypovolaemia and abnormalities of colloid pressure caused by the disease; indiscriminate treatment with diuretics may further aggravate the process and so are contra-indicated. Pulmonary oedema is the only indication for diuretics and in this situation the advice of a cardiologist should be sought urgently. The use of colloid infusion in patients with hypovolaemia is currently under investigation.

Timing and Method of Delivery

The objective of treatment is to allow the pregnancy to continue towards term, consistent with maternal health. Knowledge of the intact survival rates related to birth weight and gestational age help in deciding when delivery should take place (Chapter 4). If preterm delivery is likely, betamethasone may be given to accelerate lung maturation if the fetus is extremely immature. In the acute case with imminent eclampsia, the pregnancy should be terminated in the maternal interest with a minimum of delay.

Delivery in the most severe cases should be by Caesarean section, especially if the gestational age is less than 32 weeks and where there is evidence of fetal compromise. Other factors such as advanced maternal age and other complicating medical problems have to be taken into consideration. Where the fetus is appropriately grown and is of more than 32 weeks maturity, an attempt should be made to achieve vaginal delivery by induction of labour together with continuous fetal heart rate monitoring. Epidural analgesia in labour is recommended since it abolishes pain and anxiety which may increase hypertension. When there is evidence of intravascular coagulation or if the patient has required magnesium sulphate to prevent or control convulsions, epidural analgesia is absolutely contra-indicated (Chapter 2). Ergometrine is a powerful vasoconstrictor and should be avoided in the management of the third stage unless required for the control of haemorrhage.

Observation and treatment should be continued for the first 48 hr after delivery to prevent postpartum eclampsia. After this time the maternal condition improves very rapidly and there will be a marked, spontaneous diuresis.

Eclampsia

The transition from an apparently normal pregnancy or one with only mild hypertension to the eclamptic state can be extremely rapid. This condition may threaten the life of the mother by causing a cerebral haemorrhage or disseminated intravascular coagulopathy and also may cause fetal death. Since the condition is so dangerous, these patients should be managed in the labour ward which is usually well staffed with facilities for intensive monitoring.

The main objectives are to control seizures and to reduce the blood pressure. Seizures are controlled by giving either intravenous diazepam or intravenous magnesium sulphate. Intravenous diazepam (20 mg) is given initially and should be continued as an infusion, of 40 mg in 500 ml of dextrose. Magnesium sulphate is given in an initial dose of 2–4 g and continued as an infusion of 1–1.5 g/hr which is stopped if there is respiratory depression, if the urinary output falls below 100 ml in 4 hr, or if the patellar reflex cannot be elicited. The effects of magnesium sulphate are reversed by calcium gluconate. If the diastolic blood pressure exceeds 110 mmHg, a test dose of 10 mg of hydrallazine is given intravenously and the blood pressure is measured every 5 min. If the diastolic pressure does not fall to between 90 and 100 mmHg within 20 min, a further 10 mg should be administered. This dose is repeated at 20-min intervals until the required effect is achieved and is maintained either by continuous intravenous infusion of 40 mg hydrallazine in 500 ml of 5% dextrose/saline solution or by repeated intravenous injections.

Blood should be grouped and cross-matched and, because there is a risk of disseminated intravascular coagulopathy, it is necessary to perform a blood coagulation analysis.

When effective control of the convulsions and hypertension has been achieved, the mother should be delivered. In most cases, delivery should be by Caesarean section if the fetal heartbeat is still present. Vaginal delivery may be considered if the cervix is extremely favourable. In such circumstances fetal heart rate monitoring is necessary and the second stage of labour should be shortened by timely forceps delivery. Anticonvulsants and anti-hypertensive therapy must continue for 48 hr after delivery to prevent the recurrence of convulsions. After this time, they may safely be discontinued.

Future Pregnancies

A full discussion of the implications of severe pre-eclampsia or eclampsia for future pregnancies should take place at the postnatal visit. If the blood pressure has returned to normal and there are no detectable abnormalities of the renal or endocrine systems, the mother can be advised that the risk of a recurrence is about 30% but that future disease is usually mild.

CHRONIC HYPERTENSION COMPLICATING PREGNANCY

The appropriate management of the patient with hypertension complicating pregnancy depends upon the identification of any underlying cause, the assessment of any organ involvement in the mother and an evaluation of any effects on the fetus.

If a woman is found to be hypertensive in the first half of pregnancy or a history of hypertension is obtained, the cause should be sought. Some of these women have already been investigated and information is available from the relevant hospital records, but it is surprising how often this is ignored in a busy antenatal clinic.

The commonest causes in this age group are essential hypertension, renal or adrenal disease (p. 207), connective tissue disorder (p. 224) or coarctation of the aorta. Evidence of such diseases may be obtained from personal and family histories and hypertension may have occurred in previous pregnancies.

The examination of the hypertensive patient should include a specific search for such causes and for evidence of the effects of hypertension, such as left ventricular enlargement or ocular fundal changes.

A short hospital admission for 48–72 hr should be advised unless the patient has been previously investigated or the disease is mild. The purpose of this is to observe blood pressure patterns, collect 24-hr urine specimens for catecholamines, glomerular filtration rate and protein excretion, and to perform any other appropriate tests. These observations serve as a baseline against which to assess the clinical progress and to compare subsequent investigations.

The decision to treat chronic hypertension complicating pregnancy is still a matter of debate. In general, treatment should be continued in those whose blood pressure required treatment before pregnancy, but the drugs used may need to be changed to those that are considered safe for the developing embryo. When the elevation of the blood pressure is discovered for the first time at the antenatal examination, treatment is given if average diastolic pressure is in excess of 100 mmHg.

Methyldopa is generally recommended as the drug of choice because experience of its use is greatest. However, some prefer to use labetalol because of the high incidence of maternal side-effects with methyldopa.

In general, the fetus is not compromised, but regular assessments should be carried out and it is customary for labour to be induced at 38 weeks.

Chronic renal disease is not an uncommon occurrence in women of childbearing age and the outcome of pregnancy depends upon the type of renal disease (Table 9.1) Impairment of renal function reduces the likelihood of a successful outcome more than the hypertension itself. The one essential of management is the establishment of co-operation between the obstetrician and

Table 9.1 Prognosis of pregnancy in chronic renal disease

Normal expectation of successful pregnancy	*Decreased expectancy of successful pregnancy*

1. Polycystic disease of kidney
2. Renal stone disease
3. Medullary cystic disease (medullary sponge kidneys with stone disease)
4. Chronic pyelonephritis without renal failure
5. Hydronephrosis
6. Congenital renal anomalies
   (a) Duplex kidney/kidneys
   (b) Solitary kidney
   (c) Horseshoe kidney
   (d) Crossed ectopic kidney
	1. Glomerulonephritis
	2. Chronic pyelonephritis with impaired renal function
	3. Systemic lupus erythematosus
	4. After urinary diversion
	5. After renal transplantation
	6. During regular dialysis therapy

McGeown and Houston (1982).

the nephrologist, preferably in a tertiary-care unit with all the facilities to cope with the complications that may arise in the mother and to perform fetal assessment. If there is significant deterioration in renal function, the pregnancy should be terminated. Similarly, if there is evidence of a deterioration in the fetal condition, the mother should be delivered (Chapter 3).

Pre-pregnancy counselling of all women with chronic renal disease may help improve the chance of a successful outcome. Risks can be explained and it may be possible to gain better patient compliance with dietary restrictions and medication.

CHRONIC HYPERTENSION WITH SUPERIMPOSED PREGNANCY-INDUCED HYPERTENSION

Superimposed pre-eclampsia in a patient with chronic hypertension is diagnosed when hypertension occurs before or early in pregnancy (before 20 weeks) and then proteinuria and/or oedema develops with a further rise in the blood pressure of 30 mmHg systolic pressure or 15 mmHg diastolic pressure.

The risk of a pregnant woman with chronic hypertensive disease developing pre-eclampsia is at least three times that of the normotensive woman. The disease is usually severe and often occurs at an earlier stage of pregnancy. The woman with chronic hypertension should have been identified either before or early in pregnancy so that baseline information about fetal maturity, the blood pressure and its control and the renal function can be obtained. Superimposed pre-eclampsia can then be identified more easily. Since the risk of developing early, severe disease is high, these women should be seen frequently at the antenatal clinic and regular fetal assessments performed so that any deterioration in the clinical condition of either the mother or the fetus may be detected early. If severe disease occurs, further management is as for pre-eclampsia.

LATE OR TRANSIENT HYPERTENSION

Frequently women are seen at the antenatal clinic late in pregnancy with elevated blood pressure. This is usually transient and requires no treatment. If hypertension persists, early delivery should be arranged and the mother treated if her diastolic pressure is greater than 110 mmHg or if she has symptoms. The fetus is rarely affected.

THE NEWBORN OF THE HYPERTENSIVE MOTHER

The fetus or newborn baby of the hypertensive mother may be affected by perinatal asphyxia, intrauterine growth retardation, immaturity and the effects of the drugs given to the mother to control her hypertension.

Perinatal Asphyxia (Chapter 3)

Infants with perinatal asphyxia withstand labour relatively poorly because of their limited growth, diminished energy reserves and immaturity. Additionally the mother may need to be given medications, such as diazepam, to protect her; this may depress neonatal respiration. Finally, placental abruption may occur (Chapter 11).

Intrauterine Growth Retardation (Chapter 5)

Infants whose mothers have significant pre-eclampsia may be growth retarded.

Such infants are particularly prone to develop polycythaemia since placental insufficiency causes fetal hypoxaemia which stimulates erythropoietin production leading to an increase in the fetal red cell mass. There is also evidence that the fetus suffers from intravascular dehydration. Since polycythaemia may be a threat to the infant, it is important that the umbilical cord should be clamped quickly at birth in order to reduce the amount of placental transfusion.

Pulmonary Haemorrhage

Pulmonary haemorrhage has been classically associated with the growth-retarded infant, but the frequency of this condition has diminished over the past two decades. It is seen particularly frequently in those infants with asphyxia, hypothermia and hypoglycaemia. Thrombocytopenia and disseminated intravascular coagulopathy also occur in babies of mothers with severe pre-eclampsia.

The haemorrhage usually occurs in the first 48 hr of life and presents with sudden onset of cyanosis, tachypnoea and increasing subcostal recession. On occasions, the infant may dramatically produce a foamy, bright-red haemoptysis with a sudden deterioration in the clinical condition. Chest radiographs may show coarse, patchy consolidation which may be localized or generalized. The infants often require ventilatory assistance and blood transfusion and the condition may be fatal.

Pulmonary haemorrhage has become increasingly uncommon in small-for-dates infants and now is more frequently seen in infants with profound hypothermia and acidosis or those who are infected.

Hypoglycaemia

Growth-retarded babies are at risk of developing hypoglycaemia because of their poor hepatic glycogen reserves. In addition, gluconeogenesis and the adrenal medullary response to hypoglycaemia are impaired. Further, these infants are prone to develop asphyxia and hypothermia which further increases the likelihood of developing hypoglycaemia (Chapter 5).

Hypocalcaemia

This is often found coincidentally on routine biochemical monitoring but may give rise to clinical symptoms in a minority of infants who develop jitteriness or brief seizures. If the infant is symptomatic and the serum calcium is less than 1.2 mmol/l, calcium gluconate is given intravenously. Extreme care should be taken to avoid inadvertent subcutaneous extravasation of this solution as it may cause severe sloughing of the surrounding tissues. If seizures are absent and serum calcium is below 1.6 mmol/l, then oral calcium supplements are given.

Problems of Immaturity

In addition to the problems of growth retardation, these babies may also be preterm and so may suffer from those diseases associated with immaturity (Chapter 4). Respiratory distress syndrome may be absent or mild because the stress of pregnancy may have accelerated fetal lung maturation.

Maternal Medication

Most of the drugs used to treat the hypertensive mother also affect the baby. Magnesium sulphate may lead to hypotonia and respiratory depression in the baby, but this usually only occurs when large amounts have been given to the mother. Diazepam may cause hypotonia, apnoeic spells and respiratory depression if either large amounts of the drug have been used in a short period of time or if there has been chronic administration. These effects may take several days to disappear and occasionally infants require ventilatory assistance. Barbiturates are now infrequently used. They may also cause respiratory depression, hypotonia, hypothermia, poor feeding and may worsen respiratory distress. However, they do have the benefit that they may help to prevent hyperbilirubinaemia.

Beta-adrenergic blocking drugs like labetalol cause hypoglycaemia and bradycardia which may persist for at least 24 hr after delivery. They may also reduce the infant's ability to respond to acute events such as asphyxia, acute blood loss or apnoea, although these are theoretical rather than proven disadvantages. It has also been suggested that they contribute to intrauterine fetal growth retardation but this is difficult to confirm.

LONG-TERM GROWTH AND DEVELOPMENT

There is considerable debate about the effects of growth retardation caused by maternal hypertension on fetal cerebral growth. The third trimester of pregnancy and first year of life are the periods of critical brain growth, when the brain is rapidly changing at both the cellular and the biochemical level. Malnutrition may have deleterious effects, but it appears that if the baby escapes acute insults, such as severe hypoxia or hypoglycaemia, during the perinatal period, major cerebral problems do not occur. There may be a higher incidence of minimal cerebral dysfunction in these children, presumably caused by intrauterine malnutrition.

Somatic growth also tends to be impaired. The children tend to be smaller and lighter than would be expected but many catch up in the first year and grow within the normal range. Others fail to do this and remain small as adults.

FURTHER READING

Chesley, L. C. (1978) *Hypertensive Disorders in Pregnancy.* Appleton Century Crofts, New York.

Ihle, B. U., Long, P. and Oats, J. (1987) Early onset pre-eclampsia: recognition of underlying renal disease. *Br. Med. J.* **294**: 79.

Jones, R. A. K. and Robertson, N. R. C. (1984) Problems of the small for-date baby. *Clin. Obstet. Gynaecol.* **11**: 499.

McGeown, M. and Houston, K. (1982) Chronic renal disease in pregnancy. *Clin. Obstet. Gynaecol.* **9**: 101.

MacGillivray, I. (1983) *Pre-eclampsia.* W. B. Saunders, London.

Pritchard, J. A. and Pritchard, S. A. (1975) Standardized treatment of 154 consecutive cases of eclampsia. *Am. J. Obstet. Gynecol.* **123**: 543.

10

Blood Group Incompatibility

RHESUS HAEMOLYTIC DISEASE

In the past several decades, the cause of rhesus haemolytic disease has been identified and effective treatment has been devised. The disease has now been virtually eradicated by prophylaxis. This has been one of the major advances in medicine of recent times. The significance of these changes is often difficult to understand for those not in clinical practice prior to their occurrence. In previous generations, many babies died before or after birth or became handicapped because of this disease. Subsequently, exchange transfusion was used to treat neonatal anaemia and jaundice with the result that many infants survived and were normal, although some still died. Amniocentesis allowed prenatal diagnosis, and intrauterine transfusion afforded a technique of prenatal treatment of the severely affected fetus. Finally, prophylaxis with anti-D immunoglobulin was developed and the disease virtually disappeared.

Although the frequency of this condition has been radically altered, there are still some women who are affected either because they began their reproductive lives before prophylaxis was available, prophylaxis failed or was not given or they were sensitized by 'silent' prenatal feto-maternal transfusion.

Aetiology and Pathogenesis

The basic problem in rhesus haemolytic disease is an incompatibility of fetal and maternal blood. If fetal cells pass into the maternal circulation, they are recognized as being foreign and antibodies are formed. These in turn cross the placenta and attack fetal red cells causing haemolysis. The fetus attempts to compensate for this by producing more red cells under the influence of erthropoietin. The sites of erythropoiesis are the fetal liver and spleen; these organs may therefore enlarge. If the fetus fails to compensate for the haemolysis, anaemia occurs; fetal jaundice is not a problem since the bilirubin is excreted by the placenta. If the fetal anaemia is profound, cardiac failure may occur, tissue hypoxia may lead to the development of widespread oedema, ascites and pleural effusion. In addition, gross hepatosplenomegaly may occur as the result of haemolysis and cardiac failure. Hepatic failure may occur and the associated hypoalbuminaemia exacerbates fetal oedema. This overall clinical condition is called hydrops fetalis.

There are two major problems in babies born with rhesus haemolytic disease: anaemia and jaundice. Anaemia is now relatively uncommon but may be severe enough to lead to tissue hypoxia and may be life-threatening. Jaundice is also important because of the risk of kernicterus. When bilirubin is formed by haemolysis, it is transported to the liver in the blood bound to albumin. Bilirubin that is not bound to albumin is free and may pass into the brain, interfere with phosphorylation, destroy cytochromic oxidase and damage the basal ganglia and VIIIth nerve causing subsequent athetoid cerebral palsy and deafness.

Table 10.1 Events associated with transplacental transfusion

1. Vaginal delivery
2. Spontaneous abortion (4% risk)
3. Therapeutic abortion (5.5% risk)
4. Antepartum haemorrhage
5. Fulminant pre-eclampsia
6. External cephalic version
7. Amniocentesis
8. Caesarean section
9. Manual removal of the placenta
10. Multiple pregnancy

The rhesus system consists of six paired antigens – C, D, E, c, d and e – and incompatibility can occur on any pair or combination of pairs. Conventionally, people are referred to as 'rhesus positive' if they are D positive and 'rhesus negative' if they are D negative. Incompatibility on the D antigen is the most common and severe.

Sensitization of a rhesus-negative mother usually occurs at the birth of her first rhesus-positive child as this is the most likely time when fetal cells pass into her circulation. However, there may occasionally be silent transfusions of small amounts of blood during pregnancy and sensitization can also occur in other situations (Table 10.1). In a subsequent pregnancy, if the fetus is rhesus positive, maternal antibody production is greater because of previous exposure to antigen so the disease tends to become more severe with increasing parity.

Defences in Rhesus Disease

The zygosity of the father is of great importance. If he is homozygous rhesus positive, every child he fathers will be rhesus positive. If he is heterozygous, i.e. D/d, only 50% of his offspring will be rhesus positive and the rhesus-negative fetus will be unaffected.

Some rhesus-negative mothers do not produce antibody, either because the placental integrity is so good as to prevent contact between fetal cells and the maternal circulation, or the maternal reticuloendothelial system will not produce anti-rhesus antibody.

ABO blood group incompatibility also confers some protection to the fetus. In this situation, fetal cells entering the maternal circulation are recognized and destroyed by naturally occurring anti-A and anti-B antibodies before sensitization of the rhesus system can occur.

MANAGEMENT OF RHESUS-NEGATIVE MOTHERS

All women should have their blood groups ascertained at the first antenatal visit. A full obstetric and medical history should be taken with particular reference to blood transfusions and any neonatal problems. If the patient in rhesus negative, the antibody titre should be measured. All patients should be tested for other antibodies such as anti-c and anti-E.

Unsensitized Mothers

The aim is to prevent sensitization and to detect the appearance of antibodies. Sensitization may occur at delivery or with those conditions listed in Table 10.1. On these occasions any transfusion of fetal red cells should be destroyed rapidly by immunizing the mother passively with anti-D antibody. An injection of anti-D antibody lyses fetal cells and prevents them from stimulating the maternal reticuloendothelial system. The injected anti-D is then catabolized by the mother, restoring her to the unsensitized state.

Fetal cells are detected in the maternal circulation by the Kleihauer test. In this test, fresh blood slides are fixed with ethanol and incubated in an acid–citrate–phosphate buffer. Cells with fetal haemoglobin (HbF) retain their colour but those without HbF appear as colourless ghosts. If fetal cells are detected up to 16 weeks of pregnancy, 250 µg of anti-D should be given; if cells are detected after 16 weeks, the dose is 500 µg. After birth, the blood group of the baby should be determined and if rhesus positive, 500 µg of anti-D should be given to the mother. If the Kleihauer test is strongly positive (more than 80 fetal cells/50 low power field) an increased dose should be given (1000–1500 µg).

Efficacy of Anti-D

The use of anti-D has radically changed the management and prognosis for the rhesus-negative woman. Its use has led to a dramatic reduction of about 98% in the number of rhesus-sensitized patients. Further, it retains its effectiveness from pregnancy to pregnancy. These effects are seen in both mortality and morbidity statistics – deaths from rhesus incompatibility are now rare events and exchange transfusions for rhesus disease are also unusual. This dramatic change has radically altered the work done in baby units. In 1970 in the Royal Maternity Hospital, Belfast, over 300 exchange transfusions for rhesus isoimmunization were carried out, by 1986 this number had dropped to 15.

Some women still develop antibodies. This may occur because of silent feto-maternal transfusions, and sensitization of this group of women may be reduced by routinely giving anti-D to unsensitized mothers at 28 and 34 weeks. Others may have become sensitized previously but have produced antibody levels so low as to be undetectable by normal laboratory methods. Occasionally, anti-D may have been inadvertently omitted or may have been given in an inadequate dosage.

The Sensitized Mother

The aim is to detect fetal haemolysis and to plan treatment either by intrauterine blood transfusion or delivery before the fetus becomes severely affected.

Anti-rhesus antibodies should be sought in all pregnant rhesus-negative patients at booking, 28 weeks, 34 weeks and 38 weeks. If antibodies are detected, and this is the first affected pregnancy, the serum antibody nitrogen should be measured. This is a direct estimation of anti-D antibody. No action need be taken if this stays below 0.5 mg/l. If the antibody nitrogen rises, an amniocentesis should be performed unless the gestational age is greater than 36 weeks when the woman should be delivered. At amniocentesis, a sample of fluid is obtained and the bilirubin content is measured spectrophotometrically as the optical density rise at 450 nm. This result is plotted against gestational age on a graph such as that in Fig. 10.1. Liley's lines divide the figure into three zones based upon the severity of the isoimmunization. The curved line is Whitfield's Action Line and was drawn retrospectively separating babies who lived from those who died. If the bilirubin level is very low or undetectable (Liley zone 1), the amniocentesis should not be repeated and the pregnancy should be allowed to progress to term unless there is a significant rise in the blood antibody nitrogen level.

If the bilirubin level is raised (Liley zone 2 or 3), the amniocentesis should be repeated after three weeks to determine whether the level is rising, staying constant or falling. The two points are plotted and extrapolated to intersect with the 'action line' allowing a decision to be made either to treat the fetus by blood transfusion or by early delivery.

If this is not the first affected pregnancy, amniocentesis should be performed if the antibody nitrogen rises to more than 0.3 mg/l, or may be carried out at a gestational age of 10 weeks earlier than when a previous fetus or infant was severely affected; for example, if a previously affected baby was born at 37 weeks, the amniocentesis should be performed at 27 weeks. Subsequent management should be the same as for first affected pregnancy bearing in mind that the fetus is likely to be more severely affected than previous babies.

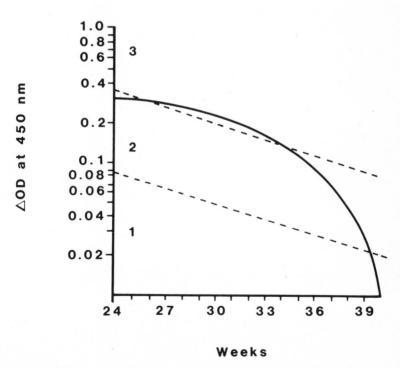

Figure 10.1 Rise in optical density (Δ OD) at 450 nm plotted against gestational age in weeks. The solid curved line is the Whitfield Action Line (Whitfield, 1976), and the straight broken lines form Liley's zones 1, 2 and 3 (Liley, 1961).

Treatment *in utero*

Treatment of severely affected fetuses should only take place in major centres. The decision to treat *in utero* depends upon the gestational age, the fetal lung maturity, severity of the haemolytic process and the expertise available.

The gestational age at which it is safe to deliver a fetus will vary from hospital to hospital and an accurate knowledge of local statistics is vital in making this decision. In most large units, it is usually safe to deliver infants at about 32 weeks. This decision may be clarified by measuring the lecithin/sphingomyelin area ratio (LSAR) and PG to estimate fetal lung maturity (Chapter 4).

If the fetus is less than 32 weeks, in utero treatment may be necessary. The degree of haemolysis will be reflected by the amniotic fluid bilirubin content. An estimate of fetal well-being may be obtained ultrasonically by estimation of the fetal weight and amniotic fluid volume together with the detection of fetal subcutaneous or pulmonary oedema or the presence of ascites. If the fetal condition is poor, blood transfusion may be given. In a few centres, cordocentesis and direct transfusion is available as early as 18–24 weeks gestation but it should be stressed that this technique, although often successful, requires great expertise and may require to be repeated.

Most centres do not have this technique available but rely on intrauterine intraperitoneal fetal transfusion. In this technique, a cannula is placed into the fetal abdominal cavity under radiographic or ultrasonic imaging, and a transfusion of group O rhesus-negative concentrated blood is given.

Neither of these techniques is free from hazard. Trauma and accidental termination of pregnancy may occur so they should only be undertaken when it is felt that the possibility of survival without such treatment is poor.

Two other methods of attempting to suppress haemolysis in rhesus disease, have been used. Promethazine (phenergan) reduces rhesus antibody coating of fetal red cells and lessens phagocytosis. It may also improve bilirubin conjugation and excretion in the neonate. Fetal T-cell suppression is a potentially serious side-effect so that this method of treatment has not generally found favour with obstetricians. Secondly, plasma exchange has been reputed to lessen the severity of rhesus isoimmunization by removal of maternal anti-D antibody. Failure of this treatment, rebound after 26 weeks and cost have ensured that its place in the treatment of severe rhesus disease is limited.

Phenobarbitone has been used to induce fetal liver enzymes in the belief that this would lessen the severity of jaundice after birth. Nowadays this drug is rarely used.

Delivery

The method of delivery is determined by the severity of the disease. If the disease is mild or moderate, vaginal delivery should be performed with fetal monitoring because of the risks of birth asphyxia. If the fetus is severely affected, delivery should be by elective Caesarean section. At birth, the cord should be clamped early to prevent circulatory overload and further antibody transfusion.

Antibodies other than D

Antibodies other than D are assuming relatively increased importance as the number of patients with anti-D antibody diminishes. Anti-c, anti-E and anti-Kell antibodies may on occasion be associated with severe disease in the fetus. All blood group antibodies should be tested for at booking and, if detected, these pregnancies should be carefully monitored and evidence of fetal compromise regularly sought.

ABO incompatibility rarely causes problems prior to delivery for three main reasons. Women of A or B blood groups have naturally occurring anti-A or anti-B antibodies which are mainly IgM and therefore do not cross the placenta. Antibody levels stay constant from pregnancy to pregnancy as there is no intrapartum 'boosting'. In addition, A and B antigens are present in many tissues; thus antibody may bind to these and not just the red cell surface, so reducing the amount of haemolysis.

However, some mothers of blood group O have anti-A and anti-B antibodies which are IgG type and may cross the placenta. For this reason, ABO incompatibility is usually seen where the mother is group O and the fetus is A or B.

NEONATAL CARE IN HAEMOLYTIC DISEASE

Severely affected babies may be grossly anaemic which may affect all the organ systems, with cardiac failure, pulmonary oedema and haemorrhage, cerebral hypoxia, alteration in blood clotting factors and renal insufficiency. Hyperbilirubinaemia, if untreated, may lead to kernicterus.

Severe disease in babies is caused by anti-D antibody, although on occasions similar consequences may be seen because of anti-c, anti-E, and anti-Kell antibodies. ABO incompatibility usually presents with jaundice in the first days of life although early, severe disease may occur.

Immediate Management of Severely Affected Infants

The immediate care of the severely affected infant in the labour ward is the same as any potentially asphyxiated baby requiring resuscitation, but there may be added problems. If the baby has suffered gross intrauterine haemolysis, there may be severe hypoxia, acidosis and cardiac failure. Lung expansion may be inhibited by pleural effusions, ascites, intraperitoneally transfused blood or hepatosplenomegaly. If this is the case, paracentesis and/or thoracocentesis may be necessary to obtain effective ventilation. On occasion, infants are so anaemic that cyanosis may not occur, leading to an underestimation of the degree of hypoxia. However, infants in this condition are now rarely seen.

Cord blood should be sent for confirmation of the diagnosis and estimation of the severity of the disease. The direct Coomb's test is positive in rhesus incompatibility of whatever type and confirms the diagnosis. One caveat is that the test may be negative if intrauterine transfusion has been given because the blood tested is, in fact, donor blood.

Measurement of the haemoglobin level gives an indication of the severity of the disease. This is best performed on a venous blood sample from the baby as cord blood may be diluted because of cord oedema giving an erroneously low result. Estimation of bilirubin, blood grouping and the platelet count should also be carried out.

The mainstay of treatment of rhesus haemolytic disease is exchange transfusion, the aims of which are to correct anaemia, remove bilirubin and to reduce the circulating antibody level. The blood used is ABO-compatible rhesus negative and exchange transfusion is carried out soon after birth if the baby is very anaemic (i.e. haemoglobin less than 10 g/dl). It may be carried out subsequently if the bilirubin content of the blood rises towards neurotoxic levels. As mentioned before, it is free bilirubin that is neurotoxic but, in practice, this is difficult to measure. For this reason, the level of indirect-reacting bilirubin which estimates both albumin-bound and free bilirubin is used. These criteria vary from baby to baby; the smallest babies may require exchange transfusion at bilirubin levels of less than 150 mmol/l, whereas large babies may tolerate levels of 400 mmol/l. Additionally, the predisposition to kernicterus may be enhanced by acidosis or hypoglycaemia. In these situations, exchange transfusion should be carried out at lower bilirubin levels.

Traditionally the umbilical vein was used; after catheterization blood was both removed and given by this route. This may cause circulatory disturbances and therefore in recent years it has become common practice either to catheterize the umbilical vein to give blood and the umbilical artery to remove blood or, alternatively, to use peripheral veins and arteries for the procedure. A double volume exchange, i.e. 180 ml/kg is performed. If the exchange transfusion is being performed because of anaemia, semi-packed cells should be used; if for hyperbilirubinaemia, whole blood is used since this enhances bilirubin removal.

The blood used for exchange transfusion should be as fresh as possible to minimize electrolyte upsets, notably hyperkalaemia. Platelets may also have to be given as these infants are often thrombocytopenic. The blood should be buffered with 10 ml of 8.4% sodium bicarbonate in every 500 ml of blood as the pH of stored blood is often 6.8 or less and the blood should be warmed before administration.

Exchange transfusion is not without risk and since the technique is now much less commonly used than before, the expertise required to perform it is becoming less widely available. Some of these risks are listed in Table 10.2.

Phototherapy

Phototherapy reduces the number of exchange transfusions that are required by breaking down bilirubin in the skin to non-neurotoxic, water-soluble metabolites.

Other Therapy

Infants with rhesus haemolytic disease may be immature and suffer from associated diseases (Chapter 4). Severely affected infants may develop hypoglycaemia, thrombocytopenia and pulmonary haemorrhage. The cause of hypoglycaemia is neonatal hyperinsulinaemia and thrombocytopenia may be due to the haemolytic process or to exchange transfusion. These two problems of hypoglycaemia and thrombocytopenia enhance the risk of pulmonary haemorrhage.

MANAGEMENT OF OTHER BLOOD GROUP INCOMPATIBILITIES

Other blood group incompatibilities are managed in an essentially similar manner to rhesus disease, although these infants are seldom seriously ill.

Table 10.2 The risks of exchange transfusion

1. Metabolic
   Acidosis, hyperkalaemia, hypocalcaemia,
   hypoglycaemia, hypothermia
2. Cardiovascular
   Arrhythmia, overload, air embolism
3. Thrombo-embolism
4. Haemorrhage, coagulopathy
5. Sepsis
   Bacterial, viral, necrotizing enterocolitis
6. Thrombocytopenia
7. Vomiting and aspiration

ABO incompatibility is usually diagnosed when a well newborn baby is found to be jaundiced. Blood grouping reveals that the mother is group O and the baby is A or B. The direct Coomb's test is weakly positive and IgG haemolysin will be detected in the maternal blood. The treatment is by phototherapy or by exchange transfusion using group O cells resuspended in plasma of the same type as the mother.

In anti-Kell incompatibility, the Coomb's test is positive and antibody is detectable in the maternal serum. Phototherapy may be used and if exchange transfusion becomes necessary, this should be done using Kell negative cells of the same ABO group as the baby suspended in plasma of the same type as the mother.

Follow-up

Mildly affected infants require follow-up for several months to detect anaemia, which is corrected by blood transfusion. Folate and vitamin E supplements should be prescribed for preterm infants. Anaemia rarely occurs after 6–8 weeks as maternal antibody levels fall and neonatal bone-marrow activity improves. Infants who are seriously affected or who are born prematurely should be observed for several years to assess neurodevelopmental progress with particular attention to hearing.

FURTHER READING

Bowman, J. M. (1981) Blood group incompatibilities. In Iffy, L. and Kaminetzky, H. A. (eds), *Principles and Practice of Obstetrics and Perinatology*. New York.

Clarke, C. A., Donohoe, W. T. A., McConnell, R. B., Woodrow, J. C., Finn, R., Krevans, J. R. *et al.* (1963) Further experimental studies in the prevention of Rh-haemolytic disease. *Br. Med. J.* **1**: 979.

Diamond, L. K., Allen, F. H. and Thomas, W. O. (1951) Erythroblastosis fetalis. VII. Treatment with exchange transfusion. *N. Engl. J. Med.* **244**: 39.

Graham-Pole, J., Barr, W. and Willoughby, M. L. (1977) Continuous flow plasmaphoresis in management of severe rhesus disease. *Br. Med. J.* **1**: 1185.

Gusdon, S. P., Jr, Candle, M. R., Herbst, G. A. and Iannuzzi, N. P. (1976) Phagocytosis and erythroblastosis. Modification of the neonatal response by promethazine hydrochloride. *Am. J. Obstet. Gynecol.* **125**: 224.

Liley, A. W. (1961) Liquor amnii analysis in management of pregnancy complicated by rhesus immunization. *Am. J. Obstet. Gynecol.* 82: 1359.

Liley, A. W. (1963) Intrauterine transfusion of fetus in haemolytic disease. *Br. Med. J.* 2: 1107.

Odell, G. (1980) *Neonatal Hyperbilirubinemia. Monographs in Neonatology.* Grune and Stratton, New York.

O'Sullivan, J. F. (1982) Rhesus and other antibodies. *Clin. Obstet. Gynaecol.* 9: 91.

Whitfield, C. R. (1976) Rhesus haemolytic disease. *J. Clin. Pathol.* 29 (Suppl. 10): 54.

11

Antepartum Haemorrhage

INTRODUCTION

Bleeding from the genital tract which occurs after the 28th week of pregnancy is termed antepartum haemorrhage (APH). It occurs in about 3% of pregnancies. This classical definition has become somewhat less useful in recent years. The 28th week was selected because of the concept of fetal viability; babies born before the 28th week rarely survived and were often called abortuses. With current medical practice, survival of such babies is not uncommon and the definition therefore needs to be revised to bleeding from 20 weeks – in line with current practice in the USA.

The significance of APH is that it may pose a serious threat to either the mother or the fetus. Bleeding may be massive and, in addition, profound shock, disproportionate to the amount of blood loss, may be seen, especially in placental abruption. This may be further complicated by disseminated intravascular coagulation. The perinatal mortality rate is about four times higher than normal when bleeding occurs at any time in pregnancy (Chamberlain *et al.*, 1978) and this increases to about a 1 in 8 chance of perinatal death in placental abruption. In addition, APH may sensitize rhesus-negative mothers. A classification of APH is given in Table 11.1; placenta praevia, placental abruption and unexplained haemorrhage account for the vast majority of cases.

INITIAL MANAGEMENT OF APH

APH is a complication of pregnancy where treatment must start before a definitive diagnosis can be made.

The first problem is that bleeding usually takes place in the patient's home and the family practitioner or midwife are the first people to attend. A distinction must be made between a 'show' and an APH. In a 'show' the blood loss is minor, is mixed with mucus and the patient shows no systemic signs of blood loss. In APH, the blood loss is greater, it is not mixed with mucus and the patient may show other signs depending on the origin of the bleeding, for example uterine tenderness (*vide infra*).

If it is decided that the patient has suffered from an APH, a careful examination for signs of blood loss and shock should be made. The 'flying squad'

Table 11.1 Classification of antepartum haemorrhage

1. Placenta praevia
2. Placental abruption
3. Extraplacental causes, e.g. cervical and vaginal lesion
4. Vasa praevia
5. Circumvallate placenta
6. Unexplained

should be summoned; this consists of a doctor, midwife and ambulance driver with facilities for resuscitation, pain relief, intravenous fluid administration and a supply of group O rhesus-negative blood. All patients with APH, no matter how mild, require admission to hospital because of the risk of further bleeding.

In hospital, the first requirements are to assess the mother's general condition and to correct shock by blood transfusion. The presence of pre-eclampsia should be noted and the fetal heart auscultated. If there is blood in the vagina, it should be tested to see if the blood is maternal or fetal (Apt's test, see p. 189); the latter is associated with vasa praevia which although rare may lead to fetal exsanguination and death.

When the condition of the patient is stable, a definitive diagnosis of the cause of the bleeding should be attempted by clinical and ultrasonic examination.

Placenta Praevia

In this condition, the placenta lies wholly or partially in the lower uterine segment. Different types of placenta praevia are distinguished depending upon the degree of encroachment of the lower uterine segment (Table 11.2; Fig. 11.1).

Types I and II placenta praevia are called 'minor' degree, types III and IV are 'major' degree, but it must be recognized that a 'minor' degree may be associated with significant and recurrent bleeding.

Bleeding occurs in the third trimester of pregnancy as the lower uterine segment forms, leading to shearing between the placenta and maternal venous sinuses.

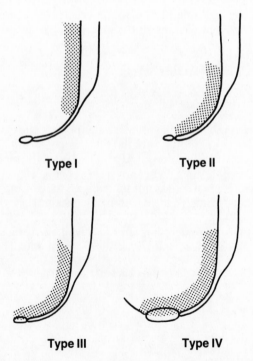

Type I **Type II**

Type III **Type IV**

Figure 11.1 Types of placenta praevia (for description, see Table 11.2).

Table 11.2 Types of placenta praevia

I	The placenta encroaches on the lower uterine segment but does not reach the internal cervical os
II	The placenta reaches but does not cross the os
III	The placenta crosses the undilated os
IV	The placenta crosses the fully dilated cervix

Clinical Presentation of Placenta Praevia

Placenta praevia is characterized by painless, apparently causeless, recurrent vaginal bleeding. The initial loss is usually slight but may be severe. In 60% of cases, the bleeding occurs after the 36th week. The uterus is soft and non-contracting unless labour has begun but there may be some degree of tenderness over the lower uterine segment if the patient is examined soon after bleeding has occurred.

Investigation

The investigation of APH is the same in all cases, irrespective of clinical presentation. The site of the placenta should be localized ultrasonically and in placenta praevia, it will be seen encroaching on the lower segment. If a type II placenta praevia lies posteriorly, this may be difficult to see because of intervening fetal parts. In placental abruption, varying sizes of blood clot may be seen separating a normally situated placenta from the uterine wall.

If the ultrasonic examination fails to reveal the cause of bleeding, a gentle speculum examination should be performed to exclude local causes. In addition, if the mother is rhesus negative, the Kleihauer test should be performed and anti-D given if necessary. Any blood in the vagina should be tested to determine whether it is maternal or fetal in origin (Apt's test). In this test, a sample of blood from the vagina is added to 5 ml of water in a test tube; 1 ml of 1% sodium hydroxide is added, and if the blood remains pink, it is of fetal origin; if maternal blood, it will turn a brown-yellow colour after 1–2 min.

Management of Placenta Praevia

Conservative management remains the mainstay of treatment with the primary objective of maintaining the pregnancy until the 37th week consistent with maternal and fetal well-being. Patients with minor degrees of placenta praevia may be allowed home when the bleeding has stopped for one week; those with major placenta praevia should remain in hospital. Since bleeding may occur at any time, blood transfusion and the ability to effect delivery by Caesarean section must be available at all times. Some patients bleed from a low-lying placenta in the second trimester. They should be admitted to hospital and the placental site regularly scanned. In many cases, as the lower segment forms and elongates, the placenta comes to lie totally in the upper segment. This phenomenon is termed 'placental migration', which is a misnomer since the placenta does not move, the apparent change in position being caused by the formation of the lower segment. When this occurs the patient should be allowed home; if it does not, the patient should remain in hospital. If maternal anaemia is present it should be treated vigorously by transfusion, if necessary, to lessen the risks of postpartum haemorrhage.

Delivery

Most patients with placenta praevia should be delivered by elective Caesarean section. Those with minor degrees may have an examination under anaesthesia performed in a theatre prepared for Caesarean section. If the placenta is felt vaginally, Caesarean section should be performed. If the placenta is not felt and the head can be pushed into the pelvic brim, amniotomy may be performed and a fetal scalp electrode applied. The labour should be carefully observed because of the high risk of problems such as cord prolapse. Perinatal mortality in placenta praevia should not exceed 5% and the major causes of death are prematurity and fetal abnormality.

Placental Abruption

In placental abruption the placenta is normally situated but, for some reason, becomes separated from the uterine wall leading to bleeding (Fig. 11.2). The

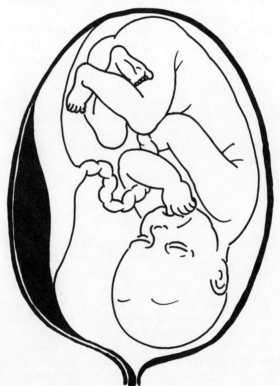

Figure 11.2 Placental abruption. A large retroplacental clot is shown in black with blood trickling through the cervical os.

condition is divided into mild, moderate and severe forms depending on the amount of separation.

The aetiology of the condition is unknown. Some cases recur in subsequent pregnancies and other risk factors are grande multiparity and hypertensive disorders. In pre-eclampsia, arterial spasm of the uterine vessels may lead to ischaemia of the placental bed with subsequent haemorrhage into this region. Blood may escape into the vagina but some may collect between the placenta and the uterus leading to further placental separation. In severe cases, blood may be extravasated into the uterine wall (Couvelaire uterus).

Clinical Presentation of Placental Abruption

Clinical presentation is variable depending upon the extent of the haemorrhage. In mild cases where the haemorrhage is small, there may be some vaginal blood loss and there may be no pain. The uterus is soft, fetal parts are easily palpable and the fetal heart can be heard. Clearly, this condition is difficult to distinguish from placenta praevia or a 'show'.

In moderate haemorrhage, the patient complains of abdominal pain and the uterus is tender and firm. Contractions may be present and the uterus does not relax between them. The fetal parts are difficult to palpate and the fetal heartbeat, although present, may be difficult to hear. Severe haemorrhage may occur later as an extension of this but may also occur *de novo* and be accompanied by oliguria, shock and disseminated intravascular coagulopathy. In this situation, the fetal heart is usually absent.

Investigation (see p. 189)

Management of Placental Abruption

Severe bleeding may threaten the life of the mother and frequently kill the fetus. The mother's life may be threatened by the triple threats of shock, renal failure and disseminated intravascular coagulation. The blood pressure may give no indication of the degree of shock since the pre-haemorrhage blood pressure may have been high due to pre-eclampsia.

The blood volume should be restored quickly, giving sufficient blood to keep the central venous pressure, as measured by a central venous catheter, above 10 cm water pressure. When this is achieved, the aim is to deliver the mother as soon as possible and to prevent further complications. If the fetus is dead or the cervix is favourable an amniotomy is performed and an oxytocin infusion commenced. A urinary catheter is inserted and the output is measured every 2 hr, but oliguria may persist until delivery when a diuresis usually occurs. Blood coagulation studies should be performed every 2 hr to detect any coagulation defect although these may not occur especially if fresh, whole blood is used to restore the circulatory blood volume.

If fetal heart activity is present, delivery by Caesarean section should be considered. This decision will depend largely on the condition of the mother after stabilization, the presence of any coagulation defect and the gestational age and state of the fetus.

In less severe cases where the abruption is minor and the bleeding stops after a short period in hospital, the patient may be allowed home. However, those patients with co-existing hypertension, pre-eclampsia or diabetes mellitus should remain in hospital because of the risk of further bleeding. If patients are allowed home, regular outpatient assessment is required. Induction of labour should be performed at 38 weeks and labour should be monitored carefully.

Fetal loss in cases of placental abruption remains high with death being due to immaturity, asphyxia, shock and congenital abnormality.

Extraplacental Causes

Bleeding is caused by some local conditions of the cervix or vagina. Blood loss is usually slight and painless, may follow coitus and the patient will have no signs of systemic upset.

Vasa Praevia

In vasa praevia, blood loss is from a *fetal* blood vessel running close to or across the internal cervical os. This may happen with a velamentous insertion of the cord where vessels transverse the membranes rather than inserting directly into the placenta or with a succenturiate lobe which is an accessory lobe of the placenta. Multiple pregnancy increases the risk of vasa praevia.

Blood loss is painless and often occurs when the membranes rupture. Although the blood loss is usually not excessive, the fetus is in danger because his blood volume is small.

If there are signs of fetal distress, clinical or cardiotocographic, out of keeping with the amount of blood loss, then an Apt's test must be performed and if this is positive, the pregnancy must be terminated at once.

Circumvallate Placenta (Placenta Extrachorialis)

In circumvallate placenta, the chorionic plate of the placenta is smaller than the basal plate. This leads to rolling of the edge of the placenta which may cause its separation from the uterine wall at the placental margin. This may lead to painless APH not dissimilar from placenta praevia, although the bleeding is usually of a lesser degree. Circumvallate placenta may also cause growth retardation and premature onset of labour. It is unlikely to be diagnosed prior to delivery.

POSTPARTUM HAEMORRHAGE AS A SEQUEL TO APH

The patient who has lost blood due to either a placenta praevia or abruption is in a poor condition to withstand further blood loss. There are four conditions which contribute to the occurrence of postpartum haemorrhage: unsatisfactory retractility and contractility of the lower uterine segment, the presence of large uterine vessels at the placental site, abnormal adherence (*placenta accreta*) of a portion of the placenta and maternal anaemia. Extra vigilance during and after the third stage of labour is very important.

In addition, the patient who has had a placental abruption should be warned that this may recur in subsequent pregnancies.

CARE OF THE NEWBORN AFTER APH

The baby may be born by elective delivery at 38 weeks gestation, some considerable time after the APH. In this case, the baby should do very well and generally suffers no deleterious effects.

In other cases, delivery is performed as an emergency because of risks to the mother or fetus. In these situations, the baby faces the risks of severe birth asphyxia and shock, and may be preterm. The management of birth asphyxia and of the preterm baby are discussed elsewhere but it should be noted that there is an increased risk of respiratory distress syndrome in these babies. Further, neural tube defects may be more common in babies born after placenta praevia.

Fetal and Neonatal Shock

Babies born after maternal APH are often severely shocked as a result of fetal blood loss and asphyxia. Blood loss may often occur after vasa praevia or placental abruption. In placenta praevia, especially if anterior, blood loss may occur at the time of Caesarean section due to placental incision. Severely affected babies are usually relatively easy to diagnose. The baby is pale and under-perfused, responds relatively poorly to conventional resuscitation techniques, has a tachycardia and is hypotensive. Less severely shocked babies may only look rather pale and may appear to be mildly asphyxiated.

The principle aim is to correct shock and restore the circulatory blood volume after support of respiration and, if necessary, cardiac massage (Chapter 3). If this is not done, perfusion to the brain, heart, lung, kidney and gut will remain low and permanent damage may develop. The essence of treatment is to infuse a fluid that stays in the vascular space, that is a colloid solution such as salt-poor albumin, plasma or whole blood in a dose of 10–30 ml/kg. It should be noted that the decision to infuse these fluids should be based on the infant's clinical condition at or shortly after birth and not on haematological indices such as haemoglobin or haematocrit which may take some hours to fall following haemorrhage.

Overtransfusion with blood is extremely unlikely but may lead to cardiac failure, polycythaemia and hyperbilirubinaemia. These possible risks should be set against the baby's clinical condition.

One logistical problem is obtaining suitable blood for immediate transfusion. One way to deal with this is for the obstetrician to obtain blood from the fetal side of the placenta by aspirating blood into a lightly heparinized syringe from a large fetal vessel. Alternatively, donor blood should be used, i.e. group O rhesus negative.

After resuscitation, these babies should be admitted to a neonatal intensive-care unit for further observation and management. They will need aftercare for asphyxia (Chapter 3), and if preterm are likely to develop severe respiratory distress syndrome (Chapter 4). Respiratory, cardiovascular, cerebral and renal function may all be abnormal and volume expansion and correction of acidosis with sodium bicarbonate may be needed after arrival at the intensive-care unit.

Long-term follow up of surviving infants is, of course, essential as they are at increased risk of developing sequelae.

FURTHER READING

Chamberlain, G., Phillip, E., Howlett, B. and Masters, K. (1978) *British Births 1970*, Vol. 2. *Obstetric Care*. Heinemann Medical, London.

Creasy, J. D. and Resnick, R. B. (1984) *Maternal–Fetal Medicine*. W. B. Saunders, Philadelphia.

Donald, I. (1979) *Practical Obstetric Problems*. Lloyd-Luke, London.

Halliday, H. L., McClure, G. and Reid, M. McC. (1985) *Handbook of Neonatal Intensive Care*, 2nd edn. Baillière Tindall, London.

Knupple, K. and Drukker, O. (1986) *High Risk Pregnancy: A Team Approach*. W. B. Saunders, Philadelphia.

12

Metabolic and Endocrine Disorders

Disorders of the endocrine glands can have profound effects upon the pregnant woman and her baby, although many of these disorders are associated with low rates of fertility so that pregnancy among these women is less common than in the normal population.

DIABETES MELLITUS

The successful outcome of pregnancy in women with diabetes mellitus depends on the careful control of blood glucose prior to conception and throughout pregnancy. Over the last 25 years the perinatal mortality rate for insulin-dependent diabetic patients attending the metabolic/antenatal clinic at the Royal Maternity Hospital, Belfast, has been reduced from 20% to less than 2%. The most significant factor contributing to perinatal mortality in diabetic pregnancies is now congenital abnormality which occurs in up to 10% of infants and accounts for more than half of the perinatal deaths.

Definitions

Diabetes mellitus is due to a deficiency of insulin secretion from the beta cells of the islets of Langherhans in the pancreas. In the past, many definitions have been used to classify diabetes in pregnancy, but currently the World Health Organization criteria are widely accepted.

Diabetes Mellitus

The patient usually has symptoms such as thirst and polyuria. A glucose tolerance test using 75 g of glucose taken orally should demonstrate, 2 hr later, a

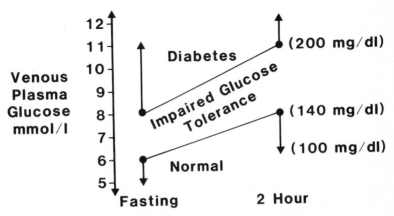

Figure 12.1 Glucose tolerance test in pregnancy.

blood glucose level greater than 11 mmol/l (Fig. 12.1). The patient usually requires treatment with diet and/or insulin or oral hypoglycaemic drugs.

Impaired Glucose Tolerance

These patients are usually asymptomatic and require no treatment. The fasting blood glucose level is less than 8 mmol/l and after a 75-g oral glucose load, the blood glucose level is between 8 and 11 mmol/l after 2 hr (Fig. 12.1).

Gestational Diabetes

This refers to an abnormal glucose tolerance test during pregnancy fulfilling the WHO criteria for diabetes mellitus. Such patients frequently need insulin but, immediately after confinement, their requirements fall rapidly and within a few days insulin treatment is no longer necessary.

Potential Diabetes

This is a condition where the mother exhibits one or more of several criteria known to be associated with increased risk of developing diabetes in later life (Table 12.1). All women with potential diabetes should be given a 75-g oral glucose tolerance test at 32 weeks.

The best-known classification of insulin-dependent diabetes in pregnancy is that of White (1971), in which patients were classified according to the duration and age of onset of their diabetes with further subgrouping depending upon the presence of vascular disease involving the eyes and kidneys. Although widely used, this classification remains of limited prognostic value since fetal outcome varies little amongst the groups, even if vascular involvement is severe. Other factors likely to adversely affect the fetal outcome include poor preconceptional and antenatal blood sugar control, pyelonephritis and pre-eclampsia.

Carbohydrate Metabolism in Pregnancy

During normal pregnancy, carbohydrate metabolism is influenced by placental transfer of glucose to the fetus and loss of glucose in the urine because of a lowered renal threshold. Additionally, there is degradation of insulin by the placenta, and, further, the effects of insulin are opposed by higher circulatory amounts of glucocorticoids and human placental lactogen which account for the phenomenon of 'insulin resistance'.

Table 12.1 Criteria for potential diabetes

---

1. Glycosuria on two occasions in the antenatal period or random blood glucose greater than 8 mmol/l.
2. Diabetes mellitus in first degree relative.
3. Weight greater than 90 kg.
4. Abnormal glucose tolerance test in a previous pregnancy.
5. Unexplained perinatal death or fetal abnormality.
6. Previous baby weighing more than 4.5 kg.

In the diabetic woman, with limited or no insulin reserve, blood glucose levels will rise during pregnancy unless exogenous insulin is administered in increasing amounts. The fetal blood glucose level closely follows that of the mother so that failure to control the maternal level results in frequent episodes of fetal hyperglycaemia with subsequent hyperinsulinaemia due to fetal pancreatic beta cell hyperplasia. The elevated level of fetal insulin is the most probable cause of the typical heavy-for-dates baby with macrosomia, i.e. enlargement of organs such as liver and heart.

This 'hyperglycaemia–hyperinsulinaemia theory' of Pedersen may also account for the prevalence of sudden, unexplained intrauterine death which remains a major problem in the poorly controlled pregnant diabetic. It is thought that following an episode of maternal hyperglycaemia, the resultant fetal hyperglycaemia causes overproduction of insulin from the pancreas which results in profound fetal hypoglycaemia and subsequent death. It is also possible that death occurs as a result of fetal arrhythmia arising from the markedly hypertrophied myocardium which may be seen in such pregnancies.

Poor control of the blood glucose prior to and in the early weeks of pregnancy is associated with a high incidence of fetal anomaly. Blood glucose control at this time may be assessed by retrospective measurement of serum glycosylated haemoglobin (HbA_1) at booking (Table 12.2).

Obstetric Complications

There are no obstetric complications that are unique to diabetic pregnancy but several occur more frequently than in normal pregnancy.

Pre-eclampsia

The reported incidence of pre-eclampsia varies from 8 to 20% and it is more common and more severe when the diabetes is of longer duration or when there is renal involvement. Pre-eclampsia is associated with an increased perinatal mortality rate.

Polyhydramnios

The volume of amniotic fluid is increased significantly in approximately 20% of diabetic pregnancies. Improved diabetic control and bed rest may reduce the amniotic fluid volume and relieve any associated pressure symptoms.

Table 12.2 Relationship between congenital malformation and HbA_1 level at booking in diabetic pregnancy

HbA_1	Newborn no.	Major malformations	Minor malformations
≥10	25	6 (24%)	1 (4%)
8–9.9	44	5 (11%)	1 (2%)
<8	58	2 (3%)	1 (2%)
Total	127	13 (10%)	3 (2%)
Normal population		2%	2%

Infection

As a result of frequent episodes of glycosuria, urinary tract infection is more common than in the non-diabetic and usually involves the lower urinary tract, but pyelonephritis may occur. The presence of such infection makes diabetic control more difficult and is a recognized cause of preterm labour. As in the non-pregnant diabetic, monilial vaginitis is common.

Diabetic Complications and Pregnancy

Renal Disease

There is no evidence that pregnancy has an adverse effect on severe diabetic nephropathy, but if urinary infection does occur, it is essential to treat it vigorously and to culture the urine at each subsequent visit.

Retinal Disease

In the past, it was widely held that since proliferative diabetic retinopathy could deteriorate during pregnancy and the fetal prognosis was so poor, termination of pregnancy should be recommended. Recently, careful ophthalmological assessment of all diabetics has shown that pregnancy has no significant effect on early proliferative retinopathy. If laser photocoagulation is necessary for severe retinopathy, the response is not affected adversely by pregnancy.

Cardiovascular Disease

Severe cardiovascular involvement is uncommon in the pregnant diabetic even when the diabetes is of long standing. In the older patient, however, the presence of ischaemic heart disease or severe large vessel atheroma represents a considerable maternal risk due to the increased demands of pregnancy on the cardiovascular system.

Diabetic Control

Insulin requirements are generally increased from the end of the first trimester. However, good pre-pregnancy counselling increases maternal awareness of the risk to the fetus of poor blood glucose control and so improves compliance considerably. Frequent visits to the antenatal clinic, careful self-monitoring of blood glucose levels and the use of a twice-daily insulin regimen usually results in better control being achieved than in the non-pregnant state. In a few women, control may be made difficult in early pregnancy by nausea and vomiting or urinary tract infection.

Management of Pregnancy

Ideally the diabetic patient should have been counselled adequately prior to conception so that her blood glucose levels are within the normal range (5–7 mmol/l). However, pre-pregnancy clinics are underused and the best alternative is to see the patient at a combined antenatal clinic (obstetrician/diabetic physician) as soon as pregnancy is confirmed, usually in the 6–8th week. The routine antenatal physical examination and investigations (Chapter 2) are performed. The patient is admitted to hospital for stabilization and instruction in self-monitoring, preferably using a reflectance meter to monitor pre-prandial capillary blood glucose four times daily. Fetal maturity is confirmed by ultrasound assessment at 14–16 weeks and further scans at 4-week intervals may help to detect any major fetal abnormality. After the initial hospital admission, the patient is seen at the combined clinic at 2-week intervals when the physician reviews her record of blood glucose results since the previous visit. These values and those of the serum HbA_1, which is measured on each occasion to give an indication of longer-term control, allow the physician to adjust the insulin dose as needed. Diabetic women should be admitted to hospital if the blood glucose levels are difficult to control or if there is pre-eclampsia or polyhydramnios.

In the past, it was common practice to deliver the diabetic patient at 36–38 weeks in order to reduce the still birth rate. This is no longer felt to be necessary except where there are complications such as pre-eclampsia. If early delivery is planned, the lecithin/sphingomyelin area ratio (LSAR) is measured, but two things must be borne in mind: in diabetic pregnancy there may be a reduced production of sphingomyelin which will give an erroneously high ratio, and there may be a qualitative difference in the surfactant produced. For these reasons, delivery should be delayed until the LSAR is greater than 2.5 and there is phosphatidyl glycerol in the liquor.

Management of diabetes immediately prior to delivery involves close liaison with the diabetic physician to ensure normoglycaemia during labour or Caesarean section. During labour an infusion of 5% dextrose, containing 5 units of insulin, is maintained and adjusted according to the hourly estimation of capillary blood glucose. Careful blood glucose control during labour reduces the incidence of neonatal hypoglycaemia. Following delivery, maternal insulin requirements fall dramatically and the dose is adjusted on the basis of regular capillary blood glucose estimation. After discharge, mothers are seen at the combined clinic so that advice can be given about contraception, subsequent pregnancy and the value of good preconception blood glucose control for subsequent pregnancies.

Management of the Infant of the Diabetic Mother

Better control of the diabetic state in pregnancy has greatly reduced the frequency and severity of the problems faced by the baby. However, difficulties still arise and are shown in Table 12.3.

The perinatal management is designed to prevent or to recognize early any of these complications. The paediatrician should be present in the labour ward to assess the baby and to decide whether admission to the special-care baby unit is necessary. Most babies can be observed for a few hours beside their mothers in the delivery room where the nurses can monitor the vital signs and can measure the blood glucose regularly. In addition, the attending paediatrician can detect polycythaemia by measuring the haematocrit.

Table 12.3 Problems of the infant of a diabetic mother

1. Respiratory distress syndrome
2. Hypoglycaemia
3. Macrosomia
4. Congenital anomalies and hypertrophic cardiomyopathy
5. Polycythaemia
6. Jaundice
7. Hypocalcaemia
8. Transient tachypnoea of the newborn
9. Small-for-dates (long-standing diabetes)

Respiratory Distress Syndrome

Respiratory distress syndrome is more common in infants of diabetic mothers than in the normal population for the reasons given above. Allowing diabetic pregnancies to continue to 38–40 weeks with correct interpretation of the amniotic fluid LSARs has considerably reduced the frequency of this problem. Management of respiratory distress syndrome is discussed in Chapter 4.

Hypoglycaemia

Hypoglycaemia is caused by fetal hyperinsulinaemia as a result of poor control of maternal blood glucose levels. The infants most likely to be affected are often macrosomic and the lowest blood glucose levels are found about 0.5–1 hr after birth. If infants develop hypoglycaemic convulsions, permanent brain damage may occur, but asymptomatic hypoglycaemia appears to be benign. Hypoglycaemia should be prevented by giving early feeds but if the blood glucose becomes low (less than 1.4 mmol/l) in spite of this, or the baby develops symptoms, intravenous glucose should be given.

Macrosomia

Macrosomia occurs mainly because of fetal hyperinsulinaemia, insulin being the growth hormone of the fetus. If macrosomia is marked, there may be obstetrical problems at delivery, such as cephalopelvic disproportion, shoulder dystocia with brachial plexus damage and fracture of the clavicle, or birth asphyxia and intrapartum death (Chapter 7).

Congenital Anomalies

Congenital abnormalities are associated with poor blood glucose control at the time of conception. The commonest abnormalities are ventricular septal defects, neural tube defects, caudal regression syndrome and small left colon syndrome.

Hypertrophic cardiomyopathy is seen in about 20% of infants of diabetic mothers. This is a form of asymmetrical ventricular septal hypertrophy associated with poor maternal blood glucose control. Although the infants may be very ill at birth with an obstructive form of cardiomyopathy, pulmonary hypertension and respiratory distress, the condition is usually self-limiting and the hypertrophy reverts to normal within about 6 months. Treatment with digoxin can make this form of cardiac failure worse but beta-blockers such as propranolol may be effective. It is therefore necessary that any infant of a diabetic mother with signs of cardiac failure should have an echocardiogram performed to distinguish the cardiomyopathy from other structural defects prior to starting treatment.

Polycythaemia

It was formerly believed that polycythaemia was due solely to chronic intrauterine hypoxia, but it is now known that insulin stimulates erythropoietin release. If the haematocrit is above 70%, the risk of venous thrombosis, for example of the renal vein, is increased significantly, and partial exchange transfusion with plasma should be performed (Chapter 5).

Jaundice

The infant of the diabetic mother is at increased risk of jaundice because of the relative immaturity of the hepatic mechanisms for dealing with bilirubin, increased production of bilirubin because of polycythaemia, and hypoglycaemia, which may impair conjugation.

Hypocalcaemia

Hypocalcaemia arises because of relative hypoparathyroidism and may be further exacerbated by birth asphyxia or prematurity. Hypocalcaemia may be persistent and requires calcium supplements when the serum level is below 1.6 mmol/l. A few infants who fail to respond may require vitamin D.

Transient Tachypnoea of the Newborn

Transient tachypnoea is more common in the infant of the diabetic mother and may be a manifestation of a slight deficiency of surfactant. It is also associated with polycythaemia, mild asphyxia and delivery by Caesarean section.

Small-for-dates

This is an uncommon complication of diabetic pregnancy, occurring in women with long-standing diabetes and microvascular disease.

Long-term Follow Up

If infants of diabetic mothers are normally formed and neonatal problems are successfully avoided or treated, the prognosis is excellent as they achieve normal physical and intellectual growth. About 1% will subsequently become diabetic.

THYROID DISORDERS

Disorders of thyroid function are among the commonest endocrine problems encountered during pregnancy. Although they do not account for as much perinatal morbidity and mortality as diabetes mellitus, inadequately treated or unrecognized thyroid disease can affect the fetus adversely and cause long-term sequelae.

Physiology

The thyroid hormones, thyroxine (T_4) and tri-iodothyronine (T_3) are transported in the blood bound to plasma proteins; approximately 85% are bound to thyroxine-binding globulin (TBG) and 15% to thyroxine-binding pre-albumin (TBPA). During pregnancy, elevated plasma oestrogens induce a 2-fold increase in the serum TBG level and, as a result, the measured total serum thyroxine rises, although the level of metabolically active thyroxine is unaltered. The renal loss of iodine is increased in pregnancy because of a reduced renal tubular absorption which results in a lowered plasma level of inorganic iodine. In order to maintain the absolute iodine uptake by the thyroid at non-pregnant levels, thyroid blood flow increases by 30%. In addition, human chorionic thyrotrophin (HCT), a placental glycoprotein, has TSH-like activity and this, with the increased blood flow, may account for the increased size of the gland, giving rise to a goitre.

The fetal thyroid gland can take up iodine and produce thyroid hormone by 15 weeks gestation although the hypothalamo-pituitary-thyroid axis is not functional until after about 22 weeks, by which time the pituitary portal vascular system has developed. Fetal levels of both bound and free T_4 increase throughout pregnancy and, by term, approach maternal levels. In contrast, cord blood levels of T_3 and TSH are significantly lower than those in the maternal serum at term. There is a significant increase in TSH production after birth which is followed after 12–24 hr by a rise in T_4, so for the first several days of life the newborn appears to be in a relatively hyperthyroid state. TSH levels remain raised for about 2 days, whereas T_4 levels are high for up to 2 weeks. This postnatal rise in TSH and T_4 is blunted in preterm infants and those with severe respiratory distress syndrome.

Long-acting thyroid stimulator (LATS) is an immunoglobulin of the IgG class associated with some forms of thyrotoxicosis. It readily crosses the placenta and affects fetal thyroid function. Mothers who have large amounts of circulating LATS may give birth to babies who develop transient hyperthyroidism. There is no evidence to show that placental transfer of T_3 or T_4 occurs.

Thyroid Diseases in Pregnancy

Hypothyroidism

Women with significant hypothyroidism are unlikely to conceive without replacement therapy, and if conception occurs in the absence of treatment, there is a high risk of spontaneous abortion.

Pregnancy in those adequately treated should proceed without any specific problem for mother or infant.

The diagnosis of hypothyroidism may be suspected by the presence of fatigue, excessive weight gain, dry skin, hoarse voice, slow pulse and delayed relaxation of the tendon reflexes. It is confirmed if the serum TSH is more than 10 μg/ml and serum T_3 and T_4 are low for pregnancy. Replacement therapy with thyroxine is commenced and the dose adjusted to render the patient euthyroid with a normal serum TSH level. Regular clinical assessment and measurement of TSH, T_3 and T_4 throughout the antenatal period is necessary.

Hyperthyroidism

This condition, which is usually a result of Graves' disease, occurs in approximately 1 in 500 pregnant patients, in most of whom the diagnosis will have been made and treatment begun prior to pregnancy. Whether or not the patient is on treatment, there is an increased risk of abortion, preterm labour and pre-eclampsia.

Clinically, the diagnosis of mild hyperthyroidism is difficult to make because the signs resemble those of normal pregnancy, such as warm extremities, with peripheral vasodilatation, and tachycardia. More reliable features include failure to gain weight, high sleeping pulse rate and the presence of eye signs such as exophthalmos. The diagnosis may be confirmed by finding a raised T_4 and free T_4 index.

Treatment is most cases is medical, subtotal thyroidectomy being reserved for those patients in whom there is a large goitre with airway obstruction or when medical treatment has failed or has caused an adverse reaction. Medical treatment consists of a low dose of any anti-thyroid drug, carbimazole or propylthiouracil. As the severity of Graves' disease tends to fluctuate, the addition of thyroxine is advocated by some to produce a more steady maternal thyroid state. It is important to avoid hypothyroidism and to remember that anti-thyroid drugs cross the placenta and may cause hypothyroidism in the fetus. Propranolol may be necessary to control symptoms while awaiting the full effect of the anti-thyroid drugs. Radio-iodine compounds are strictly contraindicated in pregnancy as they cause permanent fetal hypothyroidism and may increase the risk of thyroid carcinoma in later life.

Neonatal Assessment. If the mother remains euthyroid or slightly hypothyroid, there is little evidence of increased fetal morbidity. However, the baby may have a goitre, exophthalmos or congenital thyrotoxicosis as a result of placental transfer of thyroid-stimulating antibody. This is particularly likely in the mother who has high levels of circulating LATS.

All infants of mothers with hyperthyroidism should be screened carefully by measuring cord blood for TSH and thyroxine. Similarly, patients who are euthyroid and have a history of Graves' disease which remitted spontaneously or after medical or surgical treatment may still have circulating thyroid-stimulating antibodies so neonatal assessment is equally important. Thyrotoxicosis in the neonate is usually transient. The infants are very active, restless and have voracious appetites, in spite of which they lose weight. Anti-thyroid drugs are required for only a short period of time. Propranolol has been used to control the associated tachycardia but should be avoided in the presence of heart failure.

Maternal thyroid disease is not a contraindication to breast feeding. Antithyroid drugs are secreted in breast milk but in small amounts. However, it is advisable to review the infant's thyroid function until he is weaned.

Simple Goitre

Enlargement of the thyroid gland is normal in pregnancy and the diagnosis of goitre is made frequently. Since some goitres are due to compensated hypothyroidism, such a finding warrants investigation of thyroid function. Endemic goitre, which is due to severe iodine deficiency, is rarely seen but has been associated with endemic cretinism, so that both mother and infant require investigation.

Carcinoma of the Thyroid Gland

Carcinoma of the thyroid gland is rare during pregnancy and, if suspected, surgical exploration of the neck is essential. Pregnancy is not contraindicated in patients who have undergone a thyroidectomy for this condition and are having treatment with thyroxine.

Thyroiditis

Subacute thyroiditis is a rare condition in pregnancy. It presents with diffuse painful swelling of the gland and, occasionally, signs of mild hypothyroidism. The treatment of choice is steroid therapy. Chronic lymphocytic thyroiditis is also rare in pregnancy and the gland may be enlarged and firm with associated hypothyroidism. Diagnosis is confirmed by the presence of thyroid autoantibodies and treatment is with thyroxine.

THE ADRENAL GLAND

During pregnancy, oestrogen stimulates a rise in corticosteroid-binding globulin, resulting in progressively rising serum levels of cortisol, mostly in the bound form, from 12–14 weeks onwards. Towards term, free cortisol is also increased and there is a reduced diurnal variation.

Aldosterone levels rise from early in the first trimester, possibly due to an increase in angiotensin II. This compensates for the normal increase in urine sodium loss due to increased glomerular filtration. Plasma levels of catecholamines differ little from the non-pregnant state.

Adrenal Disorders in Pregnancy

Addison's Disease

Addison's disease is due to an autoimmune condition; tuberculosis of the adrenal gland is now rarely seen. Classically, Addison's disease presents with vomiting, hypotension, pigmentation and muscle weakness. Pregnancy is rare in untreated cases because of infertility, but with hydrocortisone therapy, fertility is restored unless there is associated autoimmune ovarian failure. Should pregnancy occur, the maternal risks are minimal and mainly relate to nausea and vomiting in early pregnancy, urinary tract infections and stress of labour or of Caesarean section. At such times, additional hydrocortisone is essential, with gradual reduction in the dose over several days after the stressful event. There is no significant risk to the fetus.

At birth, cord blood cortisol levels should be measured because of the theoretical risk of impaired adrenocorticotrophin hormone (ACTH) secretion; otherwise hypoglycaemia is the only recognized associated neonatal problem.

Cushing's Syndrome

Approximately 80% of all cases of Cushing's syndrome are pituitary dependent, i.e. excess ACTH is secreted from the anterior pituitary gland and results in inappropriate adrenal gland stimulation. The remaining 20% are due to adrenal tumours. Pregnancy is rare in patients with Cushing's syndrome since it causes anovulation, but should it occur the cause of the syndrome is usually an adrenal lesion. Many of the signs and symptoms of Cushing's syndrome resemble those of pregnancy itself, for example hypertension, oedema, striae, plethora, headaches and altered carbohydrate metabolism. The diagnosis should be made by estimation of the serum cortisol and ACTH level. The cortisol level will be high with loss of diurnal variation and will not be suppressed by dexamethasone.

If a pituitary adenoma is diagnosed on CAT scan, transphenoidal hypophysectomy may be carried out and subsequent replacement therapy commenced as for patients with Addison's disease.

The diagnosis of an adrenal tumour is difficult in pregnancy, but if it is suspected surgery is indicated, to confirm the diagnosis and remove the lesion, which may be a carcinoma.

For the fetus the major risks are due to maternal hypertension with associated intrauterine growth retardation and intrauterine death (Chapter 5). The incidence of abortion and preterm labour is increased. Macrosomia has been reported and, like the increased incidence of intrauterine deaths, may be attributed to maternal hyperglycaemia. Following delivery, the neonate should be observed carefully for signs of adrenal failure, although this is extremely rare.

Congenital Adrenal Hyperplasia

Congenital adrenal hyperplasia includes a number of inborn errors of metabolism which result in decreased secretion of glucocorticoid and mineralocorticoid hormones. The consequent rise in the level of serum ACTH stimulates production of a large amount of steroid precursors which may cause virilization, salt loss with hypotension, or hypertension. The most common enzyme deficiency is 21-hydroxylase (21 in Fig. 12.2), resulting in increased plasma 17-hydroxyprogesterone, measurement of which is used to confirm the diagnosis and to monitor treatment.

Congenital adrenal hyperplasia in females is usually diagnosed in infancy;

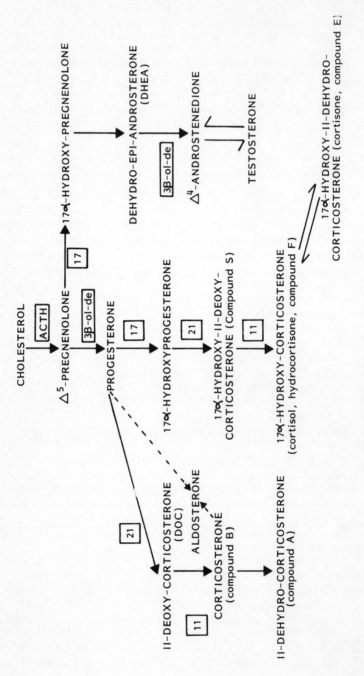

Figure 12.2 Adrenal steroid metabolism.

replacement therapy with corticosteroids, with or without mineralocorticoid, permits puberty to occur with normal ovarian function and fertility. In pregnancy, it is usually not necessary to increase the dose but intramuscular hydrocortisone should be given to cover the stress of labour or Caesarean section.

There is a theoretical, but extremely unlikely, risk that congenital adrenal hyperplasia may occur in the baby since the condition is inherited as an autosomal recessive. After birth, the baby should be carefully inspected for signs of virilization with increased pigmentation of the breasts and genitalia. In females, clitoral enlargement is usually obvious but in male infants the diagnosis is more difficult as excessive pigmentation may be the only sign. Thirty per cent of affected babies will also suffer from excessive salt loss due to aldosterone insufficiency. The other theoretical risk is of adrenal suppression if the mother has had excessive steroid therapy.

Phaeochromocytoma

Phaeochromocytoma is a tumour of argentaffin origin, usually affecting the adrenal medulla, and is associated with considerable maternal and fetal morbidity and mortality. Patients present most commonly with palpitations, sweating, flushes and intermittent episodes of hypertension and tachycardia. Although these tumours are rare, they are sometimes discovered during pregnancy because of hypertension which may be sustained. In pregnancy, these tumours may also present with convulsions or with sudden collapse and death.

The diagnosis is confirmed by finding elevated levels of plasma catecholamines and of urinary metabolites of catecholamines in a 24-hr collection. Radiological localization of the tumour may be deferred until after the patient is delivered.

During pregnancy, alpha-adrenergic blocking drugs with or without beta-blocking drugs are used to control the blood pressure. If this is accomplished, the pregnancy is allowed to continue, with careful monitoring of fetal well-being, until the 38th week.

If the blood pressure in early pregnancy proves difficult to control, radiological identification and surgical removal of the tumour is necessary. Should this situation arise in the third trimester, the pregnancy may be terminated by Caesarean section and the tumour removed at that time.

Babies born to mothers with a phaeochromocytoma have often suffered from intrauterine growth retardation as a result of maternal hypertension (Chapter 5).

THE PITUITARY GLAND

Hypopituitarism

Hypopituitarism is usually the result of destruction of the anterior pituitary by a tumour or by its treatment with radiotherapy or surgical ablation. Panhypopituitarism secondary to postpartum pituitary necrosis following severe haemorrhage is known as Sheehan's syndrome but is now extremely uncommon.

Pregnancy is rare in hypopituitarism because of failure of gonadotrophin secretion which leads to anovulation. However, multiple hormone replacement therapy results in a return of fertility with no detrimental effect on either subsequent pregnancy or the fetus.

Hyperprolactinaemia

Prolactin is produced by the chromophobe cells of the anterior pituitary and its subsequent release is suppressed by dopamine. Hyperprolactinaemia (blood level greater than 350 mU/l) leads to infertility as a result of anovulation or, less frequently, an inadequate luteal phase. Hyperprolactinaemia is usually due to a pituitary tumour, most commonly a chromophobe adenoma, but may also occur with hypothyroidism, renal disease, psychotrophic drugs and chest wall lesions such as herpes zoster. After exclusion of these causes, treatment is with bromocriptine, a dopamine agonist which rapidly lowers the serum prolactin levels with resumption of spontaneous ovulation in the majority of cases. Should pregnancy occur, there is a small but real risk to the mother of an expansion of the adenoma because of the direct effect of oestrogen. This may lead to severe headaches, visual disturbance or diabetes insipidus. Such symptoms usually regress promptly after delivery or treatment with bromocriptine.

This drug is known to cross the placenta but no significant fetal risk has been demonstrated in patients who conceived while taking this drug and who remained on it throughout pregnancy. Low fetal prolactin levels are said to be associated with development of the respiratory distress syndrome, but no increased risk has been shown when the mother has received bromocriptine during pregnancy. However, all babies born to mothers with hyperprolactin-aemia should be examined after birth by a paediatrician. Breast feeding does not accelerate tumour growth and mothers may continue to breast feed while taking bromocriptine.

Acromegaly

Pregnancy is rare in patients with active acromegaly because of the associated ovulation disorders. Should pregnancy occur in a mild case or following treatment, a normal pregnancy is to be expected.

Diabetes Insipidus

Diabetes insipidus should be more correctly considered as a hypothalamic disorder due to a lesion in the supraoptic nuclei, associated with partial or complete failure of antidiuretic hormone (ADH) secretion. It can be a congenital disorder or secondary to trauma, infection or neoplasm. If congenital in origin, the inheritance is dominant so that the infant has a 1:2 risk of developing the disease. Treatment with a synthetic pitressin compound is usually administered as an intranasal spray. No specific complications during pregnancy occur in patients with this condition. The infants should be carefully monitored in the neonatal period in case they develop diabetes insipidus.

PARATHYROID GLANDS

In pregnancy, the daily maternal calcium requirements are increased by 50% to replace losses due to increased extracellular fluid volume, increased glomerular filtration rate and uptake of calcium by the fetus.

The measured total serum calcium level falls during pregnancy, secondary to the normal physiological hypoalbuminaemia, but the ionized calcium level remains normal. Parathyroid hormone secretion may increase in the second and third trimesters, stimulating bone resorption and promoting urinary phosphate excretion. Increased levels of the active vitamin D metabolite 1,25-dihydroxy-cholecalciferol also occur.

Fetal serum calcium levels are higher than those in the mother since the placenta actively transports calcium ions to the fetus against the concentration gradient. Serum parathyroid hormone (PTH) levels are lower in the fetus than in the mother and calcitonin levels are higher, a situation which favours growth of the fetal bony skeleton. After birth, the baby may have transient hypoparathyroidism leading to hypocalcaemia.

Hypoparathyroidism

Hypoparathyroidism is rare in pregnancy and when it occurs it is likely to be due to inadvertent parathyroidectomy at the time of thyroid surgery, congenital absence of the parathyroid glands or as part of the spectrum of autoimmune endocrine disorder.

The effect on the fetus is to cause a secondary hyperparathyroidism which may be severe enough to produce significant bony change. Treatment before and during pregnancy with 1-hydroxy-cholecalciferol has been shown to be effective in maintaining maternal and fetal calcium levels. This therapy may induce hypercalcaemia, hyperphosphataemia and an increase in alkaline phosphatase which must be regularly measured. After delivery the metabolic demand falls rapidly and care should be taken to reduce the dosage in the postnatal period.

Hyperparathyroidism

Hyperparathyroidism is rare in pregnancy and is usually caused by a parathyroid adenoma. The mother may complain of polyuria, polydipsia and aches and pains which mimic many of the normal symptoms of pregnancy. Renal stones may occur. The effect on maternal serum calcium levels may go unnoticed because of the normal physiological fall.

Hyperparathyroidism may be diagnosed in the mother by demonstrating increased serum levels of calcium with decreased serum phosphate. Exploration of the neck and parathyroidectomy may be performed unless the patient is close to term, in which case it is deferred until the puerperium.

The effect on the fetus is more severe and a still birth rate of 20% has been reported. After birth, neonatal tetany as a result of transient fetal hypoparathyroidism secondary to maternal hypercalcaemia is a significant problem and, in many cases, it is this condition which gives the only clue to the maternal disorder.

FURTHER READING

DeSwiet, M. (1984) *Medical Disorders in Pregnancy*. Blackwell, London.
Hadden, D. R. (1986) Diabetes and pregnancy 1985. *Diabetologia* 29: 1.
Halliday, H. L. (1981) Hypertrophic cardiomyopathy in infants of poorly-controlled diabetic mothers. *Arch. Dis. Child.* 56: 258.
Halliday, H. L., McClure, G. and Reid, M. (1985) *Handbook of Neonatal Intensive Care*, 2nd edn. Baillière Tindall, London.
Montgomery, D. A. D. and Harley, J. H. G. (1977) Endocrine disorders. *Clin. Obstet. Gynaecol.* 4: 339.
Pedersen, J. (1977) *The Pregnant Diabetic and the Newborn: Problems and Management*, 2nd edn. Munksgaard, Copenhagen.
Ritchie, J. W. K. (1986) Obstetrics for the neonatologist. In Roberton, N. R. C. (ed.), *Textbook of Neonatology*. Churchill Livingstone, Edinburgh, pp. 97–102.
White, P. (1971) Pregnancy and diabetes. In Marble, A., White, P., Bradley, R. F. and Kroll, L. P. (eds), *Joslin's Diabetes Mellitus*. Lea and Feibiger, Philadelphia.
World Health Organization Expert Committee on Diabetes Mellitus (1980) *Second Report*. WHO Technical Report Series 646. WHO, Geneva.

13

Medical and Surgical Disorders of Pregnancy

INTRODUCTION

Most women are entirely healthy and remain so throughout their pregnancies. A minority may have some disease process which develops before or during pregnancy. This may influence the mother's ability to conceive or may affect the pregnancy.

Major changes occur in anatomy, physiology and biochemistry in early pregnancy which may alter symptoms and signs of systemic disease and which may also change the interpretation of biochemical values. This complex interplay of pregnancy and disease must be fully understood by the patient's medical attendants. If possible, the patient should be seen before becoming pregnant so that any risks can be fully explained.

There are two major questions to be answered when these women are seen in early pregnancy. The first is to decide whether the risks of pregnancy are so great that termination should be advocated. Secondly, if the pregnancy is to continue, the effects of the pregnancy on the disease, and vice versa, have to be considered and appropriate measures planned. In many situations, this is best done when there is active co-operation between obstetrician, physician and paediatrician in a hospital where experience is available.

Obviously, the number of diseases that may occur in pregnant women are legion so this chapter will deal only with relatively common major problems not discussed elsewhere (Chapters 9, 12).

HEART DISEASE

This occurs in slightly less than 1% of pregnant women. Heart disease causes 10 maternal deaths in every million pregnancies which is similar to the mortality associated with obstetric haemorrhage. Pregnancy may induce cardiac failure and if the mother suffers from severe chronic hypoxia, fetal growth may be affected.

In the Western developed world, the incidence of rheumatic heart disease is falling and now is seen in pregnancy with the same frequency as congenital heart disease. Hypertensive cardiac disease, cardiomyopathies and ischaemic heart disease are rarely seen in pregnancy.

Changes in cardiovascular physiology occur in pregnancy. The cardiac output rises by 30–40% due to a combination of a rise in heart rate of 10 beats/min and of stroke volume. This rise occurs mainly before the 20th week and is maintained until shortly after delivery. There is a marked decrease in the peripheral vascular resistance and a rise in the plasma volume. These changes may contribute to the symptoms of breathlessness, fatigue and palpitations often experienced by normal pregnant women and may erroneously suggest cardiac disease. In addition, these physiological changes increase the amount of cardiac

Table 13.1 Severity of symptoms of heart disease in pregnancy

Grade I:	no breathlessness or pain on moderate exercise
Grade II:	breathlessness, fatigue, palpitations or pain on moderate exertion; asymptomatic at rest
Grade III:	symptoms as for II on slight exertion; no symptoms at rest
Grade IV:	symptoms at rest; inability to carry out any physical activity without discomfort

work, a demand which may prove too great in some patients with cardiac disease, and may lead to heart failure.

Antenatal care is directed at the early detection of the patient at risk and to the prevention of cardiac failure. Such patients should be identified preferably before conception or, at least, as soon as possible during pregnancy. Women with suspected heart disease should be referred to a combined clinic which has a cardiologist and an obstetrician in attendance. Here the diagnosis may be clarified and the severity of symptoms assessed and classified as in Table 13.1. Although it is customary to use this classification, there is a poor correlation between the grades and the severity of the disease process or outcome. This is especially so in mitral stenosis when pulmonary oedema can occur in women who were Grade I in early pregnancy. Pregnancy usually causes patients to increase their grade of symptoms.

In addition to this assessment the outcome of previous pregnancies and the occurrence of any episodes of cardiac failure should be determined. Table 13.2 shows the effects of pregnancy on the mother with congenital heart disease. Early in pregnancy, it is important to decide whether termination of pregnancy should be offered. This may be considered if there is evidence of pulmonary hypertension or if there have been previous episodes of cardiac failure, although the termination is not without risk.

If agreement is reached that the pregnancy should continue, factors which may increase the risk of complications such as cardiac failure should be corrected. Obesity and anaemia should be controlled and women counselled to avoid emotional and physical strain. Advice should be given about the need to restrict activities within the limits of breathlessness or fatigue. Hyperthyroidism and infection, especially of the urinary tract or teeth, should be sought and treated.

Table 13.2 Maternal congenital heart disease – effects of pregnancy

Eisenmenger's syndrome	High pulmonary vascular resistance may be dangerous
Patent ductus arteriosus	Cardiac failure
Atrial septal defect	Cardiac failure Atrial tachyarrhythmias
Fallot's tetralogy	Prognosis poor if low P_{aO_2} and high haematocrit
Aortic stenosis and pulmonary stenosis	Left ventricular failure and sudden death if severe
Coarctation of the aorta	May rupture or dissect. Risk greater with increased age of patient

The patient should be seen more frequently in the antenatal period than normal and review should certainly occur weekly after the 30th week. If any signs of cardiac failure develop, the patient should be admitted.

The treatment of cardiac failure is essentially the same as for the non-pregnant patient, with the use of diuretics, digoxin and anticoagulants if there is persistent atrial fibrillation. For a discussion of anticoagulant use in pregnancy, see the following section on thromboembolism. Most patients respond rapidly to such treatment and there is seldom need to resort to termination of pregnancy or surgical repair during pregnancy. The patient should remain in hospital for the remainder of her pregnancy although it is often possible to allow weekends to be spent at home for the woman's peace of mind. Cyanotic heart disease carries a high risk for mother and fetus. For example, in Eisenmenger's syndrome, maternal mortality is about 10–20% and perinatal mortality about 50%. The maternal risk is maximal in labour and the puerperium.

Cardiac surgery during pregnancy is seldom needed and should be reserved for patients in whom medical treatment has failed to control cardiac failure and who have intolerable symptoms. Mitral valvotomy for tight mitral stenosis is not contraindicated. Cardiopulmonary bypass surgery is associated with a 50% fetal mortality.

The presence of cardiac disease is not an indication for induction of labour. When labour occurs spontaneously, epidural analgesia should be given since pain may cause tachycardia and precipitate cardiac failure; furthermore, epidural analgesia causes a peripheral vasodilatation, thus reducing cardiac work. Antibiotics should be given at the onset of labour to patients with previous episodes of bacterial endocarditis or those with prosthetic valves, and maintained until after delivery. Care must be taken with the administration of intravenous fluid and oxytocin.

If there is delay in the second stage, delivery should be expedited; an oxytocic should be given in the third stage unless the patient is in cardiac failure. Syntocinon is preferable to ergometrine which may cause tonic uterine contractions leading to a rapid transfusion from the uterine circulation which in turn may precipitate cardiac failure. Frusemide may be administered at the same time.

Heart failure may occur in the first few days after delivery as the uterine circulation closes down. During this period, the patient should be carefully observed and ambulation gently introduced.

Occasionally, women with cardiac disease may go into premature labour. This is a difficult situation because of the risk of development of acute pulmonary oedema if arrest of labour with beta-mimetic drugs is attempted. Present evidence indicates that no attempt should be made to arrest preterm labour with these drugs (ritodrine) or to give steroids to stimulate fetal lung development.

Infants born to mothers with heart disease are usually perfectly normal, although if the mother has severe cyanotic disease, the infant may be small-for-dates and develop polycythaemia. Some drugs used to treat heart disease in pregnancy have harmful effects on the fetus. Warfarin may cause nasal hypoplasia, chondrodysplasia punctata, low birth weight and increased risk of mental retardation if given in the first 16 weeks. Its use after 36 weeks may promote bleeding in the fetus or the newborn. For these reasons warfarin should be used from 16 to 36 weeks, after which heparin is preferred. Neither warfarin nor heparin is a contraindication to breast feeding. The risk of congenital heart disease in the baby is small, but genetic counselling at the combined clinic should be given and the baby examined carefully at birth by a paediatrician.

THROMBOEMBOLISM

Venous Thrombosis

Venous thrombosis is not uncommon in pregnancy, but pulmonary embolism is rare (about 1 in 5000 pregnancies). Predisposing factors include increasing age and obesity, excessive bed rest, past history, Caesarean section, anaemia and sickle cell disease. Deep venous thrombosis presents with oedema, local tenderness and a positive Homan's sign. The diagnosis should be confirmed by a venography before treatment is started.

Pulmonary Embolism

Pulmonary embolism, which is still the second most common cause of maternal death, presents with pleuritic pain, dyspnoea and haemoptysis. The clinical picture may resemble an acute pulmonary infection and there may be no obvious predisposing venous thrombosis. Pulmonary scan with technetium-99 may be used to confirm the diagnosis. Treatment initially should be with heparin: 15 000 units intravenously followed by 10 000 units at 6-hr intervals for at least 48 hr. For long-term treatment heparin may be given subcutaneously (7500 units every 12 hr). Heparin does not cross the placenta or enter breast milk and its anticoagulant effect can be rapidly reversed by protamine sulphate. Warfarin may be used after the first trimester up to the 36th week of pregnancy. Warfarin is teratogenic and may cause neonatal haemorrhage if given up to the time of labour. Vitamin K can be used to reverse this effect but this takes place slowly. Warfarin does not pass into breast milk in significant quantities, but phenindione does and should not be given to lactating women (Table 13.12).

HAEMATOLOGICAL PROBLEMS

Anaemia

Anaemia is the commonest medical disorder encountered in pregnancy. It is arbitrarily defined as a haemoglobin concentration of less than 10.4 g/dl. The causes are shown in Table 13.3. The main risks to the mother are a reduced

Table 13.3 Classification of anaemia in pregnancy

Acquired	Iron deficiency
	Haemorrhage – acute or chronic
	Infection
	Megaloblastic
	Haemolytic
	Aplastic
Hereditary	Sickle cell disease or trait
	Thalassaemia
	Haemoglobin C
	Mixed haemoglobinopathies

ability to withstand haemorrhage and an increased risk of infection. Preterm delivery and fetal hypoxia are more common if maternal anaemia is severe. Maternal and fetal risks are considerably increased if the mother has a haemo-globinopathy such a sickle cell disease.

Iron deficiency anaemia is by far the commonest anaemia in pregnancy in the UK. The origin may be a poor diet or there may be an excessive loss of iron due to grande multiparity or menorrhagia. On occasion, anaemia is due to a poor intestinal absorption of iron. Often the women are asymptomatic, but some may complain of fatigue, giddiness or breathlessness. The condition may be avoided by using prophylactic iron taken as a daily tablet, but many patients are either intolerant of this or are forgetful. The diagnosis is suspected by the observation of a hypochromic, microcytic anaemia and confirmed by measurement of the serum ferritin which will be low. Treatment is with oral or parenteral iron, the latter being given as an iron/dextran infusion.

Folic acid deficiency may lead to megaloblastic anaemia. It may be encoun-tered in malnourished women or in alcohol abusers. It occasionally occurs in women with excessive vomiting or with malabsorption. Epileptic patients may develop megaloblastic anaemia if they are treated with primidone or pheno-barbitone. The condition also occurs in multiple pregnancy because of the extra fetal demand. The diagnosis is confirmed by measurement of the serum folic acid level and the patients usually respond to oral therapy.

Megaloblastic anaemia due to vitamin B_{12} deficiency is very rare in pregnancy since the condition is usually seen in people over 40 years of age and also may be associated with infertility.

Anaemia may also be caused by a number of subacute or chronic infections, notably of the urinary tract, and may also be seen in connective tissue disorders or neoplasia. In these situations, the anaemia is normochromic and normocytic, caused by reduced red cell production, though in pyelonephritis there is also evidence of increased red cell destruction.

Haemolysis may occur in pregnant women for a variety of reasons. In black women and those from Mediterranean countries, haemolysis may be due to a deficiency of red cell glucose-6-phosphate dehydrogenase (G-6-PD). Haemolysis may be initiated by the use of drugs such as sulphonamides, nitrofurantoin or aspirin. Usually all that is necessary is for affected women to avoid these drugs. The inheritance is X-linked with boys more likely to be affected.

Occasionally, haemolysis may be precipitated by drugs such as penicillin in women who have normal red cells. This is due to activation of an antibody by the drug.

Women with acquired autoimmune haemolysis with a positive direct Coomb's test may suffer from rapid deterioration in pregnancy. Fortunately, corticosteroids are effective in treatment of both the anaemia and thrombocy-topenia which frequently occurs in this condition.

Aplastic anaemia is rarely seen in pregnancy. The prognosis is extremely poor, although if the anaemia has developed in pregnancy, termination may result in remission.

Sickle cell disease is seen in the black population. It is an inherited derange-ment of synthesis of the β side-chain of haemoglobin. Homozygous patients suffer from sickle cell disease, heterozygotes suffer from sickle cell trait. Sickle cell disease is an extremely serious illness with a high childhood mortality; the fertility of survivors is impaired. The maternal condition in pregnancy may be extremely poor with exquisite bone, joint and abdominal pains caused by microinfarctions, infections of lung and kidney and an increased risk of pulmonary embolism. Abdominal pain is common and may be attributed incorrectly to the disease while other causes of such pains are ignored. If these patients are seen early in pregnancy, termination should be considered. If the pregnancy continues, infection and nutritional deficiency should be assiduously sought and treated. Folic acid requirements are high because of the increase in erythropoiesis and the extra demands of pregnancy. The abortion and death rate in these pregnancies is high. Spontaneous premature labour is common; in addition, elective preterm delivery may be necessary because of fetal growth retardation and maternal hypertension.

Labour should be closely observed and the haemoglobin concentration should be at least 10 g/dl at the onset; blood should always be available. These women are at risk of cardiac failure which may be exacerbated by severe hypertension. Maternal hypoxia, infection or dehydration may precipitate haemolytic crises and should be avoided. Fetal distress and consequent birth asphyxia are obvious neonatal risks, and these births must therefore be attended by an experienced paediatrician.

In addition to the problems of prematurity and growth retardation, the haemoglobin type of the infant should be ascertained. It should be noted that it may be impossible to decide if the baby is affected for about 3 months after birth. This is because the haemoglobin of the newborn infant is primarily haemoglobin F and it may take some months for the abnormal haemoglobin S to be produced in sufficient amounts to be detectable.

In contrast to sickle cell disease, the trait is relatively benign in its effects. There is an increased incidence of bacteriuria in pregnancy but there are no significant differences from the normal population in complications of pregnancy, the perinatal mortality rate, the incidence of birth asphyxia or the mean birth weight.

The thalassaemic syndromes are a group of haemoglobinopathies where either the α- or β-side-chains of haemoglobin are not formed. β-Thalassaemia is a disease seen in those of Mediterranean stock. The disease is subdivided into those with thalassaemia minor who are heterozygous, have mild microcytic, hypochromic anaemia and who have increased levels of HbA_2, and those with thalassaemia major, which is the homozygous form of the disease. These patients suffer from severe anaemia, hepatosplenomegaly, have high levels of HbF and require frequent blood transfusions.

Thalassaemia minor has little effect on pregnancy or on the infants. In contrast, patients with thalassaemia major rarely survive to the third decade, fertility is impaired and pregnancy is uncommon.

In α-thalassaemia, there is impaired synthesis of the α-chains with the result that γ-chains are formed (Hb Barts). Homozygous and heterozygous forms of α-thalassaemia are seen in those from the Far East. The heterozygous form is mild, but if such women marry men who are also heterozygous, the fetus may be homozygous and develop gross intrauterine haemolysis and hydrops fetalis. Only occasionally do homozygous infants survive birth.

A major advance in the treatment of these haemoglobinopathies has been the ability to assess the fetal haemoglobin level in early pregnancy and to correct low levels by intrauterine umbilical vein blood transfusion. This technique has afforded hope to prospective parents and in many cases such treatment has been successful. However, it is difficult and carries a 5% risk of spontaneous abortion; it should therefore be performed only in supraregional centres.

Perhaps of more practical importance is prepregnancy counselling of women who are known carriers of haemoglobinopathies. In this situation, haemoglobin electrophoresis should be performed on the partners to determine their status.

Treatment of haemoglobinopathies is with folic acid and repeated blood transfusions; iron therapy is avoided and desferrioxamine may be used as a chelating agent.

Coagulation Problems

There is a tendency for the platelet count to fall in normal pregnancy so that values as low as 150 000 per mm^3 may be regarded as normal. Thrombocytopenia may arise as a complication of such conditions as pre-eclampsia, infection, folate deficiency or collagen disease. It may also be drug induced.

Idiopathic thrombocytopenia purpura (ITP) is a disease caused by an anti-platelet antibody, which in pregnancy may cross the placenta leading to neonatal thrombocytopenia. In the majority of cases, maternal ITP begins before pregnancy and has been controlled by the use of steroids or by splenectomy. In these situations, although the mother is well, transplacental passage of antibody can still occur and cause fetal thrombocytopenia. Neonatal thrombocytopenia is more likely to occur when the mother is thrombocytopenic at the time of delivery; 50–70% of babies may be affected. It has been suggested that in such circumstances, delivery should be by Caesarean section to prevent neonatal intracranial bleeding, but if labour is well controlled, vaginal delivery can be carried out safely and this reduces maternal complications. In the infants, it is necessary to measure the platelet count regularly until it rises above 50 000 per mm^3. Haemorrhage is infrequent and steroids are seldom needed. Platelet transfusions are sometimes given in the first few days if the platelet count is dangerously low (less than 20 000 per mm^3). Treatment with immunoglobulin has recently been shown to be very effective and it is thought that it acts as a blocking antibody.

Disseminated intravascular coagulation (DIC) may occur in pregnancy in the situations listed in Table 13.4. Thromboplastins released into the circulation cause depletion of clotting factors, especially fibrinogen and factors V and VIII. Thrombocytopenia also occurs and fibrin degradation products are increased, resulting in a vicious cycle of anticoagulation and haemorrhage. Fresh blood transfusions and fresh frozen plasma or cryoprecipitate are used to treat DIC. Earlier intervention to terminate pregnancy after fetal death, reduction in precipitate or prolonged labour and careful assessment of clotting abnormalities in cases of abruption have helped to reduce the incidence of DIC in pregnancy. (For management of the neonate see Chapter 11.)

RENAL AND URINARY TRACT PROBLEMS (see also Chapter 9)

During pregnancy, the renal collecting system and ureters dilate under the influence of progesterone. Renal function changes with an increase in the glomerular filtration rate of 50% during the first and second trimesters and a subsequent fall in the third trimester. These changes, in association with

Table 13.4 Causes of disseminated intravascular coagulation in pregnancy

Placental abruption
Fulminant pre-eclampsia
Eclampsia
Amniotic fluid embolism
Intrauterine death, e.g. twins

increasing circulating blood volume, lead to a progressive reduction of the blood urea to 3.0 mmol/l and an increase of creatinine clearance to 130–150 ml/min by the third trimester. These physiological changes affect the interpretation of laboratory results.

Urinary Tract Infection

Asymptomatic bacteriuria is seen in about 5% of pregnant women. The most common organism is *Escherichia coli* and a count of greater than 10^5 organisms/ml is significant. Thirty per cent of such patients will develop clinical infection if they are untreated. Urinary cultures are performed routinely at the booking clinic and at 28 weeks. Those with a history of previous infection, renal disease or hypertension should have a urine culture done at each visit. If a significant bacteriuria is detected, the culture should be repeated and if this is positive, antibiotics should be given for 2 weeks. Further urine cultures should be done to confirm that the treatment has been effective. If the patient relapses, treatment should be repeated and a full investigation of the urinary tract should be performed in the postnatal period since a proportion (30–40%) of such women will have structural abnormalities.

Acute pyelonephritis is uncommon in pregnancy. The patient suffers burning and frequency of micturition, loin pain, vomiting, fever and dehydration. Hospital admission is required for treatment with intravenous antibiotics and fluids, and systemic analgesics.

Maternal urinary tract infection may cause premature labour and the newborn is also at increased risk of developing congenital or early-onset sepsis.

Chronic Renal Disease (see Chapter 9)

Pregnancy may be associated with the renal diseases, some of which are listed in Table 13.5. For a review of this topic, see McGeown (1977).

Table 13.5 Renal disease and pregnancy

Glomerulonephritis
Systemic lupus erythematosus
Chronic pyelonephritis
Renal stones
Nephrotic syndrome
Polycystic disease
Diabetic nephropathy
Ureteric diversion
Renal transplantation

ABDOMINAL PAIN IN PREGNANCY

Abdominal pain occurs fairly frequently in pregnancy and can cause great difficulty with diagnosis. Acute appendicitis occurs in about 1 in 1500 pregnancies and carries a higher mortality than in non-pregnant patients since the diagnosis may be delayed and the appendix may perforate. The diagnosis may be unclear since the symptoms of pain and vomiting may be confused with other conditions. Further diagnostic difficulties arise because the appendix is pushed upwards and laterally by the gravid uterus and the distended abdominal wall is unlikely to exhibit guarding or rigidity. Also, since the omentum is also displaced upwards, its ability to surround the inflamed appendix is reduced, thus allowing spread of infection. If the diagnosis is suspected, laparotomy should be carried out. Antibiotics should be given and the operation site should be drained if the appendix is gangrenous. The main risks to the fetus are premature onset of labour and infection.

Intestinal obstruction rarely occurs in pregnancy. The obstruction is usually of the small bowel secondary to adhesions from previous surgery. Colicky abdominal pain, particularly in the periumbilical region, is suggestive in a patient with persistent vomiting and constipation. An abdominal radiograph performed with the patient in the erect position will reveal gas-filled loops of bowel with fluid levels. Treatment is with fluid replacement, analgesia and surgery.

Acute cholecystitis occurs in approximately 1 in 4000 pregnancies. The pain is colicky, is in the right-upper abdominal quadrant and is associated with vomiting. Fever may be present and there may be a history of previous episodes. An ultrasonic scan may reveal a thickened gall bladder wall or gallstones. Treatment is with analgesics, antibiotics and fluids.

Acute pancreatitis is also uncommon in pregnancy, occurring in about 1 in 3000 pregnancies. The condition may be extremely severe, leading to maternal death or more commonly to perinatal death which occurs in about 50% of cases. The condition is strongly associated with biliary tract disease and 1–4% of patients have been found to be alcohol abusers. Infections such as mumps may also cause pancreatitis and there is an association with pre-eclampsia. The symptoms and signs of acute pancreatitis are the same as in non-pregnant patients but the diagnosis may be more difficult due to the lack of change in the enzyme patterns; the amylase, lipase and the ratio of amylase to creatinine may be in the normal range. The management of pancreatitis is supportive with intravenous fluids and bowel rest. The condition may affect all body systems and complications such as hypovolaemia, pulmonary oedema and renal failure should be prevented or corrected. There appears to be little value in termination of pregnancy and the benefit of premature induction of labour remains in doubt.

Acute abdominal pain may also occur because of some complication of the pregnancy or disease of the reproductive organs. Abortion and ectopic pregnancy may cause abdominal pain in early pregnancy, as may a retroverted uterus. Uterine fibroids may undergo red degeneration or torsion, or a vessel overlying a fibroid may rupture. These fibroid-associated complications present with abdominal pain and a tender mass may be palpable close to the uterus. In red degeneration, the condition will subside with bed rest and analgesics, but when a torsion has occurred, surgery is necessary. Ovarian tumours may also cause abdominal pain. The tumour can be seen on ultrasound and should be removed if it is greater than 6 cm in diameter. If the tumour is less than 10 cm in diameter and asymptomatic in the first trimester of pregnancy, surgery is delayed till about 16 weeks in order to avoid disturbance of the pregnancy.

In uterine rupture, the patient presents with acute abdominal pain and signs of circulatory failure. There may be a history of previous Caesarean section and localized tenderness of the uterus may be felt. Vaginal blood loss is much less than that expected from the severity of shock. Rupture may occur before the onset of labour if there has been a previous classical Caesarean section; lower segment scars usually rupture in labour. Treatment is by surgical repair of the uterus with sterilization, or hysterectomy. Somewhat surprisingly, the babies are often well, although some may suffer from the effects of shock and asphyxia and some may be stillborn.

Acute polyhydramnios may cause abdominal pain. It may be associated with multiple pregnancy or malformation of the fetus, particularly anencephaly or an atresia within the alimentary system. The uterus is large and there may be a fluid thrill. An ultrasonic examination is useful to confirm the excess volume of fluid and to detect multiple pregnancy and fetal abnormality. Amniocentesis with slow release of amniotic fluid provides only temporary relief and is seldom performed because of the risk of placental separation. Premature labour may occur and the prognosis for the infant depends on the degree of prematurity or the type of abnormality, the most common of which are oesophageal or high intestinal atresia (Chapter 6).

Liver Disease Specific to Pregnancy

The causes of jaundice are shown in Table 13.6.

Cholestatic jaundice is uncommon but may affect successive pregnancies. The disease usually occurs in the third trimester and the dominant feature is pruritis with mild jaundice developing later. The liver function tests show slight elevation of the serum bilirubin and plasma alkaline phosphatase. Liver histology is unrevealing apart from centrilobular cholestasis. Cholestyramine may be used to treat patients and prenatal vitamin K should be given to correct any coagulation disorder. The prognosis for mother and infant is usually

Table 13.6 The causes of jaundice in pregnancy

Viral hepatitis
Haemolytic anaemia
Drugs
   Chlorpromazine
Recurrent cholestatic jaundice
Acute fatty liver
Hyperemesis gravidarum
Severe pre-eclampsia
Cholelithiasis
Others
   Chronic active hepatitis
   Primary biliary cirrhosis
   Gilbert's syndrome
   Dubin–Johnson syndrome

excellent with the pruritis disappearing shortly after delivery. The cause is unknown but, interestingly, similar problems have been experienced by women on the pill or at menstruation so that oestrogen has been implicated. In some cases late still birth or preterm labour occur and perinatal mortality is slightly increased.

In sharp contrast to the above condition, acute fatty liver of pregnancy is associated with death of the majority of women and their fetuses. The aetiology is unknown but there is an association with pre-eclampsia. The disease, which is fortunately rare, occurs usually in obese women with pre-eclampsia. Abdominal pain is followed by vomiting, jaundice, liver and renal failure and coagulopathy. The clinical picture resembles that of Reye's syndrome – an acute hepatic disorder with encephalopathy seen in children and young adults. Laboratory investigations show an increase in the white cell count and renal and coagulation failure. Liver function tests may be less deranged with slight elevation of the serum bilirubin, serum aspartate amino-transferase (AST) and plasma alkaline phosphatase. Management is a complex process involving correction of hepatic and renal failure but there is no specific treatment for the primary condition. The pregnancy should be terminated in the maternal interest as soon as the coagulopathy is controlled.

NEUROLOGICAL DISORDERS

It is unusual to see neurological problems in women of childbearing age but epilepsy is the commonest. Seizures may become more frequent during pregnancy for a variety of reasons. Interestingly, women carrying a male fetus are twice as likely to deteriorate in pregnancy as those with a female fetus. The overall fluid volume of the patient is increased so that a higher dose of anticonvulsant is required to maintain a therapeutic serum level. Compliance may be poor as mothers may have fears of taking tablets when pregnant. Further, the intestinal absorption of drugs such as phenytoin may be reduced. Liver metabolism and renal clearance of these drugs may also be altered. For these reasons it is important that pregnant women with epilepsy attend a combined clinic (obstetrician and neurologist) and have the dose of anticonvulsant adjusted according to clinical findings and serum levels of the drug.

The choice of anticonvulsant drug is important since some are associated with increased risk of congenital malformation in the fetus. There is some debate as to whether these malformations are due to the maternal epilepsy or to the anticonvulsant drugs. Drugs such as troxidone should not be used at any time in pregnancy, and sodium valproate should be avoided in early pregnancy. Hydantoin (phenytoin) may cause a syndrome with cleft palate, reduced intelligence and small fingers. Phenobarbitone taken late in pregnancy may depress the baby's central nervous and respiratory systems, which may be followed by barbiturate withdrawal symptoms such as hyperexcitability and tremulousness.

Infants of epileptic parents are about five times more likely to develop epilepsy than the general population. This is particularly so with petit mal epilepsy.

Breast feeding is not contraindicated in mothers with epilepsy. Phenobarbitone in large doses may cause drowsiness and can be substituted if the mother wishes to breast feed.

Multiple Sclerosis

Multiple sclerosis is occasionally seen in pregnant women. The main problem is that relapse is three times as likely in the puerperal period than in the non-pregnant state. Termination should therefore be considered, taking into account the degree of debility at the beginning of the pregnancy.

Myasthenia Gravis

Myasthenia gravis is an autoimmune neuromuscular disorder presenting clinically as weakness and easy fatiguability of muscles, particularly of the face and limbs. The basic pathological abnormality is a deficiency of postsynaptic acetyl choline receptor protein at the motor end-plate caused by an autoantibody. Myasthenia gravis is associated with a number of other autoimmune disorders, for example rheumatoid arthritis, systemic lupus erythematosus, thyroiditis, polymyositis and pernicious anaemia.

Anticholinesterase drugs are used to treat myasthenia gravis – neostigmine and pyridostigmine being the most commonly employed. Pregnancy has an effect on myasthenia gravis (Table 13.7) and the myasthenia affects the pregnancy (Table 13.8).

Apart from anticholinesterase drugs, the mother may need treatment with steroids, plasmapheresis or thymectomy. Myasthenic crisis may occur during pregnancy with profound weakness and mechanical ventilation may be necessary. Such crises may be exacerbated by the stress of surgery, labour or infection. Drugs known to enhance muscle weakness in myasthenia include barbiturates, inhalation anaesthetics, magnesium sulphate, beta-adenergic agents, aminoglycosides and propranolol. These should be avoided during pregnancy and use of ritodrine to delay preterm labour is also contraindicated.

Table 13.7 Maternal outcome of pregnancy in myasthenia gravis

Worsening during pregnancy	40%
Remission during pregnancy	30%
No change in pregnancy	30%
Post-partum worsening	30%
Maternal death	3%

Neonatal Myasthenia Gravis

Neonatal myasthenia gravis occurs in 10–20% of babies born to mothers with myasthenia gravis. It is characterized by weakness, a feeble cry and respiratory

Table 13.8 Fetal outcome when mother has myasthenia gravis

Abortion	12%
Perinatal death	8%
Still birth	3%
Neonatal death	5%
Neonatal myasthenia	10–20%

distress. The onset is usually 12–48 hr after birth and the duration ranges from 1 to 15 weeks with a mean of about 3 weeks. Neonatal myasthenia is probably due to the passive transfer of maternal anti-acetyl choline receptor antibodies to the fetus. Some babies have been born with joint contractures (arthrogryposis). Babies who develop muscle weakness should be treated with anticholinesterase drugs. Edrophonium is short acting and may be used as a diagnostic test for the condition.

RESPIRATORY DISEASE

Oxygen consumption during pregnancy rises by about 20%. This is achieved by an increase in the tidal volume without a significant change in the respiratory rate. The arterial carbon dioxide tension is lowered. The stimulus to this respiratory drive is progesterone.

A sensation of breathlessness is felt by many women in pregnancy and is maximal at about 30 weeks. The significance of this phenomenon is that it must not be confused with pathological dyspnoea seen, for example, in patients with cardiac or respiratory disease.

Asthma

Asthma is a fairly common condition. The effects of pregnancy on asthma are unpredictable, some patients improve, some deteriorate and the rest are unaffected. The effect of asthma on the fetus is minimal unless the mother is so severely ill as to be chronically hypoxic which may cause the fetus to suffer from growth retardation. Acute asthmatic attacks can occur in labour and lead to acute fetal distress.

The management of asthma in pregnancy is the same as for non-pregnant patients. β_2-Sympathomimetic inhalers such as salbutamol and inhalations of betamethasone can be used safely. Oral steroids should be used with caution in early pregnancy because of the risk of cleft palate in the fetus.

The one major risk is of status asthmaticus, the severity of which may be underestimated. In such an attack, the patient uses the accessory muscles of respiration, the respiratory rate increases and there is significant tachycardia: she should be seen by a physician and admitted to hospital urgently for control.

Asthma is uncommon in labour but should respond to drugs such as salbutamol. If the patient has previously been treated with steroids, hydrocortisone should be given in labour. Asthma is not a contraindication to breast feeding.

Other Respiratory Diseases

Tuberculosis is very uncommon in the UK but may be seen occasionally in recent immigrants from the developing world. Pregnancy appears to have little effect on tuberculosis and vice versa and the main problem is in deciding which drugs to use. Isoniazid and ethambutol should be used in early pregnancy with rifampicin introduced after the period of organogenesis (8 weeks).

After birth, if the bacterium is isoniazid resistant, the baby should be given BCG vaccine and isolated from the mother until the Mantoux test converts. If the bacterium is sensitive, isoniazid and isoniazid-resistant BCG should be given to the baby. Follow up of the baby is advised to check for conversion and to exclude disseminated infection. If the baby is infected at birth, then hepatomegaly is usually present.

Connective Tissue Disorders

Systemic lupus erythematosus (SLE) is not uncommon in young women, especially in blacks. SLE is usually unaffected by pregnancy but there may be exacerbation of the disease, particularly in the puerperium, and renal disease may ensue. There are three main ways by which SLE may affect the fetus. The abortion rate is high, possibly due to an immune reaction or alternatively by alteration of the maternal coagulation pathway. An inhibitor has been found which causes prolongation of the partial thromboplastin and prothrombin times. SLE increases the risk of hypertension and renal insufficiency in pregnancy and this is associated with growth retardation and still birth; if hypertension develops the fetus must be regularly assessed. Steroids are used in the management of SLE in pregnancy in as low a dose as possible. If azathioprine is used, 40% of the babies will be small for gestational age. The ESR is an inaccurate guide to the activity of the disease since this normally increases in pregnancy. A better index of activity may be obtained by measuring C_3 complement. Finally, the condition may affect the neonate. Preterm labour may occur and the babies may be small for gestational age. SLE antibodies cross the placenta and may cause congenital heart block, discoid skin lesions, transient haemolytic anaemia, leucopenia and thrombocytopenia. If heart block is present, specialist cardiology advice is needed as a pacemaker may be required. If the heart is unaffected, neonatal SLE is transient and clears up after a few weeks.

Rheumatoid Arthritis

Rheumatoid arthritis often improves in pregnancy because of the increased endogenous secretion of cortisol. The abortion and perinatal death rates are not increased and rarely will the neonate be affected, although heart block may occur. Its significance lies in that arthritis, particularly of the hip joints, may make vaginal delivery difficult and intubation of the mother for general anaesthesia may also be complicated because of cervical arthritis. Additionally, drugs that are used to alleviate the symptoms of arthritis may damage the fetus. Paracetamol and steroids may be used but prostaglandin antagonists like indomethacin are contraindicated because of the risk of premature closure of the ductus arteriosus. Antimalarial drugs also appear to be safe, but gold salts should be avoided.

NEOPLASMS IN PREGNANCY

Benign Genital Lesions

Uterine fibromyomas occur in 0.5–1% of pregnancies; the tumours, usually multiple, are more frequently seen in older childbearing women. The majority of fibromyomata do not cause clinical problems; however, if they are situated in the lower uterine segment or cervix they may interfere with engagement of the presenting part and can lead to obstructed labour. Pregnancy invariably causes a marked increase in the size of fibromyomata which can result in pressure symptoms. There is also a tendency for the tumour to undergo a form of degeneration (necrobiosis) due to an impaired blood supply. This complication can cause pain and tenderness and must be considered in the differential diagnosis of the acute abdomen in pregnancy (p. 219). Ultrasound can assist in the diagnosis of fibroids and in the majority of cases the treatment should be conservative. Myomectomy in pregnancy is a hazardous procedure and is rarely required except for torsion.

Cystic and solid tumours of the ovary may also complicate pregnancy; although the vast majority are benign, they are potentially serious because of the increased liability of complications such as torsion, haemorrhage or rupture. A symptomless ovarian swelling, greater than 5 cm diameter, detected on routine pelvic examination at the first antenatal visit can be confirmed by an ultrasonic scan. If the patient is symptom free and the lesion persists or increases in size, surgical excision by ovarian cystectomy should be postponed until the second trimester when the risk of abortion is greatly reduced. Caesarean section may be required if an ovarian tumour causes obstructed labour and in such cases the tumour can be removed at the same time. If a symptomless tumour is discovered in late pregnancy and is not in the pelvis, normal delivery should be planned and the removal of the lesion deferred until the early postpartum period. Torsion of the pedicle is a very common occurrence in the puerperium.

Malignant Disease

Malignant disease in pregnancy is fortunately an uncommon occurrence; the reported incidence is less than 1 in 1000 because cancer most commonly occurs after the reproductive years. This means that even large referral centres have little opportunity to accumulate experience on the management of specific conditions and it is difficult to evaluate properly new treatment methods by means of clinical trials. The distribution of the most common malignant lesions complicating pregnancy are found in Table 13.9.

A pregnant patient with a malignancy creates a complicated clinical problem. One must understand that the pregnancy may affect the disease process and the pregnancy. Delaying treatment may have detrimental effects while therapy may be toxic to the fetus. Other factors such as attitudes to termination of the

Table 13.9 Relative frequency of malignant disease in pregnancy

Site	Percentage
Breast	26
Cervix	26
Leukaemia	15
Lymphoma	15
Melanoma	8
Thyroid	4
Others (includes trophoblastic tumours)	11
Total	100

pregnancy, the effects on subsequent fertility and the fear of the mother that she may not survive to rear her child can also influence the case management.

Patients presenting with early breast carcinoma in the first trimester should be treated in the same manner as non-pregnant patients. There is no disadvantage in allowing the pregnancy to continue unless it is against the express wishes of the patient and her husband. However, if cytotoxic drugs are to be used then therapeutic termination should be advised because of the teratogenic effects. During late pregnancy, patients with early breast carcinoma should have surgery followed by post-partum radiotherapy. The prognosis of advanced carcinoma of the breast is poor and such patients should be advised to have termination of the pregnancy and appropriate treatment started as soon as possible. In patients found to have a breast carcinoma postpartum, lactation should be suppressed with bromocriptine and the malignancy treated. The overall survival of carcinoma of the breast in pregnancy is no worse than in non-pregnant patients with similar staged disease.

Acute leukaemia is among the most common neoplasms in young adult women; there have been approximately 300 reported cases in pregnancy. The incidence is 1 per 100 000 women per year. Termination of pregnancy is advisable and the patient referred to a haematologist for chemotherapy.

Invasive carcinoma of the cervix in pregnancy does not alter the long-term prognosis significantly, but vaginal delivery is totally contraindicated because not only can the disease disseminate through the larger cervical venous sinuses and dilated lymphatic spaces but it can also be transmitted down the vagina, resulting in metastatic disease – particularly in episiotomy sites. In the first and second trimesters the patient should be treated as in the non-pregnant state, according to the stage of the disease. After 28 weeks, elective Caesarean section should be performed followed by radical hysterectomy.

In Western societies the increasing incidence of pre-invasive cervical carcinoma is also seen in pregnant patients. An abnormal cervical smear in pregnancy should be further investigated by colposcopy and, if indicated, directed punch biopsy. If the diagnosis of cervical intraepithelial neoplasia (CIN) is confirmed, then management is conservative until after delivery, when repeat colposcopy and cone biopsy can be performed. There is no indication for Caesarean section in uncomplicated cases of pre-invasive disease of the cervix.

PSYCHIATRIC DISORDERS

Pregnancy is often an emotional and stressful period and many women suffer some mental upset. Typically, there are three emotional phases during pregnancy. The first is a period of emotional lability in the early months of pregnancy. This is scarcely surprising in view of the hormonal changes at that time which interact with the many hopes or problems which may be associated with conception. These reactions may lead to requests for termination of pregnancy on psychiatric grounds and in many cases it may be extremely difficult to distinguish a 'normal' transient phase from a more truly pathological state.

The second phase is one of stability with strong 'nesting' impulses and associated activities. Often people with established psychiatric disease such as schizophrenia improve in this phase. This stable time is followed in the final months by a more passive phase, but the mother may have an underlying anxiety about the outcome.

Superimposed upon these phenomena, there may be somewhat more pathological reactive states such as depression and anxiety. Again, this is hardly surprising since, to many families, an additional member may not be entirely welcome because of such factors as family size, legitimacy and the need for the mother to be a wage earner. The significance of these disturbances is that many pregnant women need to be able to talk about such problems to a sympathetic listener, a requirement that busy antenatal clinics or general practitioner surgeries are often inadequate to meet. This leads, all too frequently, to a ready recourse to drugs such as diazepam which are not without risk to both mother and baby.

True psychotic behaviour is seen in about 1 in 1000 pregnancies. Endogenous depression is by far the most common and usually begins in the first few months after the birth of the child. The onset is gradual with increasing feelings of unworthiness, misery, being unable to cope and frank depression or despondency. In the extreme phases, suicidal and infanticidal feelings may be felt. Clearly, the loving bonding process between mother and baby may be seriously affected which may lead to the infant failing to thrive. These mothers do not require exhortation from the inexpert to 'buck-up'; they require psychiatric help and may need to be separated temporarily from their baby for the safety of both.

Schizophrenia is relatively uncommon in pregnancy. This is the most important of the functional psychoses leading to emotional 'flattening', incongruous emotion, thought-blocking and delusions. Again, these patients require psychiatric care with preservation of the mother–infant link since this is often the only normal emotional reaction in the patient.

Anorexia nervosa is commonest in young women of childbearing age. Usually, such women are infertile but some may become pregnant. It can be extremely difficult to achieve sufficient nutrition in such women to allow for the increased demands of pregnancy. The spontaneous abortion rate is high and there is suggestive evidence that if the pregnancy continues, the fetus may suffer from growth retardation. Respiratory distress syndrome may also be more common in babies of mothers with anorexia nervosa, perhaps because of deficient intake of precursors of surfactant such as myoinositol.

HANDICAP AND BEREAVEMENT

Although the vast majority of women deliver healthy, normal babies, for a few, pregnancy ends in the death or handicap of their babies. These are the most tragic results of pregnancy and it often appears that the profession is ill-equipped to cope with them.

Miscarriage in the first weeks of pregnancy is common and most women cope with this problem very well. For many, particularly those with recurrent problems, miscarriage is frequently emotionally traumatic. Women may become depressed about the outcome, anxious about the possibility of future pregnancies or guilty, especially if the pregnancy was unplanned. Unfortunately, these emotional upsets are not discussed properly in busy gynaecological units. Clearly, the family practitioner has a major role to play in this area.

Unexplained still birth may be the most cruel outcome of pregnancy. Most people can accept the death of a fetus more readily if it has been known to be at risk. However, the sudden death of an apparently normal fetus is a major tragedy. In this situation, an explanation should be given as gently as possible by a senior obstetrician. When the diagnosis of intrauterine death is confirmed, the initial interview should not be filled with technical explanations; the mother will be unable to understand them at this time. After the initial shock, many questions have to be answered, particularly about why the death happened. Some women wonder about what is happening to the dead baby inside them. One such mother, writing in a national newspaper, wondered whether the baby was rotting inside her. There is the utmost need to explain and to listen as much as possible.

Labour in these situations may be extremely upsetting for all concerned. There can be no joyful anticipation; the labour is just a prolonged, painful experience. All that can be done is for the doctors and nurses to be sympathetic and ensure that the labour is as pain-free as possible.

After the birth of a dead baby, most mothers want to go home. Postnatal wards are full of lusty, healthy babies belonging to other women; side-wards are quieter but lonelier. There are two important aspects: the parents should be allowed to see and hold their baby in the labour ward, and it is of vital importance that they be left alone with their child for some time. In addition, photographs of the baby should be taken and kept as mementoes. The other essential is that an autopsy be carried out. Although parents will often be upset by this, the questions they will ask later can only be answered if post-mortem information is available.

The same guidelines apply with the death of a newborn infant. In this case, the blow of death may be softened by keeping the parents fully informed throughout the course of the baby's illness and, when the time comes, to allow the child to die peacefully in the arms of his parents.

The death of a baby is followed by episodes of anger, depression and guilt in the parents. Often parents will seek to blame someone for what has happened and may have these ideas reinforced by other people of their acquaintance. However, the role of the health professional is clear – to provide help for the bereaved parents. This means seeing them after the death, perhaps after an interval of 6 weeks or so, to discuss with them what happened, and how they have coped with bereavement. These discussions should take place in a quiet room, *not in the busy postnatal clinic*. Often, inadvertently, women whose babies have died are given appointments for the outpatient postnatal clinic. This may well prove to be unbearable for the mother, and unguarded comments by other parents or by the staff may prove to be excruciatingly painful.

Those parents whose children are handicapped or malformed are in a different position for a variety of reasons. The true nature and extent of the problem may not be initially clear and the outcome of the disease may be unpredictable. Further, the disease or malformation may be extremely complicated, making explanation difficult; in some cases there is a genetic basis for the problem. However, the major difference is that the parents are confronted with a major problem which will not be resolved quickly; in many cases it will require a life-long commitment from them.

There is no easy way of helping these parents to cope and it is facile to suggest that there is. The one major contribution that the doctor or nurse can make is to commit time to the parents to listen to their problems, to explain repeatedly the nature of the clinical condition and to ensure that appropriate specialist treatment is given. This may impose considerable strains on the time and emotions of the therapists but is absolutely vital if the family are to be helped.

DRUGS AND DRUG DEPENDENCE

The development of modern pharmacology has lead to the development of a wide range of powerful drugs. Some of these drugs may be safely given to pregnant women or lactating mothers, but many cannot. Many drugs are known to be teratogens, and some are thought to have teratogenic effects (Tables 13.10 and 13.11). However, there are three main rules to be applied when prescribing drugs in this period. The first is that drug therapy should be avoided if possible. If drugs are required, well-established medications should be used in the first instance.

Many drugs taken by the mother pass to the infant via the breast milk. In most cases, the amount passed is so little as to cause negligible effects. Some of these drugs and their effects are listed in Table 13.12.

Drug dependence is becoming an increasingly important problem. The drugs themselves may cause illness and there may be other associated conditions such as sexually transmitted disease, hepatitis, Aids and malnutrition. Opiate addiction is associated with growth retardation, fetal distress, prematurity, birth asphyxia and meconium aspiration syndrome. The perinatal mortality is nearly three times that of comparable non-addicted patients.

In addition to these problems, the baby may suffer from drug-withdrawal symptoms (neonatal withdrawal syndrome). These symptoms develop at a variable period of time after delivery, depending on the drug. The affected babies become hyperirritable, have diarrhoea and vomiting and may develop seizures. The treatment is with paregoric (tincture of opium) or barbiturates. Swaddling the infant may also be of benefit.

The management of such mothers is complex. There will be nutritional, infective and social problems, as well as the problems of the drugs themselves. It is generally agreed that the mothers should be managed in a methadone-maintenance programme. This reduces the risk of withdrawal symptoms in the mother and has the added advantage of putting her in contact with the social services, but withdrawal effects in the baby may be more severe than with heroin.

However, it must be realized that many addicts fail to comply with this conversion, do not attend clinics or return to their old ways after delivery.

Table 13.10 Known teratogens

Substance	Effect
Thalidomide	Limbs: phocomelia, CVS, GI tract
Tetracycline	Dental enamel hypoplasia, bones
Aminoglycosides	Ototoxicity
Antimitotic agents	Abortifacient
	Genitourinary abnormalities
Quinine	Abortifacient
	CNS, limb abnormalities
Sex hormones	
Androgens	Masculinization of female
Stilboestrol	Female: vaginal adenosis, adenocarcinoma
	Male: hypospadias
Progestogen (19 nor-testosterone derivatives)	Masculinization of female
Alcohol	Fetal alcohol syndrome
Anticoagulants	
Warfarin	Nasal hypoplasia
	Chondrodysplasia punctata
	Fetal bleeding
Anticonvulsants	
Phenytoin	Craniofacial abnormalities
	Hypoplasia, ossification of distal phalanges (fetal hydantoin syndrome)
Trimethadione	Craniofacial abnormalities
	Cardiac/renal defects
Irradiation	Microcephaly
	?Leukaemia risk
Radio-iodine	Hypothyroidism
	Thyroid carcinoma
Isotretinoin (Retinoids)	CNS malformation
Live vaccines	
Vitamin A excess	

Table 13.11 Possible teratogens and drugs which may produce neonatal complications

Category	Substance	Effect
Antibiotics	Sulphonamides	Neonatal hyperbilirubinaemia
	Novobiocin	Neonatal hyperbilirubinaemia
	Chloramphenicol	Cardiovascular collapse

Analgesics	Salicylates	Neonatal Bleeding
		  Decreased factor XII activity
		  Decreased platelet function

	Narcotics	Respiratory depression in newborn
	Phenacetin	Methaemoglobinemia/ haemolytic anaemia

Category	Substance	Effect
Anticoagulants	Warfarin	
	First trimester	Warfarin embryopathy
	Second, third trimester	Fetal haemorrhage
Anticonvulsants	Phenobarbitone	Neonatal haemorrhage
		Barbiturate withdrawal syndrome
	Diazepam	Neonatal withdrawal syndrome
		Floppy infant syndrome
Anticholinesterase	Neostigmine	Transient neonatal muscular weakness
Antidepressant	Chlorpromazine	Neonatal extrapyramidal syndrome
	Lithium	Neonatal cyanosis, hypotonia, bradycardia
Antithyroid	Carbimazole	Neonatal goitre,
	Thiouracil	hypothyroidism
	Iodine	
Antihypertensive	Propanolol	Neonatal hypoglycemia, hypotonia and bradycardia
	Hydrallazine	Transient neonatal thrombocytopenia
	Diazoxide	Hyperglycaemia, thrombocytopenia
	Labetolol	Hypoglycaemia, bradycardia
Diuretics	Thiazides	Neonatal thrombocytopenia
Hypoglycaemics	Tolbutamide	Severe neonatal hypoglycaemia
	Chlorpropamide	
Cortisone		Neonatal adrenal insufficiency
Vitamin D		Neonatal hypercalcaemia
Morphine, heroin		Neonatal respiratory depression and withdrawal syndrome

Table 13.12 Drugs secreted in breast milk: effect on neonate

Category	Substance	Effect
Analgesic	Salicylates	Bleeding tendency
Anticoagulants	Phenindione	Hypoprothrombinaemia
	Warfarin	Safe
Antibiotics	Ampicillin	Risk of oral thrush
	Chloramphenicol	Bone marrow depression
	Gentamycin	Ototoxicity
	Sulphonamide	Hyperbilirubinaemia
		Haemolytic anaemia if G6PD deficient
	Tetracycline	Teeth discolouration
Anticonvulsants	Barbiturates	Drowsiness
	Phenytoin	Methaemoglobinaemia
	Primidone	Drowsiness

Category	Substance	Effect
Antidepressant	Chlorpromazine	Drowsiness
	Diazepam	Drowsiness
	Lithium	Hypotonia
Antihypertensive	Beta-blockers	Hypoglycaemia
Anticholinergics	Atropine	'Atropine intoxication'
Antithyroid	Carbimazole	Goitre
	Iodine	Goitre
	Radioactive iodine	Hypothyroidism
Laxatives	Cascara	Diarrhoea
	Danthron	Diarrhoea
	Senna	Diarrhoea
Miscellaneous	Alcohol	Drowsiness
	Calciferol	Hypercalcaemia
Lead	Lead acetate in breast cream	Encephalopathy

FURTHER READING

British National Formulary (1988) *Prescribing in Pregnancy and Prescribing During Breast Feeding*. British Medical Association and the Pharmaceutical Society of Great Britain, London.

Department of Health and Social Security (1986) *Report on Confidential Enquiries into Maternal Births in England and Wales 1979–81*, No. 29. HMSO, London.

Gleicher, N., Midwall, J. Hochberger, D. and Jaffin, H. (1979) Eisenmenger's syndrome and pregnancy. *Obstet. Gynecol. Survey* 34: 74.

Halliday, H. L., McClure, G. and Reid, M. (1985) *Handbook of Neonatal Intensive Care*, 2nd edn. Baillière Tindall, London.

Harris, J. W. (1982) Pre-malignant and malignant disease. *Clin. Obstet. Gynaecol.* 9: 171.

Hopkins, A. (1977) Neurological disorders. *Clin. Obstet. Gynaecol.* 4: 419.

Howie, P. W. (1977) Thromboembolism *Clin. Obstet. Gynaecol.* 4: 397.

Kumar, R. (1985) Pregnancy, childbirth and mental illness. In Studd, J. (ed.), *Progress in Obstetrics and Gynaecology*. Churchill Livingstone, Edinburgh.

McGeown, M. G. (1977) Renal disorders and renal failure. *Clin. Obstet. Gynaecol.* 4: 319.

New York Heart Association Inc. (1965) *Diseases of the Heart and Blood Vessels*, 6th edn. NYHA, New York.

Ritchie, J. W. K. (1986) Obstetrics for the neonatologist. In Robertson, N. R. C. (ed.), *Textbook of Neonatology*. Churchill Livingstone, Edinburgh, pp. 90–106.

Stirrat, G. M. and Beeley, L. (1986) Prescribing in pregnancy. *Clin. Obstet. Gynaecol.* 13: 2.

De Swiet, M. (1984) *Medical Disorders in Obstetric Practice*. Blackwell Scientific, Oxford.

Tuck, S. and Studd, J. (1983) The obstetric problems in the black community. In Studd, J. (ed.), *Progress in Obstetrics and Gynaecology*. Churchill Livingstone, Edinburgh.

14

Perinatal Infections

INTRODUCTION

Infections occurring early in pregnancy are generally characterized by the relatively benign course in the mother compared with their major effects on the fetus and newborn infant. This disparity of effect is due to the immunoincompetence of the fetus and newborn which renders infected babies vulnerable since they are unable to localize and eliminate infecting organisms.

With the improving survival of low-birth-weight infants, deaths and malformations caused by infection are assuming greater importance. Further, some infants with intrauterine infections may manifest no signs at birth but may later develop sequelae. The most notable example of this is cytomegalovirus (CMV) where infection may be clinically undetectable in the neonatal period and yet the child may become obviously handicapped in later life. The incidence of some common intrauterine infections is given in Table 14.1.

Bacterial infections with or without chorio-amnionitis are generally far more common than the intrauterine TORCH infections (Table 14.2). Bacterial infections are discussed on p. 105.

ROUTES OF INFECTION

Transplacental Infection

Transplacental infections are usually viral but bacterial and protozoal infection may also occur, e.g. syphilis, toxoplasmosis.

Ascending Infection

Ascending infection is enhanced by prolonged rupture of the membranes, prolonged labour and by repeated vaginal examinations. Such infections are usually bacterial but may also be viral, for example herpes simplex.

Table 14.1 Incidence of some intrauterine infections

Infection	Mother/1000 pregnancies	Fetus	Newborn
Cytomegalovirus	50	5	5
Rubella (epidemic)	20	4	2
Toxoplasmosis	3	1	<1
Herpes simplex	10	?	0.03
Syphilis	0.04	?	?
Haemolytic streptococcus	200	?	4
Listeria monocytogenes	40	rare	rare
Acquired immuno-deficiency syndrome	?	?	?

Table 14.2 TORCH infections

T ⎫ O ⎭	Toxoplasmosis
R	Rubella
C	Cytomegalovirus
H	Herpes simplex

Infections Acquired During Delivery

These infections may be subdivided into two groups. (i) Local infections. These occur on body surfaces which come in contact with vaginal micro-organisms. The most common of these is conjunctivitis of either the inclusion or gonococcal types. (ii) Generalized infections. The micro-organism gains access to the baby, through the airway, gastrointestinal tract or via the umbilical cord. The organism may colonize the maternal genital tract (herpes simplex virus and group B streptococci) or may originate from the maternal intestinal tract (enterovirus and *Escherichia coli*).

Infections Acquired in the Neonatal Period (Nosocomial Infections)

Infections acquired in the neonatal period are extremely common, especially in those infants in high-risk nurseries. These infections are most often acquired from medical and nursing personnel; they are usually bacterial and the potential for spread within a nursery is increased by overcrowding and understaffing, with consequent reduction in care taken with handwashing and cleaning of equipment.

FACTORS INFLUENCING OUTCOME OF PREGNANCY

Type of Infection

Primary infections occurring in mothers who are non-immune are more commonly transmitted to the fetus than reinfection. The reason is that in primary infections, there is a blood-borne phase in the mother, whereas with reinfections the organism is frequently localized. One notable exception to this general rule is CMV, where fetal infections have been reported in mothers known to be previously immune.

Age of Fetus

In general, the earlier that the fetus is infected, the more extensive are the effects. The classic example of this is congenital rubella syndrome where the temporal relationship between the gestational age of infection and organ damage has been clearly demonstrated (p. 236). Other infections apparently disobey this axiom – fetal infections with syphilis and toxoplasmosis are much more commonly acquired in the second trimester (*vide infra*). The answer to this apparent paradox may be that the placenta is less permeable to some organisms in early pregnancy. It has been suggested that damage to the fetus from syphilis occurs in

234

the second trimester of pregnancy because the fetus is able to respond immuno-logically after the 18th week and it is this response which leads to fetal damage.

Virulence of the Organisms

There is evidence to suggest that the virulence of strains of micro-organisms varies, but whether this affects the human fetus is unknown at present.

RESPONSE TO INFECTION

The components of the immune system are present from early fetal life but are either present in insufficient amounts or only become activated after birth. The cells involved in the immune response are derived from the yolk sac, bone marrow and fetal liver and appear as early as the 8th or 12th week of pregnancy. These cells develop along two specific lines – the haemopoietic and the lympho-poietic system.

The haemopoietic system develops in the fetal liver and bone marrow pro-duces leucocytes, red cells and platelets. The lymphopoietic system produces two types of cell – the T-cell from the thymus and the B-cell.

The granulocytes produced by the haemopoietic system are immature leading to poor chemotaxis (migration of cells) together with poor phagocytosis and poor intracellular digestion of micro-organisms. The poor phagocytic function is made worse by deficiencies of antibody and complement.

The B-cells of the lymphopoietic series are concerned with production of antibody. These cells can produce antibody late in pregnancy but the system is generally immature, which is partly compensated for by the transplacental passage of maternal IgG. This provides most of the immunity against blood-borne organisms, including viruses, bacteria and fungi.

IgA is not present in fetal blood as it does not cross the placenta. Normally, IgA is found in body secretions where the secretory form which is produced by lymphoid aggregations, is able to localize infection. In the neonate, breast feeding provides local secretory IgA for gut protection.

IgM is the largest immunoglobulin and does not cross the placenta. The fetus can produce IgM in response to infection and this has been used as the basis of a screening test of transplacental infection (*vide infra*).

T-cells are produced by the thymus and are responsible for delayed hyper-sensitivity reactions so that absence of T-cells renders the infant susceptible to viral and fungal infections.

SPECIFIC INFECTIONS

Viral Infections – TORCH Complex

Rubella

Approximately 20% of women are non-immune to rubella and are at risk of having a baby affected with the congenital rubella syndrome. The disease is most

Table 14.3 Risk of congenital rubella syndrome by age and maternal infection

Duration of pregnancy*	Risk of severe defect (%)
First 4 weeks	33–50
5–8 weeks	20–25
9–12 weeks	5–10
13–16 weeks	1–5
17–30 weeks	<1

*Weeks from last menstrual period.

harmful when contracted in the first trimester of pregnancy when many fetuses will be infected and the effects are most severe (Table 14.3).

Diagnosis of rubella during the period of organogenesis (the first 8 weeks) is important since it has been accepted as an indication for termination of pregnancy. All women should have rubella antibody levels measured at the first antenatal visit; if rubella antibody is absent, the patient is regarded as being non-immune and should be vaccinated *in the postnatal period*. If a non-immune woman is in contact with rubella or suspected rubella in the antenatal period, the antibody level should be remeasured and, if present, she has been infected.

However, a more common problem is when a woman attends the clinic, with unknown immune status and with a history of rubella contact. The position may be clarified with knowledge of when the contact occurred and the woman's present immune status. If the woman attends within a week of contact, her antibody level should be measured. If antibodies are present, she can be reassured that she was immune prior to contact and that no harmful effects should occur, although these may happen on very rare occasions. If no rubella antibody is detected, the test should be repeated after 2 weeks; if antibody is detected, the patient has been infected.

Another problem occurs when a woman delays attending the clinic for a period of weeks, has a history of contact and also has antibody in her blood. This antibody shows that she has been infected but does not indicate when infection occurred. In such situations, the rubella specific IgM should be measured. This rises only after a recent infection and, if present, means that the fetus is at risk.

Termination of pregnancy may be considered since the effects of congenital rubella are widespread. Some children have congenital heart disease, notably pulmonary artery hypoplasia and patent ductus arteriosus. Cataracts and retinopathy are common. The haemopoietic system may also be involved, leading to thrombocytopenia and anaemia. Characteristic mulberry (blueberry muffin) spots may be seen in the skin due to dermal erythropoeisis. Jaundice may occur due to neonatal hepatitis. Perhaps most sinister, though very uncommon, a progressive encephalitis may develop during the first year of life or later, and may cause microcephaly. It should be remembered, however, that almost any organ system may be involved (Fig. 14.1). The confirmation of congenital rubella is made by measuring rubella-specific IgM in the baby.

Treatment is limited to the management of specific defects, for example removal of cataracts to avoid blindness and careful follow up to detect and

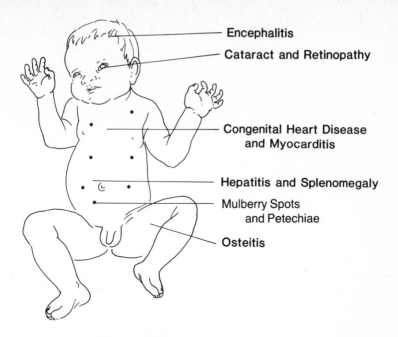

Encephalitis

Cataract and Retinopathy

Congenital Heart Disease
and Myocarditis

Hepatitis and Splenomegaly

Mulberry Spots
and Petechiae

Osteitis

Figure 14.1 Signs of congenital rubella.

ameliorate further handicaps such as deafness. The baby should be isolated from non-immune female staff as he may remain a reservoir of rubella for many months.

Prevention of rubella is now feasible by vaccination of non-immune females. There is a variety of schedules for doing this, but an effective way is to immunize girls at puberty and to revaccinate them periodically through their reproductive lives. This is logistically difficult to do and more commonly vaccination is carried out at puberty and, perhaps, postnatally. This schedule of vaccination does not give total protection but does reduce the risk. If it were possible, vaccination of all pre-school children, males and females, would remove the source of rubella in the community. This is current practice in the USA and Sweden where the incidence of congenital rubella is decreasing. It would appear that if rubella vaccination is given inadvertently in pregnancy, there are no major harmful effects on the fetus. After postnatal vaccination, contraceptive measures should be adopted for 3 months.

Cytomegalovirus (CMV) Infection

Twelve per cent of women excrete the virus during pregnancy, but the incidence of congenital infection is about 0.5%. Carriage in the mother is usually asymptomatic, although she may become infected in pregnancy and develop an influenza-like illness. In the unlikely event that systemic CMV infection is diagnosed by specific IgM testing in early pregnancy, termination may be offered. In the majority of cases, the occurrence of an infection antenatally is

Table 14.4 Symptomatic congenital cytomegalovirus infection: findings at birth

Findings	Frequency (%)
Petechiae	79
Hepatosplenomegaly	74
Jaundice	63
Microcephaly	50
SGA	41
Preterm	34
Inguinal hernia	26
Chorioretinitis	12

After Pass *et al.* (1980).

unknown, a problem which is compounded by the difficulties in diagnosing the condition in the neonatal period. About 4 in 1000 live-born infants have demonstrable IgM antibody in their sera, but in approximately 90% of cases CMV infection is not clinically apparent in the neonatal period. The condition may later become manifest with the development of mental retardation, hydrocephaly or microcephaly. In the 10% of symptomatic cases at birth the infant may present with jaundice and hepatosplenomegaly, haemolysis, thrombocytopenia and growth retardation (Table 14.4). Chorioretinitis may also be present. Radiographs of the skull may show periventricular calcification although this is usually seen only later in life (Fig. 14.2). The diagnosis may be confirmed by detection of specific IgM antibody in the blood, by isolation of the

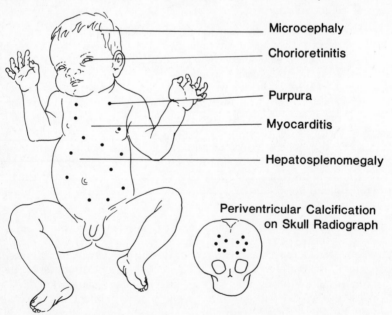

Figure 14.2 Signs of congenital cytomegalovirus infection.

virus from the throat, urine or spinal fluid or by detection of intracellular inclusion bodies in the urine. Isolation of the baby is not required, but handling by pregnant staff should be avoided.

There is no effective specific treatment of CMV infection, although new antiviral drugs are under investigation. All children should be followed up to ensure early detection of handicap (Table 14.5). It has been estimated that 10% of mental retardation in children under the age of 6 years is due to CMV infection.

Although neonatal infection usually occurs following a primary maternal infection, babies in subsequent pregnancies can be affected. As yet, there is no vaccine available. A mother with active CMV infection should not breast feed her baby. CMV negative blood should be used for all blood and exchange transfusions in neonates.

Herpes Simplex

Genital herpes is a sexually transmitted disease and is caused in 90% of cases by herpes virus hominis (HVH) Type II, and in 10% by Type I virus. Primary infection of the mother is often asymptomatic, but may produce a cluster of vesicles on the vulva or cervix which soon rupture to leave painful superficial erosions. Dysuria and inguinal lymphadenopathy may occur, together with constitutional symptoms of malaise and fever. The condition is the commonest cause of ulcerative lesions of the female genital tract in the UK and is often recurrent. The diagnosis is confirmed by viral culture from a wet ulcer or vesicle.

Infection of the fetus is thought to occur principally by direct contact during parturition. There is evidence that fetal infection will occur within 6 hr of rupture of the membranes if there is active maternal infection. Transplacental passage of the virus is rare, but there are reports linking genital tract infection at the time of conception and in the first trimester with spontaneous abortion (30–50% of cases) and with congenital malformations.

Infants are usually asymptomatic for the first few days, but they may develop non-specific signs of sepsis with lethargy, poor feeding, jaundice with hepatomegaly and disseminated intravascular coagulopathy. Classical cutaneous lesions of herpes may also be present, making the diagnosis relatively simple, but their absence does not exclude the disease. It is disseminated infection with central nervous system involvement that has severe implications for the newborn (Table 14.6). In the rare cases of prenatal infection, the infant may have

Table 14.5 Long-term outcome of infants with symptomatic congenital cytomegalovirus infection

Defect	Frequency (%)
Microcephaly	70
Low IQ	61
Seizures/cerebral palsy	35
Hearing loss	30
Visual loss	22
Total handicap rate	91

After Pass *et al.* (1980).

Table 14.6 Outcome of neonatal herpes simplex viral infections

Clinical findings	%	Mortality (%)	Survivors with sequelae (%)
Disseminated			
No CNS involvement	38	94	0
CNS involvement	31	79	11
Localized			
Skin and CNS	15	43	40
Eye	3	0	50
Skin alone	11	0	32
Mouth	1	0	0
Asymptomatic	1	0	0

After Nahmias and Visintine (1976).

microcephaly with intracerebral calcification, growth retardation, chorioretinitis and micro-ophthalmia.

Virus may be isolated from the cutaneous vesicles, the throat and the urine. Multinucleated giant cells with intranuclear inclusions may be seen from the lesions and IgM antibodies may be detected in the serum. The prognosis for infected babies is very poor with 40% dying and a further 40% becoming handicapped; infants with disseminated infection are much more likely to have sequelae than those with local infection (Table 14.6).

Prevention of intranatally acquired infection is possible by elective Caesarean section in known vaginal carriers or in those with active disease if the membranes have been intact or have been ruptured for less than 6 hr. If the membranes have been ruptured for longer than this, ascending infection will have occurred and the fetus will have become infected. The use of acyclovir topically or systematically for mothers is under investigation.

Treatment of infants with herpes virus infection is possible but difficult since many of the antiviral drugs are toxic. Currently acyclovir is advocated by some, and the judicious use of such drugs is indicated when the diagnosis is proved. If the baby is not infected and the mother has active herpes, he should be isolated from the mother until her lesions heal. Topical idoxuridine may be used to treat ocular disease.

Hepatitis B

Hepatitis B virus (HBV) is distributed worldwide with particularly high HB Ag carrier rates of 10–20% in Africa and Asia. In contrast less than 1% of the population are carriers in the United Kingdom.

Transmission from mother to infant can occur during pregnancy, birth and the neonatal period, whether the mother has acute hepatitis B infection or is a chronic carrier. The risk of transmission would appear to be low (less than 5%) for Caucasians but much higher (greater than 50%) in Asians. The rate of transmission appears to be related to the presence of e antigen in the mother's blood and absence of e antibody, i.e. the virus is active. Care must be taken in handling all secretions from these mothers, especially blood and amniotic fluid.

Gloves should be worn, needles carefully disposed of and blood for laboratory investigation labelled with hazard warnings.

The risk of transmission to the baby from the mother with acute hepatitis depends upon the duration of the pregnancy. In the first trimester the rate is about 10% but is much higher when the mother is infected in the third trimester. This clearly implicates the birth process, when the fetus is in contact with maternal blood, as the major time of inoculation.

Virus has been isolated from the breast milk of mothers with hepatitis B. Although the risk of transmission of virus by this route is not known, breast feeding is probably best avoided.

Normally the infants show no sign of infection but may develop chronic subclinical hepatitis especially if they have coincidental alpha-1-anti-trypsin deficiency. Occasionally, acute fulminant hepatitis occurs which has a high fatality rate.

Infants of mothers who suffer from disease or are carriers should be immunized using inactivated hepatitis B vaccine as this has been shown to reduce the incidence of the carrier state in the babies.

Acquired Immunodeficiency Syndrome (AIDS)

AIDS was first seen in Western countries in male homosexuals in America but is now spreading to affect the heterosexual population. It has been estimated that one million Americans have been exposed, of whom 20% are women.

The aetiological agent is a retrovirus that used to be called human T-cell lymphotrophic virus type III (HLTV-III) but is now known as human immunodeficiency virus (HIV).

AIDS is the most severe manifestation of infection with HIV (Table 14.7). Many are asymptomatic carriers while others may develop a spectrum of lymphadenopathy-associated syndrome grouped as AIDS-related complex (ARC) which appears to be much more common than AIDS itself. However, it has been estimated that 2–9% of seropositive persons will develop AIDS each year.

HIV can be isolated from blood, bone marrow, spinal fluid, brain tissue, lymph nodes, skin graft, semen, saliva, tears, breast milk and cervical secretions. Transmission is usually by sexual contact but may also occur when drug-users share contaminated needles. Heterosexual and mother–child transmission also occur and infection can be acquired following transfusions of blood or blood

Table 14.7 Diagnosis of AIDS

Biopsy-proven Kaposi's sarcoma
Non-Hodgkin's lymphoma
Unusual infections, e.g.
   Protozoal
   Helminthic
   Disseminated fungal
   Disseminated atypical mycobacterial
Cellular immunodeficiency
Positive HIV antibody

Table 14.8 AIDS embryopathy

Small for gestational age
Microcephaly
Box-like head – prominent forehead
Hypertelorism
Short nose, flat bridge
Upward, outward eye slant
Long palpebral fissures
Blue sclerae
Patulous lips

products, and breast feeding. Transmission by blood transfusion should become less frequent with screening of donor blood for HIV but will not disappear since some donors with HIV are seronegative at the time of testing. Conversion may take up to 4 months.

AIDS is unusual in one other important regard. Normally, with viral infections, the presence of antibody means that the patient is immune; in the case of AIDS, the presence of antibody indicates active, current infection. Pregnancy may increase the risk of AIDS developing in HIV-positive women and termination may therefore be offered.

Two-thirds of seropositive mothers give birth to seropositive babies and about 50% of these babies will develop clinical AIDS within 2 years.

Prenatal infection of the fetus can occur, causing an embryopathy (Table 14.8). Apart from the embryopathy, affected infants may develop AIDS and present with hepatosplenomegaly, lymphadenopathy, interstitial pneumonia and recurrent infections.

The treatment of AIDS in both adults and children is supportive but the mortality is high and no vaccine is yet available. The only sure way to prevent the condition for most people is sexual fidelity; promiscuous homosexual and heterosexual contact may lead to AIDS. It has been suggested that the use of sheath contraceptives may help prevent transmission.

Women at risk (Table 14.9) should be screened antenatally after consent has been given and termination offered if they are antibody positive.

One major problem for the health professional is to avoid self-inoculation when treating a patient with HIV. There is some evidence that health personnel can develop the syndrome after accidental needle pricks with contaminated needles but not during normal nursing procedures. Clearly, if one is dealing with AIDS patients then precautions appropriate for management of patients with hepatitis B infection should be employed. (Breast feeding should be prohibited.) If infected secretions – blood or amniotic fluid – are spilt, then 1% sodium hypochlorite may be used to neutralize the virus.

Table 14.9 High-risk groups for AIDS in pregnancy

Drug addicts
Prostitutes
Central African women
Partners of bisexual men
Partners of haemophiliacs

Table 14.10 Other viral infections

Virus	Effect on fetus
Enteroviruses (Echo and Coxsackie)	Heart, genitourinary tract defects, myocarditis, hepatitis
Influenza	Abortion, preterm delivery, tumours
Mumps	Abortion, endocardial fibroelastosis ? aqueduct stenosis,
Measles	Abortion, preterm delivery
Polio	Abortion, preterm delivery, neonatal infection

Varicella

Varicella (chicken pox) infection in the first trimester may cause damage to the central nervous system, cataracts and scarring of the skin. Infection in the last 4 days of pregnancy and soon after birth can also seriously affect the baby, causing disseminated infection and death in 5%. Infection near term should be treated by giving the newborn immune globulin (Zoster Immune Globulin, or ZIG) and probably also acyclovir. Females are five times more likely to be infected than males and there is a slightly increased risk of leukaemia.

Other Viral Infections Affecting the Fetus

These are listed in Table 14.10 and are very uncommon.

Diagnosis of Torch Infections

The TORCH complex of infections comprise those due to the viruses listed in Table 14.2. These babies tend to be small for gestational age and have rashes, hepatosplenomegaly, central nervous system abnormalities, chorioretinitis and subsequent failure to thrive. Small-for-dates babies where no obvious cause is found may be screened for infections by measuring cord blood IgM which is normally less than 0.2 g/l. If there has been a recent infection, then cord IgM will be greater than 0.25 g/l in about 60% of cases. Confirmation should be made by sending appropriate blood samples for serology and viral culture.

Bacterial Infections (see also Chapter 4)

Group B beta-haemolytic Streptococcal (GBS) Infection

GBS infection is becoming increasingly worrying to obstetricians and paediatricians because of the often fulminant course of the disease in babies and the high mortality rate (around 50%). Group B streptococci may be isolated from the genital tracts or rectums of approximately 10% of pregnant women, is often asymptomatic, although some will have urinary tract infections, and is difficult to treat. Fortunately, the infection rate of neonates is low and the disease incidence in the neonatal period is about 4 per 1000. If a woman is a known carrier, she should be given penicillin or ampicillin during a labour complicated by prolonged rupture of the membranes, signs of amnionitis or occurring preterm.

Commonly, the disease presents in the immediate neonatal period with respiratory distress closely resembling hyaline membrane disease, or with shock and apnoea. The bacterium should be sought in the infant's gastric aspirate and umbilical swab and in the maternal high vaginal and rectal swabs. Alternatively, the disease may have a more insidious onset with symptoms and signs of generalized, non-specific infection such as lethargy, failure to suck and abdominal distension. In these latter cases, the diagnosis is confirmed by isolation of the bacterium from blood, urine or spinal fluid.

Treatment should be prompt because of the fulminant nature of the disease. Penicillin should be given alone or in combination with gentamicin in all cases where the organism is seen on direct microscopy; penicillin alone should be given where the disease is suspected but direct microscopy is negative. Treatment should be continued for 10–14 days or until the cultures taken prior to treatment are negative. All infants with symptoms should be treated in neonatal intensive-care units with the availability of full life-support systems. These infants require careful monitoring and may require assisted ventilation.

Syphilis

Congenital syphilis is a rare disease in the United Kingdom but may be increasing in frequency due to changing sexual habits. Serological tests for syphilis are positive in 0.42 per 1000 pregnancies.

The effects of syphilis occur mainly in the second and third trimester of pregnancy when active infection is associated with intrauterine death and congenital infection. It has been argued that in the second and third trimester the fetus can respond immunologically to the spirochaete and that it is this immune response which causes fetal damage.

Signs of infection in the mothers are scanty. The chancre in the genital tract and the rash of secondary syphilis may be unrecognized. The difficulty with the diagnosis has led to the routine measurement of the VDRL and TPHA tests at the first antenatal visit of all mothers, since detection and treatment at this stage of pregnancy may prevent fetal infection.

Congenital syphilis (Fig. 14.3) is very difficult to diagnose in the neonatal period since clinical findings are often entirely absent. There is no primary stage since the spirochaete has been introduced directly into the blood stream. Rashes may be present and may be seen on the hands, feet and face. The rash may be violaceous, maculopapular or may be bullous with clear, highly infectious fluid contents. Classical snuffles may also be seen with a clear, profuse nasal discharge and there may be interstitial pneumonitis. On occasions, periostitis may be present, giving rise to pain and pseudoparalysis of a limb (Parrot's syndrome). Hepatosplenomegaly and haemolytic anaemia may also be present.

Approximately 50% of infants with congenital syphilis will have central nervous system involvement, but in the majority of cases this is asymptomatic. However, all infants with congenital syphilis should have their spinal fluid examined since neurosyphilis carries a more guarded prognosis.

Confirmation of the diagnosis depends on serological testing. When there are cutaneous lesions, *Treponema pallidum* may be seen on dark-field microscopy, but more commonly the diagnosis is confirmed by the fluorescent treponema antibody absorption test (FTA-ABS test).

Parenteral penicillin should be given for 10 days to eliminate the spirochaete

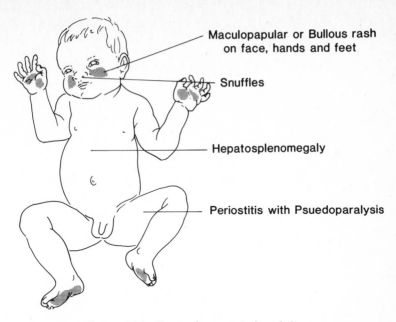

Maculopapular or Bullous rash on face, hands and feet

Snuffles

Hepatosplenomegaly

Periostitis with Psuedoparalysis

Figure 14.3 Signs of congenital syphilis.

but will clearly not affect damage caused prior to birth. Such infants should also be tested for infection with other sexually transmitted disease, such as gonorrhoea and chlamydia (Table 14.11) which usually causes conjunctivitis.

Listeriosis

Listeria monocytogenes, a Gram-positive, pleomorphic bacterium, may be isolated from the genital tract in up to 4% of pregnant women, but the incidence of neonatal infection in the UK has been estimated to be about 1 in 37 000 births, though it may occur more commonly. Transmission to the fetus may be either transplacental or by direct contamination during parturition. The organism may also be transmitted to the neonate in breast milk.

Table 14.11 Sexually transmitted diseases affecting the fetus

Infection	Effect on fetus
Syphilis	Embryopathy, pneumonitis
Gonorrhoea	Conjunctivitis
Group B streptococcus	Pneumonia, septicaemia, meningitis
Chlamydia	Conjunctivitis, pneumonitis
Herpes Simplex	Embryopathy, local and disseminated infection, encephalitis
Hepatitis B	Carrier state, hepatitis
HIV (AIDS)	Embryopathy, carrier, AIDS disease
Candida	Local or occasionally disseminated infection

Maternal listeriosis is often associated with two or more febrile episodes and may be misdiagnosed as urinary tract infection, influenza, glandular fever or gastroenteritis. Infection may cause abortion, still birth or preterm labour with offensive 'meconium-stained' liquor and this combination should alert the clinician to the possibility of *Listeria* infection.

After birth, the infant may have a fulminant widespread infection similar to that seen with streptococcal infection and, in some, a characteristic rash consisting of small erythematous papules may be seen mainly on the trunk. In a few, the onset of the disease may be delayed for some weeks and present with meningitis.

It should be noted that the isolation of *Listeria* is difficult, and unless the laboratory personnel are asked to look specifically for the micro-organism, the diagnosis will frequently be missed. The disease should be treated for 10 days with parenteral penicillin or with ampicillin and gentamicin.

Protozoal Infections

Toxoplasmosis

Toxoplasma gondii infection of adults is extremely common with about 20% of women in the UK having positive toxoplasma titres in pregnancy. Fortunately, in most cases, this indicates previous infection and the fetus is therefore not at risk. About 1 in 400 women acquire the infection for the first time in pregnancy, and of these approximately 30% will have infected fetuses. The diagnosis in the mother is difficult as many are asymptomatic, although some have influenza-like symptoms with posterior cervical lymphadenopathy. There may be a history of contact with cats and the mother may have been infected by eating undercooked meats. The risk of infection of the fetus increases with gestation, rising from 15% in the first trimester to 70% in the third trimester. Infection in subsequent pregnancies has been reported, though this is extremely rare. Infection may lead to spontaneous abortion, intrauterine death or preterm labour.

The clinical syndrome in the neonate is very similar to CMV infection with hepatosplenomegaly and chorioretinitis (Fig. 14.4). Later, hydrocephaly or microcephaly may develop with intracranial calcification which is generalized in distribution. Only a minority of affected infants can be diagnosed clinically in the neonatal period, with the majority of children appearing later with psycho-motor retardation, together with visual and auditory impairment. The diagnosis of toxoplasmosis is confirmed by the toxoplasma dye test and haemagglutinin test.

Treatment of the infected pregnant mother has not been proven to be effective, although it has been suggested that spiramycin may reduce the fetal effects. Infected neonates should be treated with pyrimethamine and sulpha-diazine with folate for 3 weeks. The prognosis for these infants is poor and the children require prolonged follow-up to ensure detection and amelioration of handicap.

CHORIO-AMNIONITIS (see also Chapter 4)

Chorio-amnionitis is said to affect about 10% of all pregnancies when careful histological examination is made. Signs of chorio-amnionitis may be found in

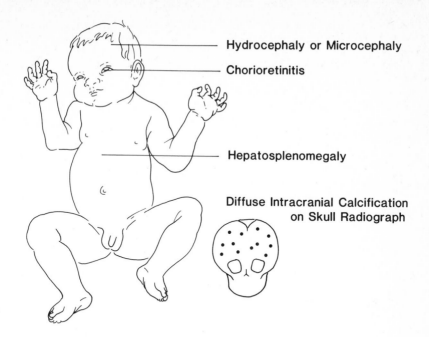

Figure 14.4 Signs of congenital toxoplasmosis.

50% of those pregnancies where the fetus weighs less than 1000 g and in 66% of mid-trimester abortions. The vast majority of these infections are not recognized before birth.

FURTHER READING

Amstey, M. S. (1984) *Virus Infections in Pregnancy. Monographs in Neonatology.* Grune and Stratton, London.

Boyer, K. M. and Gotoff, S. P. (1986) Prevention of early onset neonatal group B streptococcal disease with selective intrapartum chemoprophylaxis. *N. Engl. J. Med.* **314**: 1665.

Grossman, J. H., III (1980) Perinatal viral infections. *Clin. Perinatol.* **7**: 257.

Halliday, H. L., McClure, G. and Reid, M. (1985) *Handbook of Neonatal Intensive Care*, 2nd edn. Baillière Tindall, London.

Marion, R. W., Wiznia, A. A., Hutcheon, R. G. and Rubenstein, A. (1986) Human T-cell lymphotropic virus type III (HTLV-III) embryopathy. *Am. J. Dis. Child* **140**: 638.

Minkoff, H. L. and Schwarz, R. H. (1986) AIDS: time for obstetricians to get involved. *Obstet. Gynaecol.* **68**: 267.

Nahmias, A. J. and Visintine, A. M. (1976) Herpes simplex. In Remington, J. S. and Klein, J. O. (eds), *Infectious Diseases of the Fetus and Newborn Infant.* W. B. Saunders, Philadelphia, pp. 156–190.

Pass, R. E., Stagno, S. *et al.* (1980) Outcome of symptomatic congenital cytomegalovirus infection. *Pediatrics* **66**: 753.

Pinching, A. J. and Jeffries, D. J. (1985) AIDS and HTLV-III/QAV infection: consequences for obstetrics and perinatal medicine. *Br. J. Obstet. Gynaecol.* **92**: 121.

Sever, J. L. and Fuccillo, D. A. (1977) Perinatal infections. In Bolognese, R. J. and Schwartz, R. H. (eds), *Perinatal Medicine*. Williams and Wilkins, Baltimore, pp. 211–219.

Stirrat, G. M. (1981) *Obstetrics Pocket Consultant*. Grant McIntyre, London, pp. 121–133.

15

Future Developments

Each of the authors of this book has at some time been a student of medicine and has experienced the feeling of relief attendant upon closing a book – another subject safely tucked away, the knowledge received! We do not wish you to stop now with a sense that 'that is all you know, and all you need to know'. There are many problems still to be solved and those of us currently in practice cannot foresee their solution, so it may be left to some who read this book to respond to the challenges of perinatal medicine.

First, let us examine how we currently think about this subject. The writers were initially trained as obstetricians or as paediatricians and only later did we come together to realize that our problems were similar. This chance could only have occurred recently because our predecessors had different problems to contend with; only when they were resolved could perinatal medicine develop. This has led to a radical change in the thinking and attitudes of obstetricians and paediatricians – each learning from the other – for the benefit of their patients. Only by a combined approach to these problems can we help to understand and resolve them.

The problem of unexplained still birth remains in spite of our best efforts. These tragedies occur 'out of the blue' and, as yet, we have little idea why they happen; pathology, histology and microbiology are all unrevealing. Perhaps they represent some form of intrauterine 'cot death'. At this point in time it is difficult to see how these deaths can be understood and prevented, and it seems unlikely that there is one cause of this problem. At the moment, possible solutions are obscure but what is certain is that the current methods of fetal surveillance are inadequate.

Placental abruption accounts for a significant proportion of still births. Most occur for no obvious reason, although some are associated with maternal hypertension. It would appear likely that the basic problem is in the placental bed, possibly arising because of faulty implantation or from some local pathological process. It may be that better histology of the placental bed will prove helpful and it is conceivable that high-resolution real-time and Doppler ultrasound of this area may allow us to detect high-risk patients.

The diagnosis of the unhealthy fetus remains difficult. One problem is to detect the poorly grown fetus by a clinical screening method so that more sophisticated ultrasonic measurement of fetal size can be performed. The best clinician will have difficulty in making this diagnosis correctly in even 50% of cases. Further, we are still concentrating our efforts on measurement of fetal size and too little effort has been made to develop methods of assessment of fetal health or function. Physiological measurements are likely to be more revealing than anatomical ones.

Current methods of diagnosis of 'fetal distress' are not ideal. Even when they are applied to high-risk babies, the correct diagnosis is made in only 60% of patients and in low-risk pregnancy the false positive rate is high, leading to increasing and unnecessary use of Caesarean section. The supposition is often made that if a baby is born requiring resuscitation that there was unrecognized acute fetal distress in labour. However, many feel that some of these babies are unhealthy at the beginning of labour and are born ill because of chronic disease that occurred much earlier in pregnancy. We need a better method of assessment of fetal health, prior to the onset of labour, as well as more accurate methods of detecting fetal distress in labour when it does occur.

Fetal maturity is currently thought of by obstetricians in terms of gestational age which for most pregnancies is entirely reasonable. However, fetuses mature at different rates so that some babies born at low gestational ages will behave maturely and others born near term will appear immature. Such problems go beyond those of fetal lung maturity and probably affect all organ systems. Obviously an attempt to arrest preterm labour when the fetus is mature should be avoided.

The problem of preterm labour and its management remains a vexed question. It is of fundamental importance that we learn to understand more fully the mechanisms which trigger preterm labour because then it may be possible to prevent or arrest it more effectively.

Neonatal intensive care is reasonably successful in that most babies survive and are normal. However, intensive care is invasive, time consuming and may be extremely frightening to the parents. We need to develop means of preventing the need for intensive care. One light on the horizon is the use of surfactant replacement therapy to manage respiratory distress syndrome. The evidence is still being gathered and there are many problems still to be resolved but there is some indication that surfactant replacement may have a major role to play in prevention and treatment of respiratory distress syndrome. This would greatly lessen both acute and chronic sequelae of babies currently being managed in neonatal intensive-care units.

The problem of brain damage is one which most worries neonatal paediatricians. We are much better at detecting irreversible damage but in many we cannot be sure. There is a need to refine our current diagnostic tests and to develop new methods of assessment of neonatal cerebral function. In addition, we need to understand better what causes such damage. At the present time, alteration in cerebral blood flow would appear to be important in the pathogenesis of cerebral damage and, perhaps, as we learn how to measure neonatal cerebral blood flow accurately and continuously we will be able to correct or prevent abnormalities before cerebral damage occurs.

A major problem faced by paediatricians is whether to employ intensive care on extremely immature infants. The smaller the baby, the greater the mortality and handicap rates, so it is often difficult to know what is best to do. It would appear advisable that treatment of such babies should only occur in large centres with their increased resources and ability to evaluate options carefully until the situation becomes clearer.

The problem of congenital abnormalities is the major area where advances must be made. The prevention of neural tube defects may be possible using periconceptual vitamin supplements. Sadly, the first major study did not have a proper control group but sufficient evidence was gleaned to support the view that a randomized study should be performed. We must await the results of these studies before firm conclusions can be drawn.

Prenatal treatment also is a possibility. In recent years, surgical techniques have been applied to congenital malformations such as hydrocephaly and urethral valves. To date, the results of these operations have been disappointing, but there is potential for further developments in this area.

The whole field of prenatal diagnosis is about to explode with developments in fetal DNA analysis. The science of gene isolation is extremely difficult but it may be possible to isolate and analyse gene defects by this means. At present, chorionic villus biopsy is being used to provide fetal cells for analysis, but it may be possible to separate fetal cells from maternal blood where they appear in minute quantities in early pregnancy. This would obviate the need for invasive procedures to obtain fetal tissue and would help reduce the current abortion rate after chorionic villus sampling of 5%.

There are two other problems which we have discussed earlier in this book but which need to be considered. For many women, recurrent early pregnancy loss occurs and we have little idea as to why this happens. However, in some cases there may be rejection of fetal tissue as an antigen and it may prove possible to reduce this by injecting the woman with washed blood cells from her partner. This form of immuno-therapy is currently under investigation but has not found favour with all members of the profession. The problems of infertile couples will also affect the perinatologist notably because new techniques of treatment often lead to higher multiple births which often occur prematurely. This may well have major consequences for the neonatal intensive care units – one set of immature quadruplets will keep most units busy for several weeks!

So far in this chapter, we have been chauvinistic by mentioning only those problems which affect us in the developed world. However, we must realize that our problems are only a fraction of those faced by other members of our profession. Many hospitals in the developing world have perinatal mortality rates of 50–80/1000. In the Fourth Perinatal Lecture at the Royal Maternity Hospital in 1987, Professor Hugh Philpott addressed the theme 'Obstetrics and Poverty'. He compared two hospitals in the same town in South Africa, one serving white people and the other blacks. Their respective perinatal mortality rates were 12 and 50/1000 – the results of poverty, ignorance and disease. Such problems must be addressed by our profession, not only as doctors and nurses, but as citizens; after all, we are the great caring profession.

We have tried, in this chapter, to indicate some areas where advances in this field of medicine may take place. There are many others for example, the whole field of perinatal medicine abounds with ethical and moral dilemmas which would require a book in themselves. We have confined ourselves to the practical problems because we feel that the major ethical issues require wider debate than would be afforded in a book such as this.

The problems that we see are ours at the moment but we hope that some of you will take up the challenges of perinatal medicine and in the future solve them.

FURTHER READING

British Medical Association (1983) *Handbook of Medical Ethics*. BMA, London.
Campbell, A. G. M. (1986) Ethical problems in neonatal care. In Roberton, N. R. C. (ed.), *Textbook of Neonatology*. Churchill Livingstone, Edinburgh, pp. 35–41.
Hon, E. H. (1982) Symposium on fetal monitoring: epilogue. *Clin. Perinatol.* 9: 443.
Mutch, L. M. M. (1986) Epidemology, perinatal mortality and morbidity. In Robertson,

N. R. C. (ed.), *Textbook of Neonatology* Churchill Livingstone, Edinburgh, pp. 20–34.

Weatherall, D. (1984) On track of genetic disease. *New Scientist*, 5 April: 32–36.

Index

Note: Figures in italics refer to illustrations and tables